D0085827

HANS
HOLLEIN

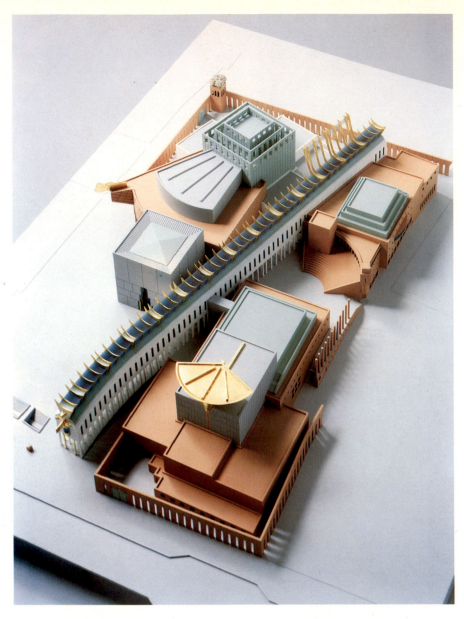

Competition New National Theatre of Japan, Tokyo, 1985-1986:
model and interior perspective sketch.

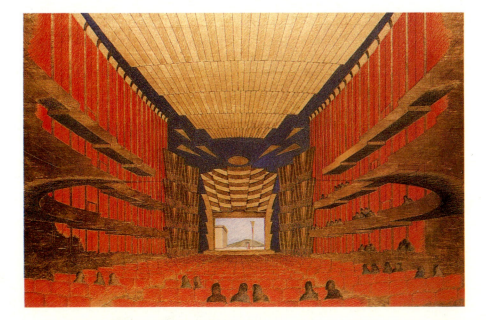

"Carillon" Tower, Tiegarten, Berlin Kulturforum, 1986.

Catalogue of the exhibition "Hans Hollein. Works 1960-1968"
Accademia delle Arti del Disegno - Firenze, Aprile-Maggio 1988
English language version

Comune di Firenze
Ordine degli Architetti di Firenze
Accademia delle Arti del Disegno

Editorial conception: Passigli Progetti
Art direction: Anthony Mathews

Design: Studio Branzi (Jim Obata)

Research, coordination, English texts: Stefania Coppi

Translations from the Italian:
Peter Boutourline Young (text by G. Pettena)
Camille Monti (index of works)

Photographic Sources
Aldo Ballo, Sina Baniahmad, Luc Bernard, Otto Breicha, Marlies Darsow, Evelyn Hofer, Hans Hollein,
Franz Hubmann, Ruth Kaiser, Peter Lehner, Norman Mc Grath, Gino Molin-Pradel,
Erich Pedevilla, Thomas Römer, Georg Riha, Lee Salem, Roberto Schezen, Jerzy Survillo, Gerard Zugmann.

Contributors

Atelier Hollein
Walter Kirpicsenko, Erich Pedevilla.
Barbara Aull, Sina Baniahmad, Marie-Paul Greisen, Madeleine Jenewein, Alexander Klose.

German texts: Hans Höger

© 1988 Idea Books Edizioni, via Vigevano 41 - Milano / 250 West 57th Street, New York, NY 10107

All rights reserved. No part of this book may be reproduced in any form by any electronic
or mechanical means (including photocopying, recording, or information storage and
retrieval) without permission in writing from the publisher.

ISBN 88-7017-035-7

Set, printed and bound in Italy.

Front cover: Jewellery Shop Schullin II, Vienna, 1981-82.
Back cover: Centerpiece for Swarowski International, 1986-87.

Gianni Pettena

HANS HOLLEIN

Works 1960-1988

IDEA BOOKS EDIZIONI

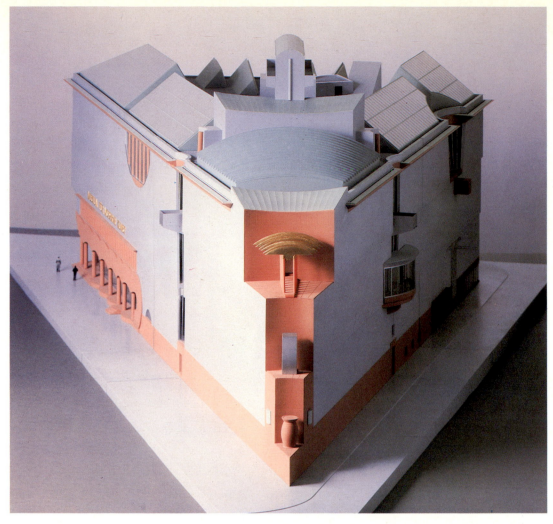

Frankfurt Museum of Modern Art, 1983: model.

Thyssen-Bornemisza Gallery Expansion Project, 1986: model.

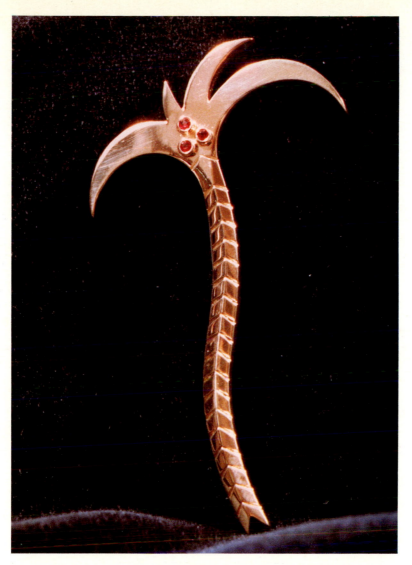

Brooch, "Kochert Collection", 1987.

Jewels, "Cleto Munari Collection", 1985.

Contents

H.H. Interview

(The conversations with Hans Hollein, which have taken place in the course of the past few years, have become even more frequent during the preparation of this book, started in 1985, together with a historic exhibition of his work. They have been very useful both in providing reciprocal understanding and in the organization of an exceptionally varied and rich collection of work, and not only in a strict "disciplinary" sense. A certain consonance of intentions and interests, and a very similar cultural education, led us to give this conversation a particular and rather more effective form or structure. This interview of March 1986 is the only one in recent years to be so complete in character and so precise in its definition of Hollein's work.)

P.: "I believe that for me personally, and for the whole architectural scene, what is most interesting about your cultural position, and about the continuity of your activity and the evolution of your work, is the fact that you not only deal simply with architecture but with at least three fields that are (according to a technical and not always correct distinction) architecture, architectural and furniture design, installations and art work. This is something that derives from your cultural origins, from the cultural debate of the early '60s in which all took part and to which, also in Italy then, we all related. What happened in Italy and especially in Florence in that period, that is 'radical architecture', had some correspondence with your work and the general situation in Vienna and in England at that time. These were our points of reference: the fact that there were no barriers between disciplines, the fact that 'everything' was and is architecture, the fact that you could temporarily suspend the strict architectural traditions that were taught in architectural schools and practise other languages instead, re-conceptualizing them in architectural terms. It was something that for many of us, and certainly for me, was extremely important: to be able to practise an architectural language or develop an architectural concept not only with a pencil and a ruler, with drawn lines, but also through other media. Movies, statements, writings or sketches that were not necessarily related to a project which, until that time, had been considered the only way of representing architecture.

This was certainly very important and I think we must point it out. Otherwise we may not understand why you are, even now, still practising as an architect (which naturally occupies most of your time because of the difficulties one encounters in realizing an architectural design) but at the same time you are no less interested in your art work. In fact I think your interests show an almost even balance between form and visual languages, how form responds to function or is important only to you yourself, and can be regarded with an emotional and not strictly rational insight.

I think that this common issue also led us to the design of furniture; a skill that nobody had ever taught us (certainly not we in Florence and perhaps not even you), was how to design a piece of furniture. We came to it naturally and I think we did so because it was an extension of our daily practice of architecture, of building a scale model (a prototype from which very often nothing followed). It was an unconscious, and sometimes conscious, need to ascertain whether our visual language could be translated onto a real scale. In fact, in the architectural schools we had until then made models on a larger scale (1 to 100 or 200 or 1 to 50, if we were lucky), but we had never tackled a model on a scale of one to one. This, together with the architectural project and the art work, related in a sort of mental and conceptual gymnastics in which I think originated the continuity and complexity of your work. Yours is the most coherent version of the European architectural avantgarde movement that began in the late '50s and early '60s. If we look at other architects and artists who began to experiment at the same time, none of them is practising today with the same complexity in the field of visual expression in space. Some of them concentrate on art work; others only on architectural projects; some just write, but none of them show in their work the same continuity and evolution of every element of poetic expression that existed when the movement began."

H.: "I think you are right for most of them: a number of those who started in the '60s with some good ideas and intentions, retreated to very narrow, defendable positions, which they continue to explore (sometimes doing interesting work), but this is what I have tried to avoid. I wanted to realize the dreams of my early years. This was the intention. I don't think that one can say at a certain point: 'Okay, those were the dreams and now comes reality, now comes life!' So, I think that what I always wanted, what you may call the continuity and what led me to take an interest in different fields, is that I had two things in mind.

First, I have always taken seriously my ideas and initial plans and have wanted to carry them on to further work and to realization. I have never done anything solely for the sake of being extravagant, utopian or isolated, just to make a beautiful picture but with no reference to earlier work or to the work of the future. This was and is a very important factor in my work. Of course, emphasis shifts and the ways of presenting things shift. Today things are more complex and integrated but, for instance in my work in the Mönchengladbach Museum but also in other works, it is possible to detect many of my early ideas.

This is one element; the other is that the variety of activities I undertake, actual architecture, fine art, installations, drawings (which are not only architectural drawings, mostly not, but architectural drawings, too), and the things I do in product design or furniture, in stage design or exhibition design, are things you cannot really isolate or separate into pigeon-holes. If I were a musician, maybe a pianist, I think then it would be one thing *or* the other (just as Sinopoli was a physician and an orchestral director and there was probably little connection between the two things). This is very important to me. Therefore I hardly have any projects or ideas of which I can say 'this was ten years ago, and now I take a completely different position'. Of course , things have changed to some extent because I have developed and I have matured, but in the process of continuity and development, my position has shifted only slightly. In the early years some of my ideas were more absolute, presented in a more absolute way, more isolated, more autonomous, because I wanted to pinpoint certain things, things that are now more integrated and in a certain sense more implicit. They are not as obvious as they were in the early years because then there was *this* project or *this* drawing or *this* manifesto or *this* piece of writing, which was very clear on certain points. It's also very clear now, but it is a step further on and it is, of course, integrated in what I do now, for instance in terms of buildings. It was always my intention to realize my plans in terms of building, of course, but also, in other terms. I never considered my architectural activity as a mere theoretical or academic exercise, or a pure production of drawings. I can draw very easily and I don't see any great achievement in just making a beautiful drawing. If I want to make beautiful drawings for a particular purpose, I do so; if you have to explain certain complex things in a simple way, you present them in the form of design or collage or any other appropriate form. But this activity would not have been sufficient to me. I have never wanted to design architecture only in order to show my work in art galleries. I must say this trend is a recent development which to me seems rather unfortunate. Of course, I have had a lot of exhibitions of my work and there are drawings and collages and other works of mine which have been bought by major museums, and this I think is very positive in terms of their *general* importance, not just because they are exhibited at Max Protetch's or elsewhere. This seems to me to be a very dangerous tendency among the young generation. You can see very clearly when the drawing is an end in itself even if some of them are very beautiful. It is enough just to look at the enormous quantity of nicely drawn projects and those absurd models, all carved and gilded..."

P.: "To cover the lack of ideas!"

H.: "Sometimes, yes. And then it no longer serves as a medium. What I mean is that a drawing, a model, or any other means of simulating reality, serves as a vehicle to convey an idea. But when one turns to the community, one is dealing with people who are unable to read a plan or imagine the spatial complexities conveyed by an architectural drawing, however simple. So, you have to deal with them in a different way. It's the same difficulty that I have, for example, when I try to read a musical score in order to imagine the sound of a symphony. I cannot hear the music in an abstract way. But I can do it very easily with a drawing: understand the nature of the space in all its details. If I look, for example, at a map of the Alps, I know exactly what the landscape looks like even without having been there or having seen photographs. There are spatial characteristics that for me indicate even the nature of the atmosphere, clearly.

I think all this has been important in my life and in my development, and I think a few of my friends have followed the same road, while others have chosen a narrower and more specific path because they wanted to avoid the difficulties that one encounters in the realization of a project. To plan a project and to realize it, and especially the projects that I design and want to design, is an enormous burden. You spend a high percentage of your time on things that are basically uninteresting and not very rewarding (not in a financial sense but in a spiritual sense), but you have to put up with them in order to get your project through, to realize it. Dealing with the authorities, with public or private clients, with the workmen and the construction companies... It's a very hard and time-consuming job and not always a pleasant life."

P.: "We have now talked about the characteristic of continuity in your work from the early years until today. There is another thing I wanted to ask you, and that is your opinion of today's architectural scene. For example, a rather simplified definition of what is going on in the States is that there is a division between Greys and Whites, the so-called Greys with their vernacular origin and the Whites with their desire to regard themselves as the only legitimate heirs of the Modern Movement.

Do you feel that today the scene is more complex? For example, how does a figure like Frank Gehry, in the States, fit into that original division between Greys and Whites? And what role do you think your work plays on the international scene, or maybe first on the European scene? It is in opposition to the work of others or in dialogue with some? Let us take, for instance, O.M. Ungers: is there something in his work that you feel you share, and do you like the way in which he visualizes his ideas or, while respecting his work, do you like somebody else's more?"

H.: "I think you have to answer that question in several parts.

First, my work never intended to oppose anything, except, naturally, reactionary tendencies in general. However, I think some people do very valid work just out of reaction against something: one needs an equally strong countercurrent in order to provide a reaction to things. I want to say something in my work and, of course, what I say is a reaction, but not really to a particular current, to a person or a philosophy. To affirm one thing is automatically to deny another, but basically there exists the wish to put forward a new proposal, to create, and not react or recreate or modify or repeat. This is not my aim and it is not what interests me.

As far as groups, schools and individuals are concerned, I think you always have a certain specific situation. Of course, the situation shifts and changes, but you do have a specific situation. There is always a tendency to form groups or to consider various people as a group because they believe in something new which is not generally accepted by society or the authorities or social leaders. This sometimes brings together rather disparate ideas and disparate people who have chosen to unite in a group or who are considered by others as forming part of a group because they are in favour of something new and progressive. I think this is, for example, the case with the New York Five. Right from the outset each of these people had quite specific characteristics but on the New York scene at that moment they were the only people who, in spite of their individual distinctions, wanted to do something different, and they were seen as a group. But as soon as you express yourself more clearly, even within a group, you have to adjust your own position. It is not like a party where you have to be faithful to a dogma, and I don't think they had a dogma; now it's very clear that the group no longer exists, or it exists only in a more informal way, that is to say that they don't meet very often, and they have very different points of view, like Graves and Richard Meier, and even Eisenman who is following a very personal path.

The question you put about Frank Gehry, where he does fit in, in this or that group, I think one must consider the isolation that exists on the West Coast; there were the Greys and a few other people and he didn't fit in because he didn't have a precise role and also because he did not attempt to make contact with others. He stands apart but I really don't think he is a lonely or solitary figure. He is one of the facets, one of the different products of the architectural debate in the United States. He is a very good architect, very interesting. I feel very close to him because many of his ideas are similar to my own approach to architecture, in terms of design and of materials, and also in terms of his involvement in the arts. There are some very interesting similarities between us and we are also good friends. I am also good friend with Richard Meier, even though I would not follow certain of his architectural tendencies and I would not accept them for myself. What I like in his work is his sincerity and the authority with which he handles spatial problems, and the complexity and originality of his use of space. On the other hand, I think many of his decisions are based on a very personal dogma which results in widely diverse and heterogeneous solutions.

Ungers, and the European scene... It is very difficult because it means talking about everybody, but... as we are talking about the current trends in the States, which I have never looked at in this way, anyway...''

P.: ''Nor me. But this distinction between Whites and Greys, is something that has been written so often!''

H.: ''All these people, of course, are people of quality. Years ago we all tried to do new things, we did new things and each of us appreciated the quality and the intentions of the others. Some people have followed the line of their original intentions and have developed them, others less so. A few have produced works of great quality, others no. The moment of truth comes when you have the opportunity of doing something and you see how to express your beliefs and use your vocabulary. At times I think that the reality of how much was realized does not always correspond with the initial intentions and with the ideas of which they spoke. They did not reach the level of quality that one foresaw, for example, in the project. This is true for a number of people. Some architects now have the problem that there are opportunities to build. At the beginning we all had problems in getting commissions, in getting something built. Now times have changed: the interest in architecture is great and there are lots of clients looking for architects, and people prepared to promote competitions.

I remember that eight years after having achieved my diploma, I was happy to have a small shop to build: today, almost every student can get a shop to build. Look at Germany, Switzerland, or even Austria, and to some extent France... and, perhaps in a different way, America: there is a lot of initiative in architecture, in the organizing of competitions, for instance. There is a new generation of officials in local administration and planning departments and they have different ideas: they want architecture and they want architects. So, today people can no longer go around saying: 'I fight for true architecture and nobody lets me build!' Suddenly, it is different.

I think this is the situation in Italy. Of course, I know that in Italy it is not that simple to build and there are too many architects.''

P.: ''There are too many architects, but there is a lack of enterprise. If you turn to Paris, for example, but above all to Germany, Berlin and Frankfurt, they are two almost unique examples on today's scene that have invited architects from all over the world to build on a specific site.''

H.: ''Yes, but they are no longer unique! In Germany there are now many communities and towns that promote similar enterprises on an international scale. I think at this moment there are about ten competitions to which architectural celebrities have been invited to contribute designs, even in small towns such as Ulm, for instance. I think there is probably a good reservoir of talented people who could be encouraged in this way both in Italy and Austria. I don't know so much about Germany. I think what helped us here in Austria (and I think it also helped in Italy), is that architectural debate has always been very lively and active. And this isn't really the case in Germany, where for decades there was no architectural debate and architectural discussion was always prompted only by a competition... If, for example, there is a school to be built, you start thinking about architecture and how to approach it only when you start to design the school. As for me, I want first to have precise ideas about architecture, then I can start to consider the specific project. I don't think that architectural competitions are really very good ways to raise the level in architecture, but today they represent one of the concrete opportunities, especially for the younger generation, of realizing an idea, even if the younger generation anyway have many more possibilities of, for example, having their work published. In America you can find $ 18 books on 'The work of 4th year students at Cornell', for example. For a small cost today they publish their work, while we were lucky if in all our years of study we could get one little picture in a magazine. Now things are very different: if a young architect is good and is well taught, he will come to the surface because there are so many opportunities to make oneself known, to demonstrate one's ideas and one's quality.''

P.: ''However, all this publicity about the 'great ones', all this talk about the world 'stars' can influence a student and undermine the development of his personal language. When we started, I remember we didn't have these great examples constantly presented to us in magazines or other publications. There were a few 'masters' to whom we could refer, such as Le Corbusier or Louis Kahn, but we felt pretty free to invent a language of our own that did not have to confront an 'established' language, and that sincerely and brilliantly expressed the culture of the time. From this point of view, it is more difficult for a student today to develop any real originality. He is constantly bombarded by information which, in the long run, *is* conditioning.''

H.: ''On the other hand, the student today, as a result of a greater availability of information, also has the example of how someone, in this case an architect, can develop his own ideas, can grow and even become a 'star'. It should be made clear how difficult this is, and that is another question, but if a student assists at a lesson or a lecture illustrating the career of one of these personalities, and understands that they began with very little, even the smallest of projects, I think that he should be encouraged by that knowledge. One can say something new even through very small jobs and, like me, you can make a statement with a fourteen-square-metre candle shop; it too can become part of architectural history. So, it is no longer essential, as was thought in the past, to have a big commission in order to create something new.

This is typical of both the Viennese and the Italian scenes: you can clearly trace a line of progress and it is an encouraging sign, at least for gifted young people.

There is a risk however of giving a mistaken idea of the role of the architect because it should be made clear that only a very limited number come to the surface. The architect cannot be seen in general as an indipendent artist, free to realize his dreams and the ideas he has conceived. Professional engagements and commitments should be less individualistic and less restricted, and must be channelled towards more common ends. The relationship between theory and practice has changed and now a continuous and active presence is demanded of the architect, whether in the professional studio, in a public planning office or in the life of the city. It seems important to me that the young understand how vital and gratifying this task can be.

In the performance of a piece of music, there must be a large orchestra and, let us say, an excellent violinist or pianist... but not everybody has the necessary gifts to become director of the orchestra! I think in music this is obvious: one studies an instrument, and the moment arrives when one becomes aware of one's own potential. One could become a great soloist, for example, or play in a large philarmonic orchestra. There are many ways of finding one's own particular path. In music it's all clearer: one makes one's decisions, very often the right ones, but in architecture there is always in the background the single, isolated individual making his own choices without any contact with other people.

It is not certain that this path is the right one, whether for reasons of reliability or of objective reality. The director of an orchestra, to return to the musical metaphor, can even choose to conduct an orchestra that plays in the park to the sparrows. Anyway, there are certain hierarchies to be confronted and certain laws that each one lays down. And this is also the case when you study. I was very struck by an example mentioned to me just recently by someone at the Academy of Music, and this comes to my mind now because we have talked about music and about the choices one has to make. To be accepted by the Academy, the students must take an entrance exam and if they wish to study, let's say, the violin, they must play that instrument at the exam. If they make one mistake in playing the piece the professor asks them to come back only when they can play it perfectly because teaching can begin only when the technicalities are fully mastered.

This seems to me to be very relevant to architecture: one can begin to teach it only when the students have all the basic knowledge and you don't have to waste time on technical problems of construction or materials. Only then you can really confront the fundamental issues and have a dialogue with the student on another level, without having to go back to the beginning every time. To me this idea is interesting. But perhaps you would like to ask me something else."

P.: "No, indeed, I would like to add something about how I deal with the students at the beginning of the academic year. Usually I tell them the titles of a few books to read and only after they read them, can we start to talk, not only about matters for academic discussion but even about their admission to the course (they can choose between two or three teachers for the same subject). Only after they have read those books can I accept their registration for the course because by then we have at least a common basis of information from which to launch any later discussions.

I wanted to ask you... for example in Italy, and in particular with regard to experiments in furniture design, it seems to me that the picture we have of its development becomes clearer with succeeding generations, clearer than it is in architecture. I would like to say that when we started to design furniture (and nobody had taught us; it was a spontaneous choice), there was one person who was really a guru for us and still is, and that is Ettore Sottsass. It is not that he conditioned our development of ideas and new languages. His way of making furniture was a point of reference, a constant example. We began without being conditioned by his presence, but we had in him an example of how we could develop our own means of expression, even design. Then after the so-called 'radicals' (Archizoom, Superstudio, Ufo, myself and others), a new generation of designers grew up in Milan which included Mendini, Navone, Puppa and Raggi. There was, and there still is, a continuous tide flowing from Florence, from the Department of architecture, towards Milan. I am thinking now of a sort of 'third generation', people like Thun, Zanini, De Lucchi, who all studied in Florence with me and with Natalini, and after their graduation they went to Milan and developed a certain conceptual and also linguistic continuity.

This is in effect the situation in the field of experimental debate in furniture design, and design in general, but there are still more young people leaving Florence to face the national and international design scene. They have either just graduated or are graduating now. In Florence life is very lively among the students. They experiment with every media, even with making cakes! But the question is this: do you think we can find the same kind of continuity on the architectural scene in Italy? It seems to me that it is more difficult to recognize a current of evolution that is carrying with it new and original contributions to the debate. And this is true not only of Italy."

H.: "I think a continuity exists, whether in Italy or in Austria, in Vienna. I must admit however, to a slight reluctance to recognize the validity of the new generation because, although they are inventing many new and original languages, the most interesting results are often just a repetition, a variation on what has already been said. Of course, there might be cases or objects (like a chair), where the basic idea is there and all you can do is a variation. Maybe now is a moment when the fundamental things have already been said and one can only refine them and make other modifications. This remains to be seen. There is a continuity, but among the young I don't see any contrast, any concrete opposition to the ideas of the people before them. It's not here yet. I don't see it in Italy, Austria, Germany or America. Perhaps it exists in France, but probably because the architectural scene in France has deteriorated in the last twenty years to a state where almost nothing interesting was happening, so all that's new (and some interesting things are happening now) creates a great stir, but only because there was nothing of interest before. It is a question of quality: if we take Philippe Starck... compared to what was happening before in France, it seems that he has brought many new ideas, and he seems to be a very good man, but seen in an international context, he is not such an original phenomenon. He seems to me to be tied to a rather narrower view of reality. But you were talking about furniture..."

P.: "I was saying that in the field of experimental design in Italy, one can see evidence of this continuity. There is a new generation every five years or so which makes its own contribution. It is not particularly original, but it is something new. In the field of experimentation new voices unexpectedly appear, and little by little acquire maturity and begin to express themselves through their own particular language. I was trying to make a comparison between the evolution of a certain type of work, which started in the late '50s and early '60s, and still continues in the design of furniture and objects, and architecture, where it seems to me more difficult to identify a particular path, such as I have done for furniture design."

H.: "We must return to the reasons for this. One is that in Italy a privileged situation exists because, in terms of furniture design, many firms are open to experimentation, and there is a constant demand for new ideas, whether from the young or from already established designers. One drawback is perhpas that many things remain at the stage of the prototype and the function of these objects is often only that of being photographed and published. There are specialist magazines that publicize immediately any new idea in the field of design, all excellently produced and photographed by the best photographers in Italy. So, they get a lot of attention and a lot of publicity.

Designing furniture is basically a way of putting into practice your own architectural ideas, your own philosophy. A few things have a long life and are produced in large numbers, others not. But, at least in Italy, this doesn't seem to be the determining factor. That is to say, if one designs a chair, as long as it works it can be produced and sold. In Austria it is different, and also in Germany, Scandinavia and the United States.

In designing furniture, and in particular chairs and sofas, you ascribe to the piece a number of other intentions. This is an old story, at least in terms of the chair: just think of the Vassily chair by Breuer! It was not only an object on which to sit but also a sort of manifesto that put forward ideas about architecture and the city. I once wrote a short article on the chair and on the spatial concepts that it often embodies. I think that to design a chair is a great temptation for every architect; it is the ideal vehicle for transmitting symbolically your own ideas on fundamental issues in architecture. The specific characteristic of the chair as an object is that it can serve almost as a model for architecture. Not like a model that reproduces an architectural plan on a smaller scale than the real thing, but as an object that has its own dimensions and at the same time refers to something on a completely different scale. It is really this ambivalence that is so seductive for the architect because your relationship with the object is one to one and this is usually impossible. Recently, I too have often felt this temptation.

On the other hand, when you do get the job of designing a chair (as we did for the Town Hall in Perchtoldsdorf, and on other occasions)... this reveals maybe my more practical side... I realize that the chair must be comfortable, easy to produce, made of materials that are technologically correct, and so on. For me personally there is always this ambivalence. Even I have designed 'impossible' chairs, like the tiled chair at the Biennale in '72, but in that case it was clear that it was intended as a theorical statement and not as an object for use."

P.: "The chair is a strange object because it manages to engage in a series of different relationships. When it is used, the chair disappears because it's behind or underneath us. When you design it or you look at it, you consider above all its function, a function which, on the other hand, does not come into use at the moment in which one's relationship with it is established. It's a conceptual relationship that doesn't concern itself with the function of use, but with a different function. They are two distinct languages neatly separated and this is the ambiguity... interesting."

H.: "Certainly. As we have said, we are talking about a conscious choice: you can make a chair as a manifesto or you can stress instead its functionality, its practicality, the comfort, the price, and so on. There are chairs that, at first sight, appear to be uncomfortable: in reality, much attention has been given to the functional aspect... to the correct sitting position and the line of the vertebrae... For instance, there's a dining room chair by F.L. Wright whose rigidity and lack of comfort are carefully calculated elements in its design because during a meal the position of the body is different. The ideal thing would be to reconcile these two aspects, and there are in fact a few chairs that combine a conceptual quality with comfort."

P.: "We were talking about the possibility of making a comparison between the world of design and the world of architecture, at least within the sphere of experimentation, and about the fact that in design you can trace a kind of continuity while it is more difficult to do so in architecture. Maybe because there are not as many opportunities as in design. In fact, you said that in Italy it is quite easy to realize a design for a piece of furniture while in architecture it's much more difficult for the new generation to acquire the necessary discipline, to create a language and to make new contributions."

H.: "I have always thought, especially as far as Italy is concerned, that there are advantages and disadvantages. Confining ourselves to design is dangerous, for one reason because it is easier to be a designer than an architect. It doesn't take a long time to design a chair... a few meetings with the client... it is certainly an easier and more comfortable life. I do not want to be moralistic but I think the architectural debate must develop on a different scale and it seems to me important to discuss not only ideas and projects but also concrete realities. Both for the sake of the debate itself (certain things can only be discussed in terms of three-dimensional reality) and for the sake of the environment, because it is absurd to know the right answers and not to use them. While there are those who suffer from these problems, others, in their ivory towers, know how to resolve them, or say they know how to. I think this is part of one's job as an architect today. I too would prefer a more comfortable life, but it's no longer possible. It is a matter of necessity."

P.: "If we think about the Renaissance, or even more recent times, architects have always had to move around a lot in order to be able to build..."

H: "Sure. And it's not only a question of having the opportunity.

I think in a way the comparison between the present and the Renaissance is very apt. The problems are twofold... what I mean is that there was always someone who commissioned work (Michelangelo had his clients), but once the work had been entrusted to the architect or the artist, whose true value was appreciated, everything was left to them. Today the situation is much more complex and confused.

The other problem is that today the construction of a building requires much more time and energy: in the last century (and this is perhaps the reason for the present nostalgia for old buildings and the tendency to build according to the methods of the nineteenth or eighteenth century) a few drawings were sufficient to illustrate the basic character of the building, and the plans were mostly concerned with its actual architecture. Today the majority of the work has to do with things that one never sees like the interior structure, the air-conditioning and the pipes. And in meetings the architect must concern himself for ninety-eight per cent of the time with problems of this sort and only the remaining two per cent with actual architecture."

P.: "As you do today, in fact."

H.: "I and many others. It draws your energy away from your potential creativity, and away from the real issues, but this is part of the whole task, and, fortunately or unfortunately, architecture today – a building rather, not architecture – is a much more complex apparatus than a building of the early nineteenth century."

P.: "And the situation in Vienna? Studying your work carefully, it seems to me that certain aspects of it and of your visual language are linked in some way to your Viennese origins. In Vienna there are forms and linguistic elements that are perfectly integrated into the characteristics present in your work right from the beginning."

H.: "For instance?"

P.: "For instance, the use of the curve. Those curved lines that do not form a complete arch, or the decorative elements that you use not only internally but also in an external architectural context. It seems to me that there is a constant dialogue between your work and some of the architecture typical of Vienna, or of people who have worked there using their own language. It is not a historical inheritance... it is rather a source of inspiration, a special attention devoted to the presence of the past, that past that in Vienna is in constant dialogue with the present."

H.: "Yes, of course. There is always something to learn from the past. I have always looked around me in an effort to learn, and I think the relationship I have with the city's history is different from other people's. In Germany, for instance, they have never devoted much attention to the past, nor have they ever looked carefully at old buildings. They concern themselves with what is new, as do books and magazines, and hardly ever give any importance to the past, and to the fact that it may be relevant to the present.

But it is clear that, more or less consciously and intentionally, you learn from the past. Here in Vienna, we learn from all that we find around us, but also from the monuments we visit and from what we see in books. If, however, you mean... for instance you talked about the curve in my work... that I want to adopt the criteria of the decorative arts or Jugendstil..."

P.: "No... it's a visual world..."

H.: "To a certain extent it derives from Baroque, and this one can clearly detect in a few of my projects. The use of the curve suggests to me a precise plan, a well-defined space. It is a fraction of a circle that can easily be completed in your mind. I think I have used this in my architecture, especially for small objects, where I wanted to create two different scales. Using a curve in a confined space, you immediately open a much larger, imaginary space and you can gauge in a very clear, almost geometrical way, the dimensions of the entire space. That is to say, one uses fragments that one completes in one's mind.

Another reason for using the curve is that the curve has a different quality from the straight line and the lines used must take into account this difference in quality. There is an infinite number of connotations and symbols, male, female, and so on... that are not, however, introduced consciously. I do not believe that my architecture is based mainly on these elements, and I don't know if it is possible to be sure about these things.

The curve then, whether part of a circle or sinoidal, has a certain length that gives you not only a precise space but also different dimensions. For practical reasons, however, one has to break the curve into a polygon because otherwise the job of making the curve is very difficult for the workmen involved and very costly to produce. My method, and I often use this internally, is to construct a series of polygons inside a larger polygon, using only straight lines to create the curve. You find these elements in all my designs, which are in reality lots of fractions of a curve: the eye reads the angles as a continuous curve, visually turning the polygon into a cylinder.

We are having an interesting experience now with the museum in Frankfurt: for a variety of reason, because of the complex nature of the geometry and the calculations, we are using a computer to make the drawings. I had already done this a few times but I still think you can do it faster by hand... The computer we use now is not programmed, for example, to use the curve and reduces every curve to a polygon. So, on the drawings they become complex polygons that look like curves and it is difficult to recognize which are truly curves and which are polygons; in fact we often have to make a new drawing in order to clarify the matter. I'm sure very soon we shall have more precise programs, even covering the use of the curve but, as you see, it's really a world of straight lines!"

P.: "The Modern Movement... so Mies has won!"

H.: "Yes, in a way. And, of course, it is certainly easier now. In the past the problem was rather that of building with perfectly straight lines. The task of every bricklayer was that of avoiding the smallest deviation, or curve, and often the wall had to be pulled down and rebuilt. Today it's the opposite: it's easy to make an absolutely straight line and it's difficult to produce a curve, mainly because of the costs involved. But, above all, it is the theoretical approach that is different. For instance, in car manufacture lots of curves are used: every car-body consists only of three-dimensional curves. Only the racing cars have tried to return to straight lines, creating simplified lines and shapes. Making a motor car is an extremely complex business, even though they are mass-produced. It is only in architecture, in the construction methods of today, that the idea of the curve is still an exception. But in the Baroque period... certainly working methods were different, it was all manual. To build a colonnade whether in a straight line or curved, as Bernini did, it was enough to have a precise plan; the execution and the materials required were the same.

Today, this is no longer the case. There are a lot of other explanations we could discuss with reference to particular projects. But this has absolutely nothing to do with Art Nouveau. I mean, Art Nouveau also used the curve, sometimes for the very reasons I have just mentioned."

P.: "The question really relates to the fact that you use the curve in a different and very original way, and for me in fact it is difficult to find a specific example as a reference."

H.: "Well, for instance in the entrance of the school in Vienna (the school in the Kohlergasse, 1979) the curve is used and its intention is to invite, to welcome the children when they enter and leave the school: so, in this case, the curve is a very strong emotional and psychological element."

P.: "Indeed. They are forms used in a way that is... fragmented is not the right word... it is if behind this fragmentation there were an emotional participation. If I think, for example, of Portoghesi... the use of the curve to quote Borromini or someone..."

H.: "No. The way in which I use the curve is completely different from that of Portoghesi."

P.: "Because it is re-invented."

H.: "His way of using the curve is fine. There is thought behind it."

P.: "Yes, but your way is very different: it comes from the quality, conceptual and emotional, that you give to those surfaces, to those fragmented elements. You never use an entire circle or a semi-circle: rather it consists of a dialogue of different curved lines."

H.: "Well, there are some complete circles..."

P.: "Yes, but never on their own!"

H.: "A curve is used to achieve what F.L. Wright called 'the destruction of the box'. Certainly for Wright it was different and much more complex. How to destroy the box cheaply is the problem. Anyway the important point is the wish to destroy the box. What I mean is that one can use straight lines and cubic elements if there is a choice, a particular wish to do so. In architecture today, however, cubic elements are used in that way because they occur of their own accord, not because there is a particular intention to use them."

P.: "Then the curve is an element in your language that repeats itself in many different versions, as you have suggested: on a surface, in the 'breaking of the box', in the almost casual materialization of an object, like your table for Memphis, there are elements of the curve. Almost from a vacuum, it seems, the table was born. The lines enclose and embrace other situations and what remains, what one sees, is a piece of design."

H.: "There are other reasons... even in the work for Memphis.

First, there is a certain dialectic between hard and soft in my work and, naturally, the curved line stands for the soft and the straight line for the hard. In other cases this hard-soft dialectic is used without resorting to the curve but anyway, in a concise version, this is the case here.

Then there are elements that are suspended, almost hanging, which I frequently use. As with suspension bridges, where one creates an accentuated curve that is entirely natural."

P.: "The curve is also a method of distributing weight."

H. "Certainly. There are functional reasons for using these elements. We have often used them in museums: in rooms with a skylight it is necessary you put in a screen because otherwise the daylight would be too bright. This screen can be soft, a strip of material suspended between two points, and at first you do not see it from below because you perceive it as flat but at the same time the light is more diffused. In high rooms this is not so important, but in low rooms it is, because there would otherwise be dark corners.

Obviously, there are many other functional reasons for using the curve. Even the problems of viability are a demonstration of this: one cannot use only straight lines in the construction of roads or railways... And yet, for instance, for the great table we made for the Town Hall in Perchtoldsdorf, I chose the curve instead of the rectangle because it creates a situation in which everybody is almost equal. It's functional because everyone can see everyone else perfectly; if the table had been circular, the equality would have been absolute, while in this case the mayor had to have a slightly more privileged position than the other members of the council. On the other hand, we are talking about a democratic community, and in the interest of greater efficiency, it is only right that everybody can be seen and identified easily...

The functional motivation is clear both in a material and a psychological sense. For instance for the interiors of the Travel Agencies, and especially the smaller ones, we have used a combination of straight lines and curves which exploits the space in the most efficient way possible. When we put forward our proposal for the agencies, the objections to it related above all to the costs. It was assumed that it would have been cheaper to produce a standard linear system for use in all the branches, with identical fixtures and fittings. This argument seemed to be well-founded, but then we conducted a very careful study of the specific functional needs of this type of office and of the spaces available. They wanted to do fifty branches at that time, and they were all in buildings that were already in existence and that had no very distinctive features.

The study set out to ascertain the difficulties involved in installing prefabricated linear fittings in these spaces. It emerged in fact that the problems would have been considerable, and that space for at least three employees who should have contact with the public would have been lost, because the prefabricated fittings permitted the use of the space in only one preordained way. By gaining space for the personnel, one compensated amply for the higher costs entailed in using a design created specifically for each space."

Introduction

"There are ages in which the rational man and the intuitive man stand next to each other, the former fearing intuition, the latter despising abstraction. The intuitive man is as irrational as the rational one si unartistic. Both wish to dominate life: the rational man because he knows how to deal with his most important and urgent needs with the help of providence, prudence and regularity; the intuitive man because he does not see, being 'the supremely joyous hero' he is, those needs, and considers real life only the one transformed by fiction into appearance and beauty... While led by concepts and abstractions he only succeeds in driving back unhappiness, without being able himself to gain happiness from his abstractions. So, while he tries as much as possible not to give way to grief, the intuitive man on the contrary, placing himself at the centre of civilization, not only obtains from his perceptions a defence against evil, but also an enlightenment, a redemption, a serenity which constantly flow up to him. Undoubtedly he suffers more when he suffers: and he suffers more often because he doesn't learn by experience and falls again and again into the same well into which he had fallen already. He is as irrational in grief as he is in happiness: he cries out aloud but doesn't find consolation."
(F. Nietzsche, "On Truth and Untruth in Extramoral Sense", from The Philosophy of the Tragic Era of the Greeks and Writings 1870-73*).*

For few others as for Hollein could this citation appear more ambiguous and at the same time more precise. His ever-increasing role in the architectural debate of the last twenty years, together with his many professional successes and achievements, rewarded both in Europe and in the USA, might divert our attention from the real nature of his success.

Hollein has represented the character of the modern intellectual, facing the post-war situation and the final phase of reconstruction with all the doubts and dissatisfactions of one who meets with the heritage of the past and discovers that the 'official' culture had presented it in an ambiguous and superficial way. But he has also interpreted fully and precisely the role of the artist-architect as it was taking shape at the beginning of the sixties, coinciding with his first experimental works and "absolute" theorizations which led to a conceptual reconstruction and to new delimitations of the architect's field of operation.

Even nowadays Hollein interprets consciously this all-embracing role: working on projects does not prevent him from working in the field of art metaphor; so, even as a critic, he continues to express himself in different ways, including as the Austrian Commissioner for the visual arts section at the Biennale in Venice.

So he has not given up the complexity and ambiguity of his origins and of his Viennese education, a composite richness which has inspired a great part of the artistic and conceptual research of this century. The coexistence of these different aspects of his work does not detract at all from the quality of the apparently separate disciplines.

And this is the same specific coexistence typical of the different theorizations and "conceptual reconstructions of the universe" which took place almost everywhere, but mostly in Europe and more precisely in Austria and Italy, from the beginning of the sixties.

So, these origins, this education, which clearly embraces work conducted according to art metaphor and work carried out on buildings, make Hollein's role so different, and so fundamental in terms of contemporary architecture. The coexistence between these integrated activities, the discussion of those elements which take part in the making of a project: dreams, emotions, and sarcasm more often than joy, testify to the constant pluralism and the possibility of lively coexistence between elements that are apparently so different.

Hollein isn't reassuring. He doesn't comfort us but, on the contrary, he provides us with doubts, with deep abysses of anxiety, moments of infinite joy and of serene contemplation. All of this gives rise to overwhelming passion but also fierce criticisms, especially on the part of those who are obliged as a result to reconstruct an interpretative outline of the world which Hollein has rendered obsolete and perhaps ridiculous.

The Origins

The early training of Hollein, who attended technical schools and the Academy of Fine Arts, indicates coexistence of interests in the young student's life that were not contradictory: the atmosphere of the Viennese artistic debate at the end of the fifties, Friedensreich Hundertwasser and his "Manifesto on moulding against rationalism in Architecture"[1], "Architecture made by hand"[2] of Markus Prachensky and Arnulf Rainer, Konrad Wachsmann's strongly technological seminars which took place in Salzburg in 1956. These are all essential elements in Hollein's education which then developed further with his American experience and his masters degree from Berkeley University.

So Hollein, between the year 1956 in which he graduated in Vienna and the end of his studies in California, was able to involve himself in a cultural and physical context which proved very useful in integrating a European point of view formed by historical events and by an exceptionally well integrated network of architectural events. We have documents covering this period right from 1957, concerning Hollein's research and creative expression; at that time he said, "...architecture is not necessarily either a shelter or a monument. But one of its principal distinctions consists in the fact that a building is constructed or produced by whatever means are appropriate... A cave is not architecture, neither is a tree, whereas every sheet of steel erected in the desert is architecture. Architecture is a creation of space, created by men and for men."[3]

His writings on Schindler show Hollein not only as an experimental artist and a theorist but also a critic, a role which he maintained right up until his recent essays, among which is the one on Otto Wagner.[4] The 1964 essay on the Pueblos perfectly concludes the young Hollein's period of education and his "observation" of the historical and physical North-American scene.

The experience of the artist-architect who temporarily emigrates to the USA is common and almost traditional for many of the most sensitive Viennese architects since the beginning of the century. In particular, the interest in the North-American Indians' original buildings and in their physical context, has several points in common with the contemporary interest of certain land artists like Long, Heizer and Smithson, who were the first exponents of a method of making art which, together with "funk architecture", was strongly to influence the architectural debate of the time.

Back in Vienna, in his lecture "Return to Architecture" (1962), Hollein already proclaims the principal points of his philosophy: "Even if architecture is a pure creation of the spirit, it's nevertheless material. Architecture consists not only of ideas but also of forms; it is not only a vacuum but also a fullness."[5]

Hollein and Pichler's 1963 exhibition at the St. Stephan Gallery in Vienna is an opportunity to confirm the attacks against functionalist conformism, against that anonymous and banal building style that used the alibi that it was rationalistic architecture. Infact, he writes: "Nowadays, when advanced science and sophisticated technology put all possible means at our disposal, for the first time in the history of humanity we are able to build what we want in the way we want it; we create an architecture which is not defined by technique, but which makes use of it – a pure and absolute architecture."[6] The tone in which both Hollein and Pichler express themselves is decidedly arrogant; but their verbal aggression is part of the history of the manifestos with which those in the historical vanguard have announced their presence on the scene right from the beginning of the century. It is a verbal tone, a visual and conceptual provocation, which expresses itself in this first exhibition by means of drawings and photomontages, which, however, would be unfair to call "violent", because this strongly shaded provocative method of expression defined by slogans and metaphors, these breaking-point speeches which only after some years will become more colloquial, are typical of that period. This is a manifestation of what

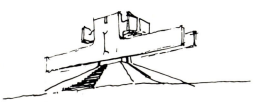

"Hollein Pichler Architektur" Exhibition, Vienna, 1963: architectural sketches.

was called at that time counter-culture: a progressive identification process of the emerging generation's experimental and ideological reality which was finding its ways of expression by means of a violent contraposition against a cultural establishment lacking in content and motivation. Successive criticisms, like the one by Ulrich Conrads[7], consider maybe unjustly Hollein's and Pichler's writings as a cynical manifesto for an architecture from which man is absent. More recently, in 1984, Michael Brix, having interpreted Pichler's mechanistic architecture as "full of sexual metaphors", defines as "arrogant" the concept of architecture expressed by Hollein: "Hollein... tries to justify his concept of architecture with man's elementary and ritual needs... he postulates an architecture which is at the same time subtle and brutal. Both warriors share the role of a Messiah, ascribed to the artist-builder as orderer of the world."[8]

These are also the premises of the rising "radical" dispute: a dispute characterized by unappealable statements and the purposeful selection of graphic provocative suggestions, using "irritating models of urban structures"[9]; but expressions like "...building is for man a fundamental need... building is ritual... architecture is sensual... form doesn't come from function... the great decision of man is to build a cube-shaped or a pyramidal structure..."[10] are maybe more a declaration of intent than élite provocative statements. It's a manifesto of intentions in architecture lacking in irony, the irony which on the contrary will be found in the following texts of "radical architecture" like "Destruction and Reappropriation of the Town", "The Shaven Gioconda" and "The Destruction of Objects" by Archizoom[11].

However Hollein introduces, at this point, the double "professional and artistic role (which) has always been somewhat complex and idiosyncratic", that is to say his constant "ambiguity", which will be, right from the beginning – as Frampton says[12] – a characteristic of his later work, indeed an element of play and enrichment of the various operating and planning dimensions. If Walter Pichler afterwards withdraws his own assertions, and his work consists nowadays of sculptures enclosed in cage-architectures, Hollein's work mantains intact, even enriched, the original elements of his poetic expression.

You may say, together with Michael Brix[13], that Hollein remains faithful to the theoretical propositions of this first exhibition. The recognition of this continuity and presence of all the original ingredients of Hollein's languages, is fundamental in distinguishing in this architect a complex personality of our time, who diplays his great mastery of architecture, interior design, scene-settings, interior decoration and works of design, as well as artistic installations, with the same rigour and intensity as ever; and the physical and conceptual scale of intervention does not condition, but on the contrary produces more precise and motivated statements.

In the above-mentioned 1963 exhibition, we find a group of works by Hollein, metal models which look like sculptures and which he calls "urban macro-structures", and drawings which show how they fit into a landscape. The zinc model, which is now in the Museum of the Twentieth Century in Vienna, is formed by a nucleus of vertical and horizontal tubes and cables, with houses spread out like wide wings, and tubes which anchor themselves to a pyramidal base leaning into a narrow valley which is meant to suggest, together with the base, the macro-structural dimensions of scale: a real city, enormous and complex, compact and exploded; an audacious creation rising from the landscape, but opposing and dominating it. It certainly is an object of enormous charm in which the multilateral, more than bilateral, symmetries, recall and cite the bilateral human symmetry. The form is at the same time precise and abstract: the technoid compactness nearly takes human forms but from the fusion of heterogeneous and almost contrasting figurations, emerges in the end also a piece of design, a refined macroform. This is how Hollein's "ambiguity" announces itself right from the beginning, by means of the numerous levels of reading to which this object-model-diagram allows itself to be submitted. The same thing happened on the other hand with the work of Pichler who, abandoning the practice of architecture, probably advances even more in this direction, producing over the years objects that are more and more formally refined and simplified, clearly quoting the contiguity between human and natural form, making architecture dependent on sculpture, even if organized according to

"Transformations", 1963: photomontages.

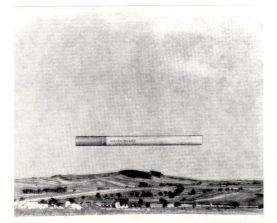

rigorous formal structures. On the contrary, Hollein's ambivalence is all contained in the project: the human forms are implied or, if quoted, elements of a statement, and significant structures of an archetypal original space which represents statements which are also archetypal.

The macrostructural dimension of these expressions ("A building which emanates power" is the title of one of his projects) introduces yet further valences. Quotations of the origins of the history of architecture, of a mythical past like that of the Maya's, together with symbologies of the same strength, which also represent power and strength, like in the later photomontages of aircraft-carriers taken as models of totally self-sufficient cities. In this case the modern technologies express power but, at the same time, set man free from need and dependence. It is an absolute architecture, building with pride the picture of a man who can finally devote himself to thought and emotion. So, as the Maya monument represents mythical original cultures, the aircraft-carrier in a landscape solves the problems of existence, emancipates man and moves him towards a time for thought and sensual creative pleasure. If there is really anything missing in this panorama, it is violence: it's wrong to think of technology, in this case represented by an aircraft-carrier, as an instrument of war. You acknowledge the aircraft-carrier's efficiency, its technological perfection, a technology which serves man's welfare, allowing him to favour reason and intuition. Perhaps for the first time in history he would not have to waste time organizing himself in order to survive, but on the contrary improve himself and produce new art and culture of great maturity.

Other projects shown in this exhibition are also related to these monumental dimensions: primitive and geomorphic drawings and models which evoke with greater precision the origins of architecture, the charm and the formal and conceptual neatness of the first structural and spatial organizations – also quoted and praised by Hollein in the "Pueblos"[14] article – where the rite of life and

"Transformations", 1963: photomontages.

22

ceremony coexist and are recognized as absolute and fundamental architectural forms. As Loos said, the monument and the sepulchre show clearly that architecture belongs to art: they are the clearest instruments of connection between different disciplines which even our times persist in keeping separate. In Holleins' artistic installations we find a planning strategy which doesn't disturb but which on the contrary enriches his conceptual communication.

The presence of death, not as a deterrent or a threat for those who live but as an element of life, an ingredient, a part of the experience of life itself, can be seen in Hollein, in Pichler, and in many Viennese artists of his time, as well as in architects who have come before him, from Hoffmann to Loos to Wagner. If Loos doesn't allow houses to provide artistic opportunities and qualifications of an artistic nature, Hollein instead tries to demonstrate the opposite with his projects, and not only with these early ones.

The projects which after 1963 go under the name of "Transformations" certainly represent a real continuation, specification and amplification of those subjects which had been synthetically suggested by means of texts and images at the nächts St. Stephan Gallery in Vienna: no longer models or drawings, but photomontages, contemporary with a planning activity expressed by means of more classical methodologies. The use of photomontage is more spectacular, and in accordance with a more definite simulation of reality. The decision to introduce at this period photomontage as a planning element is a way of avoiding architecture's long-term schedules, even those related to building, and to find the project already printed in a review. The projects-photomontages of the London Archigram are contemporary with these proposals, while the photomontages of Archizoom and Superstudio in Florence come just a bit later. The use of this technique is influenced also by the conditions of the artistic research of that time. The origins of pop art and the rising role of advertising supergraphics, of cartoons and photography in the art field render this choice virtually compulsory, adding unexpected valences to the usual methodologies of communication of the project. So the possibilities of communication amplify themselves beyond the limits of simulation of a drawing or model, but are in accordance with reality itself, which

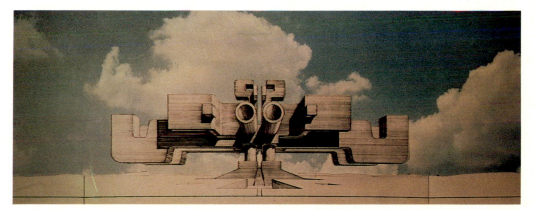

Top: "City", 1963, drawing. Bottom: "Schattenberg Castle", 1963, photomontage.

is in turn reproduced by photography. As a good part of the communication of architecture's debate was therefore produced through reviews, it's only too clear that the simulation of photomontage provided the architect with a good deal of help: even with no clients, the impossibility or at least the difficulty of building was overcome, while it began to be possible to "talk" about architecture by means of architecture. Photomontage also provides opportunities for spectactular proposals: another element which is not present in architecture's language and debate, another valence which is not available to the young architect who, at the beginning of his career, can rely only on very few assignments.

Hollein himself says that these proposals don't need to be explained, because for example the very same spectacular comparison between the Enterprise and a rural landscape introduces "...a multitude of meanings. There are many layers of a different significance as one's mind penetrates them, provoking a stream as associations."[15] The subjects, besides the Enterprise, are for example a railroad coach used as a monument, a car's spark plug presented as a vertical city, a turbine in Manhattan's Wall Street area, the Rolls Royce Skyscraper, etc.[16] Therefore these works also have a provocative component: they are industrial production objects which assume a different scale and a different conceptual role, and at the same time they reveal a careless aesthetic quality and the role of a technology which was not yet present in the production of architecture.

Now we should quote Buckminster Fuller, not for his philosophical theories but for his precise suggestions, which he introduced before the war, regarding the use of advanced technology in the construction of ships and aeroplanes: an invaluable asset which was foolishly ignored by architecture. But in Hollein's Transformations, the metaphysical elements of these transpositions seem also to quote Magritte, and at the same time to be synchronized with Claes Oldenburg's poetic expression. These are elements which are common to an architectural experimental activity, to the pop art's progressive success of this period and to many graphic ideas which one can find in manifestos, in books, in records, and in the reviews of the young generation of that time. So if the linguistical metaphor of these transformations helps us to understand the theories regarding the model of the city, Hollein on the other hand says that "today's architecture can really express our present time only if it doesn't turn against technique, but instead makes use of it, not only as an object of pure utility but also in such a way that it may show its plastic, dynamic, expressive, formal and emotional power. The objectiveness of the engineering constructions is a false myth, they are subjective and often sentimental"[17]. Nevertheless they represent proposals of self-sufficient cities, whose perfect technology makes them axiomatic monuments of which one celebrates the coincidence between aesthetic and formal perfection, a celebration which goes on pushing foward the limits of intervention to the minimum scale of the capsule, like the Intensive Box and the Helm-Kleiner Raum of Walter Pichler.

Isozaki interprets the Rolls Royce grid as "...a shrine or a sacrifice. Whichever it is, it shows the complete stationary state as a monument. The complete stationary state, the maximum value of entropy, the state of passionate death, is celebrated"[18]. This can be misleading regarding the obsession of death present and theorized in Hollein's work by Isozaki himself. Even if one can't deny the existence of this component, not only in Hollein but also in many contemporary artists of the period, the fact that in the St. Stephan exhibition, together with the plastic models and the drawings, there are launching pads for space vehicles, oil-drilling platforms, aircraft-carriers, subterraneous missile bases and anti-aircraft towers which still exist in the centre of Vienna, shown as references, doesn't depend on the war-death connection, which would be too easy to explain. It's more correct to point out that technologies, in this century more than in others, are stimulated towards development and used at first always and only for military purposes. But this is only the perverse logic which makes technique improve under the spur of the production of arms. Hollein interprets the perfection, the self-sufficiency, the beauty of an object which is technically perfect. On the contrary, these technologies are undoubtedly claimed not for man's death but for life.

Another method which is complementary and integral to the description of Hollein's first works, and the fact that they already contain many elements of his

"Hollein Pichler Architektur" Exhibition, Vienna, 1963: "Valley City".

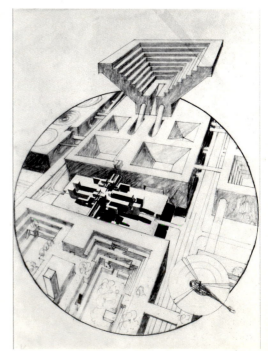

later developments, is to examine his writings covering the period between the end of his training and the beginning of his planning proposals. These writings form, however, the most important part of his activity as a critic because even though he was on Bau's editorial staff between 1965 and 1970, his theoretical works seem to have slowed down, or rather seem to have transformed themselves into projects. However, Hollein's activity as writer-critic doesn't stop. It still goes on nowadays, but Hollein transfers into projects most of his critical observations. If his first writings are published only later on in "protokolle 66", as a student in Chicago in 1957 he introduces the first elements of his theory and poetic expression. His 1960 degree thesis at Berkeley serves as the subject for a lecture which he will later publish and integrate with more analytical observations on Schindler's work and even later, in 1964, also on the Pueblos.

Hollein examines Schindler[19] in connection with his role, which at the time was unknown, as a European architect working in California, even as the anticipator of some of Le Corbusier's theories in his use of structural frames which, unlike the ones of Terragni, develop their function mainly in interiors. Having analysed Schindler's experience with Wright, Hollein examines the language and motivations of his activity as an independent architect: the modularity in the choice and inventions of private spaces goes as far as the planning of the smallest details of interior decoration, "even if many works of Schindler recall the Secession and his training with Otto Wagner, these are rather superficial influences, while the most important ones have come from Loos, Wright and the American landscape"[20].

The year 1963 saw the publication of the catalogue of the 'Hollein Pichler Architektur' exhibition, a publication containing, alternately in words and images, the complex articulations of finished projects and citations, through the use of images, of constructions and machines used as reference points. This play on the relationships between theoretical writing, projects and reference-images is important to understand that the project – more often than not never carried out other than in model form – is not sufficient to communicate the entire range of intentions; thus, the project is accompanied by theoretical-critical writings and by an exemplification of what the real project might look like. The next step towards the integration of these elements was photomontage. This technique was common to many exponents of the architectural avant-garde of those years; already, in 1960, Archigram published 'Archigram One', while it was not until 1969-70 that Archizoom and Superstudio introduced the elements of what were to become their theorizations on Non-Stop City and The Continuous Monument.

However, the first complete, organic definition of Hollein's chosen themes dealing with architecture and the city appears in 'Stadte – Brennpunkte des Lebens' (Cities – crucial points of life): "We want space without confines, created by man. We want the total city, which dominates the landscape"[21]. Already, in his 1962 lecture entitled 'Return to Architecture' which was given in Vienna, in the gallery which, a year later, was to host the 'Hollein Pichler' show, Hollein both proclaimed and pursued an architectural expression which would be technoid and, at the same time, archaicising, freed from the dominion of functionalist conformism, from false rationality and pseudo-aesthetics; an architectural expression which would take on, once again, irrational meanings; all those emotional values which had hitherto been outlawed. Thus emerges an affirmation of the architect as artist, acting on the basis of his intuitions, taking architecture back to its collective and mythological validity. "Architecture... constructed in infinite space... manifesting the spiritual force of man, material expression of his destiny, of his life"[22].

The tone of invective adopted, a veritable harangue in favour of the liberation of architecture from the lethargy of imitation, reaches the level of a manifesto on absolute architecture, in the same way in which the writings of Loos and of Le Corbusier could have been taken as manifestos: in their content, in the demand for a role for the architect as artist-builder, acting intuitively, for architecture which, through him, regains its magical roles of ambiguous irrationality. Here, Hollein reaches the most complete definition of his theory and ideology, which was later to be so effectively visualized in the St. Stephan Gallery.

But the description of Hollein's chosen problematics – this time structured

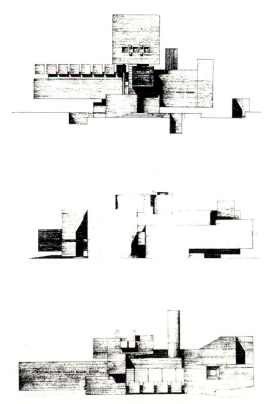

Architectural sketches, 1963.

with even greater maturity – is to be found in 'Stadte-Brennpunkte des Lebens'. Here, theoretical propositions are counterposed with the description of the aircraft-carrier as city: the *Enterprise* as the city of our time – a symptomatic choice, a didactic exemplification of the concepts he had already expressed with words and images, and were now presented in a more implicit and certainly more provocative way. The article itself is in fact divided into two parts: the first theoretical, with illustrations, and the second exemplificatory, with accurate descriptions of the workings and the various aspects of the aircraft-carrier as Ideal City.

"Pueblos", published in 1964, continues this process of exemplification of 'Ideal Cities': the compact and complex articulations of Indian villages in the southern United States are analysed, not in terms of how they function (although this is also analysed) but rather, from the viewpoint of their complex, magical integration of daily life and magical ritual. "Pueblos" can be read as a completion of the discussion already begun in the earlier article dealing with this subject in "der aufbau". The *Enterprise* had been used as a way of exalting the perfection of the machine, the myth of absolute functional perfection which, for the architecture of the time, was unattainable. "Pueblos" underlines how the function of architecture and the organisms which it creates – cities – is the representation of the whole complex of human activity, which assuredly, cannot be reduced to pure functions and rational structurings, but indeed exalts the magical and ritualistic aspects which become focal points, giving the organization its importance and structure. "...the pueblos are of the very greatest significance in today's planning and architecture... they are compact urban zones, integrated expressions in their form and content, of a community in which the social and religious structure is highly developed and complex, and the autonomy of the culture is architectonically structured in plastic-spatial compositions of unusual and interrelated articulation... the absence of external influences makes the architecture a pure example of the translation of a culture, in a way which, perhaps, exists nowhere else on earth. Therefore, they are part of an exemplary architectonic evolution"[22].

In "Zukunft der Architektur" (The Future of Architecture), published in 1965, Hollein continues his personal theorization and makes clear his thinking on the concept of the City and Architecture, illustrating it with works by himself and by Pichler, and with works by architects of the 1930s, such as Tchernikov, and visionary sketches of cities from Rietveld to Wright: "...the immense technological constructions which are necessary to make the city function possess a latent monumentality, and the architect's task is to uncover this, and to suscitate it"[23].

Still in 1965, "Technik" can be taken as the concluding article of Hollein's analytical examination of the City and Architecture, which had begun with his early theoretical propositions and had matured in this last series of essays, in which his thinking continued to be confirmed and to devote itself to technology and ideologies of the present, as well as to history and to the most lively architectural debate of the past, from the early propositions for cities of the future, from Rietveld onwards, or indeed, from Eiffel. In "Technik", Hollein concerns himself not only with flak towers, power stations, aircraft-carriers, and other primary forms of twentieth-century technology, but also with the house on the River Loue, by Ledoux, and with Le Corbusier's Villa Shodahn, which he reads as originary architectonic compositions, related, in the case of Ledoux, to the river, and in that of Le Corbusier, to light. Perhaps, as Brix notes, "Hollein was obsessed at that time with the idea of being able to make the conquests of technology usable in building, and to do so following Le Corbusier's example, respecting not only practical criteria but also artistic ones"[24]. It seems instead that these statements may be taken as intentional ones relating to Hollein's work which began to be realized in this period. His first realizations point out the necessity of a connection with experiences of the past in order to create a marriage between theory and practice, and also to supply an interpretation of his first accomplished works, which, even if small in scale, still contain intact the whole metaphor of the theory of the city. In real scale, they are still models representing more complex theories in the coincidence of an architecture which is at the same time a function, a piece of design and a manifesto.

"Transformations", 1963: photomontages.

The Beginnings

In the early Sixties, together with his ample theoretical and experimental production, Hollein starts to verify in his planning activity those concepts expressed until then by means of words and images. In the 1963-64 project for the Experimental Theatre of the Washington University in St. Louis (USA) he applies ideas of a very strong internal flexibility, adapting the structure to the most diverse scenic requirements. His use of volume is a faithful exemplification, a quotation-application of the megastructural proposals presented by means of drawings and images at the Nächst St. Stephan Gallery.

An actual transition point, as far as planning is concerned, between the theoretical phase and the first realizations in a real context is represented by the Retti Candle Shop. With this work (1964-65) Hollein's main interest and activity seems to shift from his visions of urban structures towards solutions not only more realizable but apparently also more "isolated" and individualistic, exquisitely elegant and technically perfect. Actually the Retti, which in 1966 won the

Retti Candle Shop, 1964-65: façade.

Reynolds Award for the use of aluminum, confirms instead of opposing the theoretical statements expressed until then by Hollein. The candle shop with its compact aluminum façade fits into the Kohlmarkt context like a self-sufficient shell-capsule which puts into practice the ideas of photomontage: a powerful gesture, a little presumptuous perhaps, but expressed with surprising authority through the skillful use of techniques, materials and refreshing formal originality.

In the candle shop's tiny space (16 sq. m.) Hollein creates two rooms: the first one characterized by a rombic plan by which one reaches the second square one. Continuity is obtained by the use of the same materials, especially the polished aluminum, the mirrors and the floor. The shop is a spatial enclosure, announced externally only by slits, which is given logic and self-sufficiency by its interior conceptual discipline. Even the compact steel slab at the front, which is interrupted only by the small niches at the sides of the entrance, connects itself with no interruption to the internal spatial enclosure. The narrow portal widens at the top into a large window which lets in natural light, while allowing a view from the outside of the great central lamp. Various meanings and symbols have been attributed to the Retti's façade, particularly to its portal (a burning candle, a "technological" column which holds a dialogue with the columns and the pilaster strips of the building in which the Retti is set), and this is another proof of the success of the use of photomontage in real scale. The successful combination of materials and concepts and the consequent formalizations prove the double ambiguous role which Hollein envisages for architecture: a confident and spectacular use of technology, intentions and results which are monumental, ritual, magical and exciting. The vertigo goes on in the first room which is a temple, a ceremonial site, a conceptual, emotional and physical focus. The flat external façade intentionally contrasts with the rich decoration of the historical building of which it forms a part. The two side reliefs are clefts introducing the interior. The deeper cleft is the entrance which reveals itself negatively, by subtraction; the niches inside become

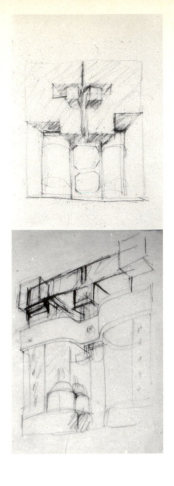

Retti Candle Shop, Vienna, 1964-65: preliminary sketches, interior and façade.

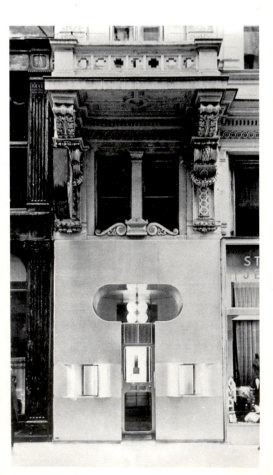

reliquary elements which participate in the ceremonial play.

The Christa Metek boutique and the project for the Svoboda showroom limit themselves to a contemporary development of the shop-sign and the façade.

As for Svoboda, the supergraphics of the name appear at one and the same time as the shop-window, the entrance and the façade; in the Christa Metek boutique "the mark is the façade"[26] and everything is defined by the geometrical functionality of the entrance in which even the air-conditioning system is set. Inside, the geometry of the modular fibreglass panels gives complete flexibility to the enclosure which is at the same time a showroom, a shop-window and a sales-room.

The Richard L. Feigen Gallery in New York, begun in 1967 and finished in 1969, confirms Hollein's already mature international reputation established by the Retti. It's a typical New York townhouse adapted inside as an art gallery on different levels which visually communicate with each other. The façade, on the outside geometrically redesigned and characterized by an almost Loosian purity, draws one's attention to the monumental entrance by means of a very simple, even if complex, opening underlined by a very high, double chrome-plated tube

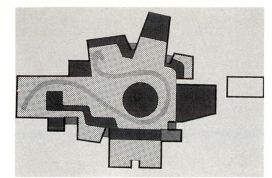

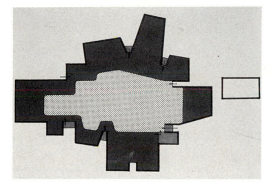

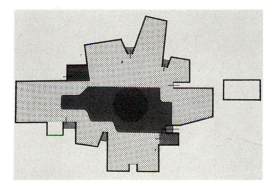

Experimental Theatre for the Washington University, St. Louis (USA), 1963-64: flexible staging and sketches for the exterior.

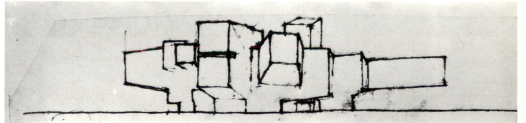

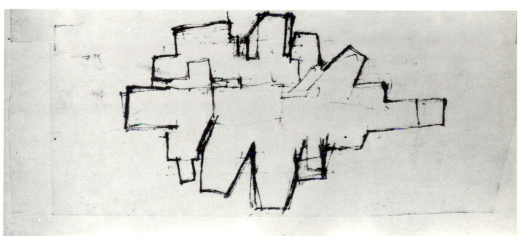

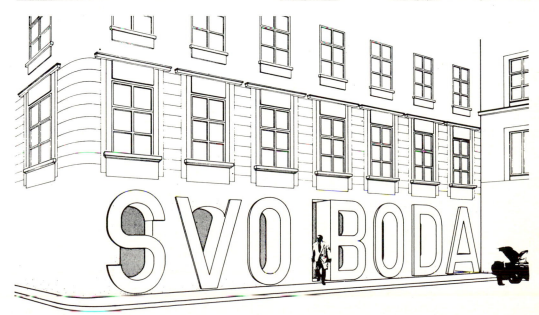

"SVOBODA" project, Vienna, 1966: façade.

which already introduces sensual themes like the ones of the double balcony inside. However, the organization of the interiors is excellent, quite magical in its alternate sequences of spatial perceptions. The lighting system not only gives continuity to this interpretation, but also underlines the various elements of technological equipment with which the gallery is provided. In an important review[27] Frampton emphasizes the building's elegance, the quality of the equipment and of the spatial organization, but at the same time he complains about the excessive integration and the spatial and metaphysical involvement. It seems that he disapproves of the richness in an art gallery which should be neutral, without interfering with the work of art. This is an old question in which many have become involved and which anyway has little validity. It's difficult to understand why the levels of interpretation of space shouldn't be numerous, the scales and the intentions different and integrated, till the utmost limit of extreme ambiguity. The visitor personally senses and organizes these different levels. In this sense Hollein educates people to perceive, to feel emotion, to enjoy a lost equilibrium slowly re-established on new parameters. Frampton also seem to complain about the fact that this technical exercise of great quality doesn't give rise to great talent and subjects itself by serving a futile purpose. But this contradicts what has been said before: the building is bare, it proceeds by subtraction, but if one complains about the building being "strong", too strong for the work of art, one doesn't understand why it should have instantly lost power in terms of man's mind and perception. The magic of the dense presences, of the altar in the ritual site, works also by means of dense absences: we should be prepared to fill our own absences, especially when the author supplies us with the reading method. So the Feigen Gallery is concerned with didactics and the perception of architecture. The key to it is less apparent, but not less important; perhaps for this reason, it is even more important. Frampton's further negative observation, which seems to complain about a decay of the optimum tension between creation and proposition in the Feigen Gallery because of the progressive professional commitments concerning work for the rich[28], is contraposed by Hollein who, foreseeing criticisms of this kind, produces two projects which were started in the same year: the experimental space for the St. Louis City Art Museum, and the first project for the

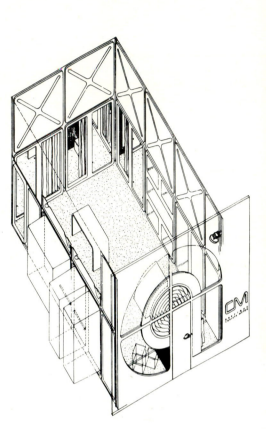

"CM" Boutique, Vienna, 1966-67: axonometric and façade.
Right: Richard L. Feigen & Co. Gallery, New York City, 1967-69: handrail.

Vienna Savings Bank at Florisdorf.

Both projects had in common a building partly below ground level (subterranean in the case of the St. Louis project), in which the extension suggested is developed mainly above the pre-existing building in order to modify and integrate spaces which require precise periods of utilization, like the St. Louis Museum, but also the Savings Bank in Vienna, both being for public use. In the St. Louis Museum the equipped area connects itself to the park, thus becoming a feature of life even during the day, while on the other hand the structure of the building is used

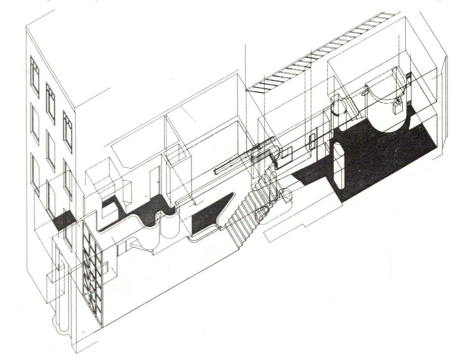

Richard L. Feigen & Co. Gallery, New York City, 1967-69: view towards the entrance from the gallery, second floor (page 32, top); interior, first floor (page 32, bottom); axonometric (right); upside of the entrance (bottom left); general view (bottom right).

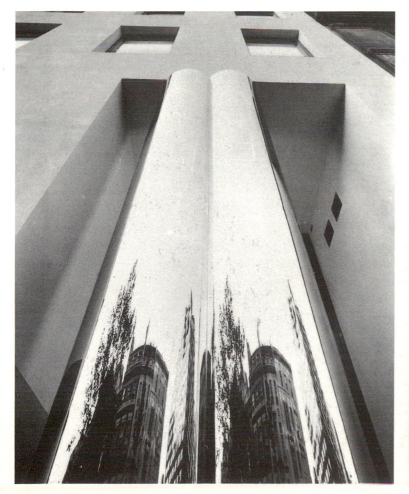

mainly at night. The Florisdorf building has a roof which is at the same time a
street and a lawn: also in this case there is an obvious wish to integrate the site
with the surroundings in a complex, total and absolute way. So the elements
tending towards a human scale of production and of spatial utilization are
exalted, theories are exemplified: the architectural "machine" can and has to
work on different levels with great efficiency. The Florisdorf building also provides a space to be used for recreation in the urban environment, while at the
same time "technical" activities may go on below. The idea of the "walk-on building", of the building reconquered for collective use and reconnected to its
surroundings, will remain an unchanging element of Hans Hollein's work, even
for his future realizations. The variation of levels and the creation of resting
places provide the building with a new, unusual valence, an emotional and intuitive way into that kind of architecture which always runs the risk of preferring
geometry and reason, and which instead in these circumstances points out
Hollein's wish for a co-existence between diverse ingredients. This is a constant

Savings Bank of the City of Vienna at Florisdorf, project I, 1966-68: axonometric.

point of reference in Hollein's projects and also in his "intentions" in architecture, which will be totally realized in the Monchengladbach Museum, where matter and artifice, nature and architecture will converse, becoming integrated but also differing one from the other.

Experimental Gallery, City Art Museum, St. Louis (USA), 1966, sketch for the exterior, model and axonometric.

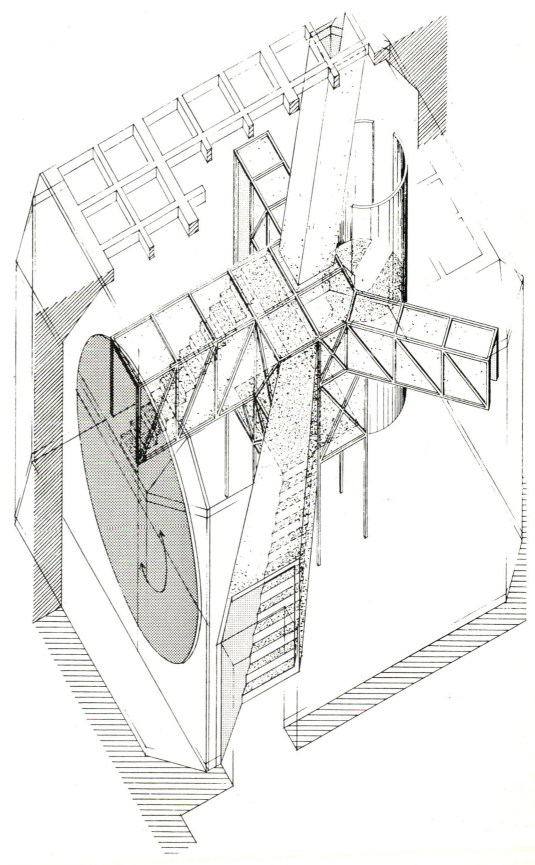

Alles ist Architektur

With the first exhibitions, projects and theoretical writings of Hans Hollein's early years come also his first realizations, which are in perfect accordance with his theory of architecture. With "Alles ist Architektur" [28 bis] Hollein amplifies and defines his thoughts with inequivocally clear statements and exemplifications. In this, as in previous writings, and also successive ones, contemporary with his collaboration with the Bau review (1965-70), Hollein slowly develops his original view that "everything is architecture": "The kernel of this notion is the talk of architecture as an 'art of space' which had become increasingly popular in the fifties and sixties, and which went back to nineteenth-century preoccupations with developing a physical and psychological description of it. It was taken up by a number of art historians before it became of great interest to artists: though Hollein's hero Schindler was well aware of it, and talked about architecture as the art of space more consciously and articulately than most of his contemporaries" [28 tris]. The sixties witnessed the debate on this matter, this way of considering architecture, which developed in the direction of more general considerations regarding the physical environment, the nature and intervention of man, and the quality and differentiation of these physical transformations[29].

Rykwert[30] calls this period a "blitzkrieg", but if it was so, it was because of the general re-examination brought about by the culture of the young by means of an often ferocious criticism of the official culture. Hollein, like Archizoom and Superstudio in Florence, and like other members of radical architecture, takes part in this counter-culture, and what's more, he develops in architecture a fundamental role of progressive thematic and idelogical maturity. "Alles ist Architektur" represents the beginnings of this "final" theoretical phase, which at this point is not any more part of a counter-culture but reaches the position of a clear articulation of a culture "against", what is nowadays our own culture. To prove that "everything is architecture", Hollein shows, by means of audiovisual aids and videotapes, how it is possible to alter one's own space and environment, changing and extending one's perception of it even in the smallest ways, by the use of a gas cannister for instance. Examples and quotations are cited of pop artists such as Oldenberg and Christo, painters like Magritte, artists like Duchamp, Lissitzky, Niki de Saint Phalle, Hudertwasser, and even others like Norman Mailer, Tom Wesselman, Beuys, Frei Otto, Wotruba. "Man creates artificial conditions. This is architecture... Architecture is a way of communicating... For thousands of years the transformation and the artificial delimitation of the environment, as well as a protection against the climate, were offered mainly by means of buildings", but "man has a brain. His senses are the basis of his perception of the environment... they are the medium for architecture... only in a few experiments has one tried to define the environment with non-physical means... Having nowadays a great number of possibilities, compared with the very few of the past, physical architecture can concern itself intensely with the quality of space and with the satisfaction of psychological and emotional needs: a quite different situation to the mere building activity which it had become. So space will acquire a more conscious awareness of tactile, optical and acoustic qualities, will provide information and will offer both conceptual and emotional pleasure" [31]. In this writing Hollein discusses the absolute liberty of reference and control over spatial conditions. The process of maximum reduction is opposed by Hollein through the use of the maximum amplification of emotions and the experimental possibilities of expressiveness.

The year 1968 saw the peak of maturity of all those elements which had appeared in the previous years and which formed the fundamental structure of the rising culture of that period, and this not only in regard to Hollein's architectural activity. 1968 sees at the same time the maturity and the death of these generalized theories which soon afterwards were to become split into specialist subcategories of research and more specific realizations. The "Austriennial", the

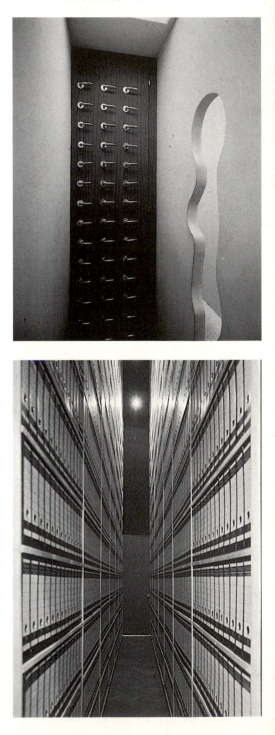

"Austriennale", Milan, 1968.

setting up for the 1968 Triennal, is Hollein's occasion to verify in real scale the complex, even if simple, theories of "Alles ist Architektur", putting at the visitor's disposal those instruments which may stimulate his sensory perception and the physical and psychic aspects of this process. Inside an apparently endless series of corridors closed by doors at both ends, the visitor was subjected to sensory impressions created by snowstorms, overcrowding, and frustration caused by disorientation. The prize offered at the end of this amusement park of perceptions and sensations consisted of a pair of rigid red and white glasses (the colours of Austria) with fixed bars. The purpose was to oblige the visitor to concentrate on an "Austrian" vision, and not only of the pavilion itself.

"This exhibition operates through physical means (through touch, hearing, smell and acoustics) but also through psychological ones. Here, not only the Great Number is represented, but also the single individual. The exhibition is individual but is offered to the people at large. On the one hand it is precise in its use of technique, but on the other it is a place of improvisation; it is clear and direct, but it also has something of Kafka and Freud. It's ambivalent, full of contradictions, like life, and being so, it's totally Austrian"[32]. The 1968 Milanese contribution to the Triennial is for Hollein a successful synthesis of elements, ingredients which, through successive specializations, will form the complex of his work: design, exhibition setting, artistic installation, architecture and theory are synthesized in this realization. It's an opportunity to say everything at the same time, to draw together in one single work the elements of one's own poetic expression and theory, and this coincides with the need to treat everything separately. Each phase of the project indicates its own definition: from now on it will be possible to subdivide Hollein's work into the above categories. Not only for the critic's convenience, but also because these sub-categories add elements of analysis, enriching the study of a complex work where everything is often so integrated that even the author is often unaware of certain connections. If in the past in various professional engagements Hollein had specialized in particular projects, only from the Austriennial onwards did this become a self-conscious need. For example, for the Austriennial some spectacles were produced, but already other pieces of design had been planned and realized, like the Roto-Desk for the Herman Miller in 1966, the Schwarzenberg Table in 1967, contemporary with the study for the Retti Exhibition system, a modular room, mountable and dismountable, reduceable and extendible and made of fibreglass. The basic element consists of a quarter of a semi-cube defined by the convergence of three axes and three surfaces: a most remarkable technological invention, and another way of verifying

"Austriennale", Milan, 1968.

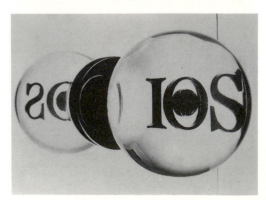

Top left: "Roto-Desk Miller", steel and formica turntable, 1966. Top right: "Roto-Desk with glass", 1968.
Bottom: Stand Retti I, Vienna, 1969.
Bottom: IOS Handles, 1969.

how Hollein can show in any scale the potentially endless possibilities of the variation of an elementary form. His design work began to specialize even more: so the 1969 IOS handle is also a sign, while the "Z" sign[33] is also a lamp. The Austriennial is also a preparation for Selection 66 (1965-66), Unipap (1967) and the Eternit Exhibition (1969). In Selection 66, together with the scene-setter, the critic intervenes and the classic representatives of modern furniture design (from Le Corbusier to Scarpa and Breuer) are re-visited with care in their unusual collocation by means of simple technical expedients. Everything is brought together, the consumer is once more stimulated towards particular perceptions, in exemplificative and demonumentalized terms.

The exhibition setting for Eternit is the occasion to show the modular tube in the most varied scales: from the pyramidal building reminiscent of Christo to the construction of an existenz-minimum inside a single tube. The Austriennial is also a very brillant project, a piece of architecture in an interior, an artistic installation, a faultless strategy of apparently unapproachable elements.

The Olivetti "Interface-Space" in Amsterdam dates from the same year. These were spaces which, according to the clients, had to overcome the traditional concept of the show-room, stimulating instead the public to test and experiment the objects on sale with the help of a specialist staff. Hollein's various and different proposals underline precisely this aspect, overlooking the formal consequences: the characteristics of sequence, of filing, of architectural organization inside architecture are, however, present, even if subjected to particular functions.

If the Svoboda Offices (1969) still answer to technical-functional needs, the Wippel House (1969) represents on the contrary a mere architectural exercise, in its small but masterly functionality and in its spatial organization of rigorous volumetries like a pure and highly specialized technological object. The 1969

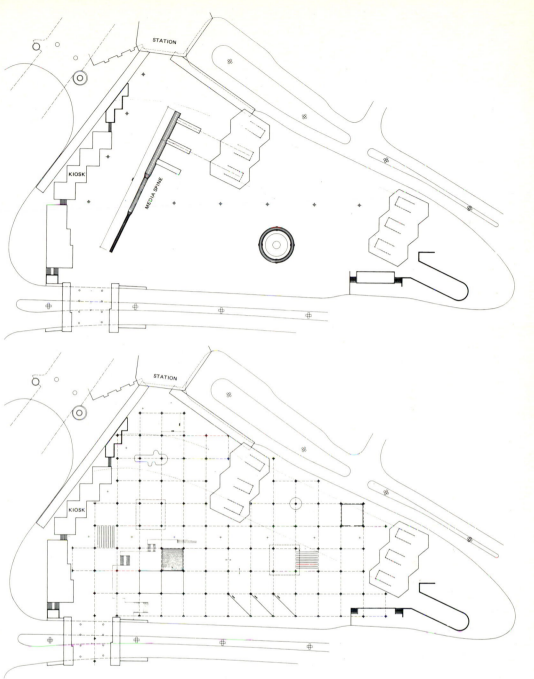

"Z" streetlamp and sign for Zentralsparkasse, Vienna, 1969: design and general view. Right: Competition for the Railroad Station Square, Ludwigshafen, 1969: project A and B.

competition for the setting of the Ludwigshafen station's service area contains elements on an urban scale which Hollein will be able to experiment with and realize in later projects, like for example the one for the Munich Olympic Village.

Among the most interesting elements are the enormous sculptures which contain the pipes for the square's artificial air-conditioning system; these spectacular works are midway between land art and Robert Morris's minimal work, and through them it's possible to understand how visual art and architecture were integrated at that time.

The commission in 1969 to transform into a museum the house in Berggasse 19 where Freud had worked and lived, seemed to represent at that time, considering the clear sexual symbology of the almost contemporary Feigen Gallery, an ideal occasion for Hollein to express ideas on themes inherent in his original training, which constantly emerged in his work, probably sometimes even unconsciously. As a matter of fact the project expresses powerfully its attempt to make accessible to a wider public the work of Freud. It was an emblematic intention to show the famous study, and even more the famous sofa, the only object contained in the whitewashed room, together with spaces with more specific functions, and with highly specialized audiovisual systems. This was therefore another example of how technique, and architecture as communication and dissemination of ideas can enrich perception and knowledge.

It's the same concept which Hollein applies the following year at the Osaka Expo '70 where, after the theme of a "Contribution to a Better Life", he realizes inside Kenzo Tange's enormous pavilion an independent spatial structure formed by industrially produced elements, containing a series of helicoidal stairs through which it was possible to see a room where audio-visual were shown. This moment, contemporary with the '68 Triennal, was for Hollein an intense period in the formation of strategical choices and of very definite realizations, in which the project exemplifies itself through a very articulated, but coherent, professional practice, with theoretical proposals put foward with a concise but complete visualization, full of implications, but more often with a project which has been completed.

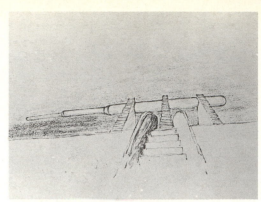

Competition for the Railroad Station Square, Ludwigshafen, 1969: sketch and model.

Sigmund Freud Museum, Vienna, 1969: floor plans, sketch and "Sigmund Freud" couch.

MODELL BERGGASSE NR. 19

The early seventies: the maturity of specialization

This period sees professional commitments growing in scale and importance. The maturity of the author's strictly professional dimension corresponds and almost opposes the most important series of Hollein's exhibitions: installations in museums, in art galleries and at the Biennial in Venice, which seem to prefer a metaphorical language. As a matter of fact, this is not true.

Hollein's professional activity specializes in planning interventions such as interior design, urban scale planning, complex interior decorations and structural integrations for the Munich Siemens AG in Bavaria.

His exhibitions, such as "Death", "Tomb of a racing driver", "Krimhild's Revenge" and "Life and Death - Everyday Situation" (an invitation to represent Austria in the visual arts section at the 1972 Venice Biennale), help to determine quite clearly Hollein's work as a visual artist. He seems to believe it necessary to establish his own character as an artist on the international scene in order to form a keypoint opposed to the one concerning his strictly professional activity. These were other ways to define clearly the conceptual and operative space in which Hollein has decided to work. The problems caused by such different commitments are solved by his exhibitions, which are characterized by a great concentration of ideas. This strategy of substitution of theoretical texts shows the same conceptual rigour expressed according to the metaphors of visual language. It therefore becomes an instrument of clarification and contraposition answering

Carl Friedrich von Siemens Foundation, Nymphenburg, 1970-72: clubroom's detail and view from the garden.

Top left: Carl Friedrich von Siemens Foundation, Nymphenburg, 1970-72: reception hall.
Top right: Siemens Casino I, Munich, 1970-75: entrance hall.
Bottom: Siemens Casino I, conference room.

a need which had already been perceived in recent years but which, on this occasion, assumed other characteristics.

The works for the Siemens AG were realized between 1970 and 1975. The plans are of various kinds: from the reconversions of antique buildings to the extension of the Siemens Foundation, from strongly characterized interior decorations to the actual invention of pieces of design. As his first commission, Hollein reconverts the small palace of the Friedrich von Siemens Foundation, inside the complex of Nymphenburg, building a new wing for the Kavalier-Haeueser used by the foundation while maintaining intact the characteristic of the baroque "scenery" inside the semi-circular walls of the complex. He also re-designs a few rooms of the palace in order to create a connection with the new structure. In the entire reconversion project, the living-meeting room assumes particularly interesting aspects. Hollein prepares the visitor for this space by placing a few signals in the rooms of the baroque building, such as a double steel column with a technoid capital. The new space is set between two pre-existing structures, and the side opposite to the entrance has a 45-degree inclination towards the building in front, in order to underline the contrast and the route which it encloses. It is placed with great sensitivity in the historical context; the opening towards the park is carefully planned and deliberately bare.

The author enriches his language especially in the interiors, with a very well-calibrated but apparently casual arrangement of meeting spaces, in order to underline a relaxed and informal atmosphere. The accents are delegated to the planning of interior design objects and to the different quality of lighting, great attention being paid to creating a particular atmosphere. This conceptual attitude was antithetical to the rationalist tradition, where interiors were a mere consequence, spaces resulting from a planning conceived entirely in connection with the organization of the exterior volumes.

In a different historical context, this time in the city itself, the Siemens AG

central office in Wittelsbacherplatz is divided into various buildings. The main one, at 1825 neoclassical work by Leo von Klenze, is placed at the end of the Odeonsplatz axis. It was rebuilt after the destruction caused by the Second World War and its accurately reproduced façade conditioned the interiors which are not original. The various aspects of Hollein's work may be summed up in this way: great care in connecting secondary spaces (corridors, halls, and interiors), the planning of a great conference room, with its strategical view over the Odeonsplatz, and of the main entrance hall of the building; the connecting spaces are handled with meticulous attention to the beautiful details, which enrich the continuity and underline their complexity. On the contrary, the conference room is a real project, an interior inside an interior, whose decoration is focused in the great oval table[34] and everything is enclosed by the formalization of the walls, which are articulated and volumetrically active. But especially in the entrance hall the author formally synthesized the spatial inventions and the conceptual propositions of an architecture of interiors. The complexity of this planning reflects the contemporary architecture of the historical town centres; it's the contribution of architecture which refrains from competing with the crystallized tissue, re-defining and criticizing it from an interior.

Siemens Casino I: entrance hall detail. Bottom: Siemens Casino II: Guests' dining facilities, room 5.

Apart from the technical details, this is the most important idea about architecture which emerges from the two different historically defined contexts of Nymphenburg and Wittelsbacherplatz, where the almost total lack of competition with the exterior expresses itself by means of external formal decision which are neutral, or characterized by a full abstention; an idea of architecture which then frees itself and focuses itself on an interior which re-defines contents, theorizes problems and distinguishes the outside as a thin archeological stratification.

In the Wittelsbacherplatz hall, space is autonomous, a diagram of distributive and volumetrical specializations, practically a quotation of an urban tissue: the metaphor is evident in the by now usual definition of the entrance as an autonomous volume, in the connotations of functions which provoke the invention of space and volumes, in the underlining of courses obtained by the diagrams of the floor and by the lighting elements, one unrelated to the other. The existing curved lines are broken, like the concentric waves of a pond, just as throwing in stones at different points provokes repeated waves which intersect and break according to the laws of physics. "The use of the curve suggests to me a precise plan, a well-defined space. It is a fraction of a circle that can easily be completed in your mind. I think I have used this in my architecture, especially for small objects where I wanted to create two different scales. Using a curve in a confined space, you immediately open a much larger, imaginary space and you can gauge in a very clear, almost geometrical way, the dimensions of the entire space. That is to say, one uses fragments that one completes in one's mind"[35].

Here Hollein's role as an anticlassicist clearly emerges, if by this definition one means the intentional absence of centralizing axes of symmetry, comforting and tranquillizing, coinciding with a schematic and reassuring vision of the world, but basically idle and passive, suitable for visualizing the images of power, the structures of classes, the confidence of a role and of a status.

Hollein says exactly the contrary, turning immediately in the opposite direction, certain as he is that the purposes of research are many, that there is not one single way (still less an unchangeable way) of interpreting the world, and that, rather, nowadays it is possible and indeed important, to affirm without anxiety and fear the complex coexistence of vital and diversified components.

In the Siemens Casino 2 Hollein's work is articulated inside a pre-existing construction built in the fifties, of which the original structural enclosure is maintained, while other spaces have provided rooms for entertaining clients, partners, managers and chiefs of state. The prevailing idea is that of the spatial enclosure, where different spaces are articulated but unified by functions and by the differentiated sequence of formal solutions and of choices of colours and materials, therefore providing a sequence that is formally and conceptually connected by means of a diversified evolution.

The complex of Hollein's work for the Siemens AG may lead to two other considerations: the first concerns the great variety of choices and the use of very diversified materials, from the most traditional ones like stucco and marble to

Siemens Casino II, Munich, 1971-72: Guests' dining facilities room 1 and general plan.

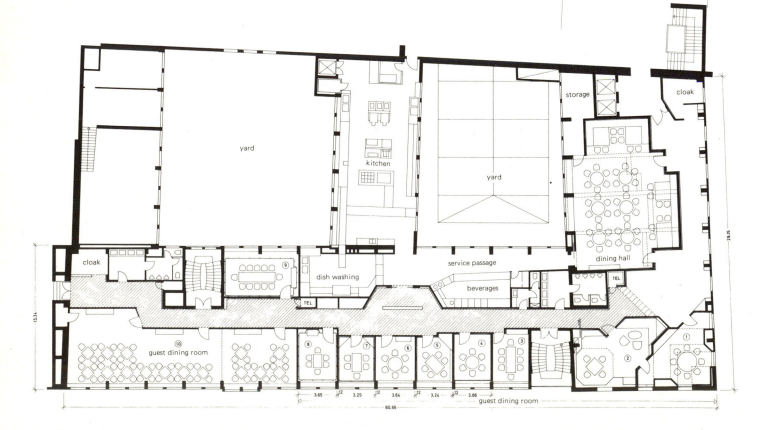

Munich Olympic Village, 1971-72. Below: "Media-linien" in Forum. Bottom left: study for the "Media-Linien" system. Bottom right: Forum detail.

chromium-plated metals, fibreglass, plastics and polyester paints; the second one concerns "the rising interest in tradition, particularly in the Viennese classico-modern period which Hollein has cautiously approached in some of the spaces of the Siemens' main office"[36]. From Loos to Wagner to Hoffmann, quotations become more and more clear and explicit: interior design objects often take on the importance of sculptures, of symbol-diagrams, synthesis and conceptual propositions.

Hollein's almost obsessional interest in technology and the continuous updating of contemporary software, lead him to win the first prize in the 1971 competition for the design of the signs and the technical equipment of the Munich Olympic Village central area: light, sound, colour, multimedia communication, realized in order to be used also after the Olympic Games. Hollein's suggestions, chosen for the correspondence between technology and communication, were used for the whole village. This so-called "Media Linien" system is formed by tubular elements on steel supports containing the electrical equipment, which is adaptable to any kind of urban and even climatic situation, because one can connect to it panels, screens, objects, posters, protective tents and fibreglass roofings. The Media Linien represent a great novelty in urban fittings, being multifunctional and at the same time a supporting structure, a visual and conceptual frame, a connection between different aspects of a fragmented and composite urban tissue, which redeems itself from its general anonymity and acquires a new quality through the superimposition of this "rescue", which provides continuity while also underlining its diversity. A real architectural project, apparently bare, obtained through the rarefaction and the intensification of the basic modular structure which bears perfectly the weight of the whole operation. Looking at its plan, in project as well as in reality, one is reminded of the setting up of the Austriennial exhibition, where the language of architecture was present both in the form of project and in that of spatial intervention, together with annotations of details and strong symbolic contents. The modular element holds a dialogue with the context while also using fittings and decorations designed by Hollein himself.

Another project of the same period concerning rearrangement and functional re-vitalization is the competition for the resettlement of the Rathausplatz in Vienna. The project deals with the visual-functional reorganization of an urban space exactly in the same way, both conceptually and in its planning strategy, as the project for the Munich Olympic Village. The context is obviously different, as Munich represented a reinterpretation and a linking of contemporary interventions, while Vienna represents a relationship with an urban tissue and with an

historically defined condition, full of spectacular and representative valences. The Vienna project proposes, as does the Munich one, an organization of lighting and air-conditioning systems, as well as the covering of the inner courtyard of the Town Hall and the widening of the already existing parking area. Hollein's intention is to reorganize the area according to its present use. These spaces, which had always had a representative function, but had been used for example by the students of the nearby university, are claimed back for a collective and popular use, for free time and entertainment activities, in the same way as in the projects for the St. Louis Museum and the Bank at Florisdorf.

The purpose of the work for these projects, the one for the Town Hall square in Vienna also being an architectural project, is the functional "correction" of those areas of urban tissue and architecture which are reacquired for public use. Hollein[37] reminds us that, for example, the Opera House in Vienna belongs, as a public space, to a "regal" past, adding that "This solution would have offered something more in the way of new thoughts and ideas"[38]. An architectural idea that once more relates to a pre-existing context, is revisited and adapted to contemporary demands, either focusing function and meanings or, alternatively, distributing them more widely.

In this same period, almost to verify the continuous change between different scales of intervention, Hollein completes the Section N shop in the Schulerstrasse, and just a bit later the first jewellery shop in the Graben, one of Vienna's most central and elegant streets. Section N is a shop dealing with furniture, interior design and experimental design objects. Here, Hollein refrains from creating a new internal enclosure, independent of the structure of the building (like in the Retti shop and the Christa Metek boutique), maintaining and exalting the characteristics of the rather fragmented interiors in the courses and the different levels, some of which he had added himself. There is a sensitive and deductive interpretation, both for façade and interiors, an attitude that is virtually opposite to the one shown in the previous shops and later on in the Schullin I jewellery shop. Hollein's attention, almost an archeological inspection, is concentrated on the characteristics of the interiors, of which various interpretations are given. Thus, he obtains very flexible neutral spaces, suitable for the different combinations of the objects and the furniture on show. As in the other interiors, the entrance is an independent episode, a hinge, a filter standing volumetrically by itself, a "gate" between inside and outside, a short entry route obtained at the back of the corner pillar of the building. The thick plastered walls and the original vaults act also as reflecting surfaces for the various lighting points. Therefore, with Section N, a further valence is introduced: the project is simplified, concentrated on independent elements which serve as instruments for the interpretation of a pre-existing structure.

"Section N" Showrooms, Vienna, 1971: looking-down view of the entrance (top), staircase and section.

The Schullin jewellery shop in the Graben reminds us, ten years later, of the Retti shop. Just as the Retti had represented a diagram in real scale of the theories that Hollein had enunciated in the sixties, the Schullin shop is a way of both verifying and updating those ideas: a diagnosis of the evolution of a mental process and of the consequent formal propositions. Hollein's language is more re-

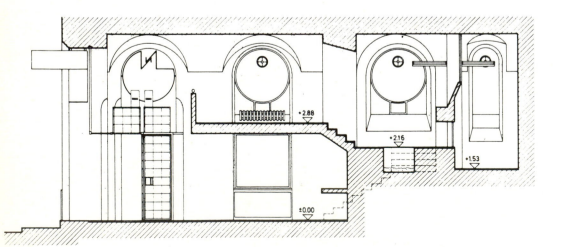

laxed. The aim is no longer a "manifesto" but a deeper attention to the analysis of his own emotions, his intellectual interests and their physical consequences. In his language one now finds history: recognizable, although filtered, quotations of the Viennese tradition of the beginning of the century, whose heritage Hollein feels on himself. Loos and Hoffman come together with all the elements of Hollein's original poetic expression and, what's more, an extremely elegant way of theorizing about artifice and nature. The façade is spectacular but not overdone; it is still a diagram of the various layers of the ambiguous co-existence of thoughts, ideas and emotions which establish their formalization and their rational discipline but at the same time strongly claim their original physical expression.

We shall find other formulations, in widely different scales, of these intentions and of Hollein's complexity as a protagonist of the cultural debate more than simply as an architect. He clearly tells us about his own evolution, displaying a comparison between elements which may seem to be contrasting but, on the contrary, generate a creative tension.

Jewellery Store Schullin I, Vienna, 1972: detail of the door (outside), sketch and façade.

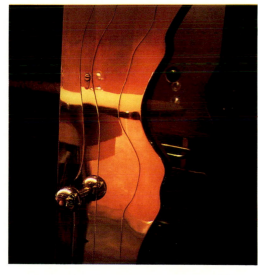

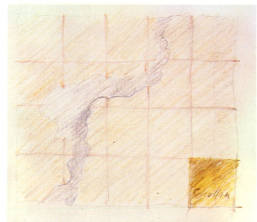

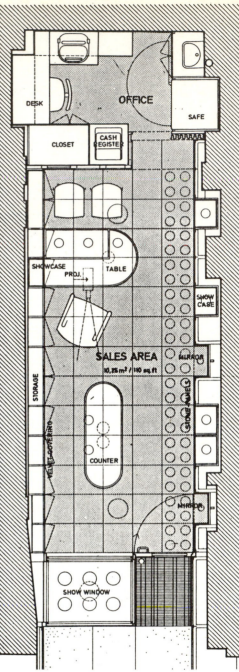

Jewellery Store Schullin I, Vienna: view towards the entrance and plan.

"It is almost as small as the candle shop, and much more varied, both in material and in colour; again the materials are precise and precious. The granite façade has a deep, low recess but its upper part is 'broken' by a rift whose interstices of brass sheet configure themselves into onion-like layers transfixed by a group of steel tubes of varying section: an image of geology, machinery and even archaeology"[39].

We should add to Rykwert's description that the façade is a rectangle in which the opening-entrance, slightly out of axis, is square, and that the cleft is realized on various levels, penetrating progressively into the depths of the façade; a quotation also of a mine open to the sky, the "description" of which, obtained by means of contours, reaches the doorway which is contaminated by this process, being itself a sequence of descending levels. Anyway one has the feeling of being attracted, sucked towards the interior, a perfect enclosure with a ceiling on three different levels and a longitudinal built-in cupboard covered with velvet facing a granite wall, reflections and iridescences emphasizing the feeling of magic and preciousness.

Schullin I, realized between 1972 and 1974, contemporary with some spaces

48

for the Siemens AG, records the "stimulating effect produced by the Viennese tradition more than any other work of Hollein. The work shows very clear references to the famous shops of Adolf Loos who, in architecture as a discipline, had created new avant-garde advertising aspects. Even Loos often had to deal with very small shops. In the am Graben square, almost in front of the Schullin, there still exists the Knize clothes shop, while the Steiner Feather shop in the Karntnerstrasse has been destroyed"[40].

"Hollein has always looked upon Loos as the most important reference in the gallery of ancestors of the Viennese artists... while he was particularly fascinated by Hoffman's planning method, characterized by a universally geometric design"[41].

To these two quotations one has only to add that the diagram of the façade is also, and perhaps mainly, a superimposition, once more diagramatic, of the co-existence in Hollein of the two inseparable aspects of the artists and the architect which are for the first time so clearly and brilliantly quoted. This is the real element of novelty: Hollein's truly original contribution, even from a conceptual point of view, to the contemporary architectural debate. The modern history of architecture, even the Viennese one which is present in the form of quotation, had not yet integrated these two aspects, and certainly not in this way. On the contrary it had kept them rigorously separated: Le Corbusier himself used to distinguish the artist from the architect conceptually and formally in his buildings.

The treatment of the theme of death, of the rituals connected with it, of recollections, and memory, emerge clearly in Hollein's work during this period. One should also say that at this time many Viennese artists were dealing with this subject, which also influenced Hollein: first of all Walter Pichler whose evolution constantly verifies in detail and in the most different valences, the relation between life and death, rituals, emotions, elements of continuity, and of an end which always gives birth to a beginning. Moreover, one shouldn't forget that the art of behaviour assumes, especially in Vienna, obsessive aspects through the work of very many artists for whom the "cerimony" of death, and the rite of sacrifice are common themes. Hans Hollein is also physically present in his work, but often only through memories, or rather recollections. Perhaps it's the most extreme limit, a purely conceptual presence, whilst most artists and artists-architects enter into the image, the installations, with their physical presence, contextual to the evolution of their work.

"Death" Exhibition, 1970: flower arrangement and "death garment".

"Death", the exhibition at Mönchengladbach in 1970, sums up the rituals, the elements through which Hollein intends to deal with the theme. Hollein's exhibition can be read as a manifesto on this subject which he will later develop in other ways in other exhibitions. In "Death", objects and phenomenologies are enumerated:

"A very strange old museum
Archaeological sites – burial grounds
    On the site you can dig and find objects and money
    (in a large room of the museum)
Discoveries
Tombs, offerings
Reconstruction – erroneously identified objects
    a broken bottle is meticolously put together again – with a few pieces missing –
    and exhibited in a showcase
Objects are identified wrongly as we know, but rightly as
one with another background would assume
the grave of the warrior – hard hat and golf club
various hats in a showcase – a cook's hat or bishop's
mitre?

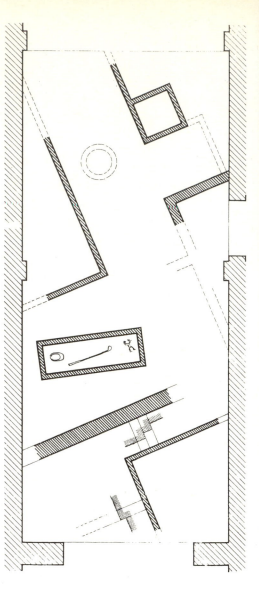

"Death" Exhibition, 1970: general plan of the exhibition and "tomb of the warrior".

50

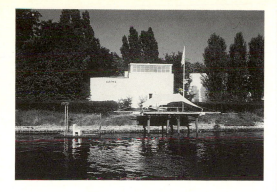

"Work and Behaviour-Life and Death-Everyday Situations" Exhibition, Venice Biennale, 1972: view from the canal and plan of the exhibition.
Bottom: "Tomb of the racing driver", Graz, 1970.

Death rites
    Rites for dying in our time and civilization
    The existing (non-existing) ones. New ones.
Death bed
    Today you die on the corridor of a hospital
Death garments
Flowers
    A room full of beautiful, colourful flowers, smelling,
    slowly disintegrating during the course of the exhibition, smelling sweeter,
    disintegrating, smelling rotten.
Altars
    Burning candles in a space defined by four walls
    penetrable anywhere – no doors. Immaterial."[42]

Together with the description of the exhibition, this text sums up the elements of analysis which will be specified also on further occasions. However, the theme is brought forth without risking a neurotic involvement or an obsessive persistence, feelings which instead are present in the works of many Viennese artists dealing with this subject[43].

These installations show an almost studious attitude, and the above quoted text is subtly pervaded by various feelings, including a slight irony. Isozaki, in his 1975 essay on this particular theme of Hollein, remarks that: "Although having been closed in a patient room by his hospitalization he was compelled to face death, that may not be the reason for him to carry it to the level where it becomes the theme of his works. To the extent that it becomes the theme, it is 'Death' as an idea. It is not merely the daily biological termination of functioning, but as he talks about the ritual in Maya, it is 'death' which sustains everyday life... Here, we can remember that Freud was from Vienna... his research was done in that city... Wittgenstein was also born here... It is a city full of the image of death to such an extent that it is rather not necessary to talk about it... Perhaps the shrine of Maya and the products of monstruous technology, being mediated by many monuments scattered in Vienna, are combined together towards the most contemporary commemorative character, that is, destruction, death and exctinction. To bring about death (Thanatos) directly means from time immemorial to bring about life (Eros) as the substantial moment. I think that it is theoretical conclusion that Hollein's work began to express physical characteristics similar to Baroque or an invisible spiritual substance. That is nothing but to perceive the relations between the object and the flesh as Eros"[44].

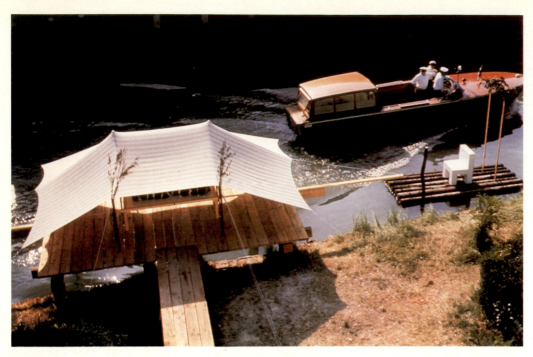

"Work and Behaviour" Exhibition, Venice Biennale, 1972: view towards the canal, vehicle and "everyday situations" room.

Chronologically, the Graz 1970 exhibition "Tomb of the Racing-driver" comes after the Mönchengladbach exhibition; a work less exactly philologic, a notation in which the four bicycle wheels , quoting the wheels of racing cars, have an obvious ironical purpose. But, once and for all, one should remember that irony, as a classic element of the ancient Viennese culture, is not a basic element but only an ingredient, a method of interpretation. This component[45] is considered as a reference point by many critics who have dealt with Hollein's work: a superficial point of view to those who think that the making of culture necessarily implies severity, coolness, sacrifice and pain; thus suggesting the impossibility of producing art and culture while being ironical or even having fun.

Hollein, representing Austria at the 1972 Biennial in Venice in the area of Hoffmann's Pavilion, divides his treatment into various episodes. The theme "Work and Behaviour – Life and Death – Everyday Situations" was represented in several ways. The room of "Everyday Situations" displayed a few objects and pieces of furniture which were white and tiled, perfectly geometrical, uniform and minimalist. Only one of them, the tiled grid, was marked by a trace of blood (which Hollein explains as recalling the altars used for sacrifices that he had seen in Mexico, with blood running in the crevices). The oppression of this aseptic space was amplified by a high and narrow door on an axis with the building, through which one could see the corpse-mummy laid on a stretcher on a platform on piles which was placed between the earth and the channel. The gap in the wall is a way out towards myth and memory; a wooden walkway physically connects the opening with the channel and the platform. At the back of the pavilion a geometrical chair faces the throne formed by interlaced branches, and the entire composition is immersed in a "natural" setting which can be observed from another gap in the wall of the pavilion.

"The contrasts between inside and outside, civilization and nature, rationality and myth, underlined the extremes through which life itself flows; only apparently one could choose different possibilities. In this case, the clinical-macabre space is not meant for rest, but for death; there's only one way out (the gap in the wall), an escape towards the archaic"[46]. The "strategy" of this project is complex, as in a real work of architecture expressed by means of episodes and "stations" which adapt the project to the role of metaphorical communication. Only an architect, when engaged in this kind of work in which, unlike in projects, simbology and metaphorical communication are preferred, can deal with such complex situations: different levels of interpretation organized according to a planimetrical rigour which shows a magic and simplified vision, at the same time emotional and rational, simple and complex.

"Krimhild's Revenge", in the Essen 1972 exhibition "Myth and Reality", ends this recognition-route on death and its rituals. It's a sequence of episodes

"Paper" Exhibition, Design Center, Vienna, 1971-72.

expressed with the greatest simplicity, essential and bare in form, although very rich in intentions and ideas. Also in this exhibition Hollein symbolically refers to the eternal dualism of life and death: a narrow corridor obstructed by a corpse lying down, over which one has to step in order to reach a second obstacle, a garment-armour formed by metal tiles, whose disturbing geometry is interrupted by the lack of just one square and by a bloodstain.

"Paper" has to be considered an installation more than an exhibition: it doesn't have a didactic purpose, even if it does stimulate the visitor, with its associations, towards an autonomous process of mental connections. In "Paper" the use of metaphor is "organized" almost like in a fairytale. The technique of associations and evocations is very clearly exemplified, almost in a provocative manner. The stimulation towards an active participation in this process of knowledge is very clear: in the center of the exhibition Hollein had placed a paper screen which had to be pierced at the opening of the exhibition, and then left on show. So, it is by now obvious that Hollein prefers to express himself by means of metaphors and associations. In his exhibitions as an artist, Hollein talks about himself and the flowing of ghosts, obsessions, emotions and intentions. In "Paper" he talks about things, events, aspects of development and knowledge, using the same forms of expression, but adopting and reducing them to a more simplified form of communication, without loosing however that sense of association and ambiguity that informs the whole of his communication method. Therefore Hollein's architecture at this period, if compared to his first works, is more specific, dealing with buildings and interiors which seem to be set, like autonomous structures, "inside" a pre-existing architecture. For the first time design assumes a connotation which may be extrapolated from the context in which the object of interior decoration is being placed. In "Paper" Hollein's aesthetics take on unusual details, forms and colour characterized by the utmost quality and autonomy. His exhibitions as an artist and his installations belong to that part of his work in which he has stressed more communication than proposition, the latter being a characteristic of the operative part of the project. However, these two aspects are always present in Hollein's poetic expression, and only the prevalence of one of them over the other permits the making of an installation instead of a project. It's difficult to find such a complexity in other artists and architects of the same period, and even in the ones belonging to the recent past or to the history of modern architecture. Anyway, this is not an element of "diversion", as Hollein deals correctly with all kinds of specializations; and not even an element of dispersion, as Hollein gathers in a single proposition all the aspects of his poetic expression in order to express them by means of the same language. The Mönchengladbach Museum is for in-

"Paper" Exhibition: interior and axonometric.

54

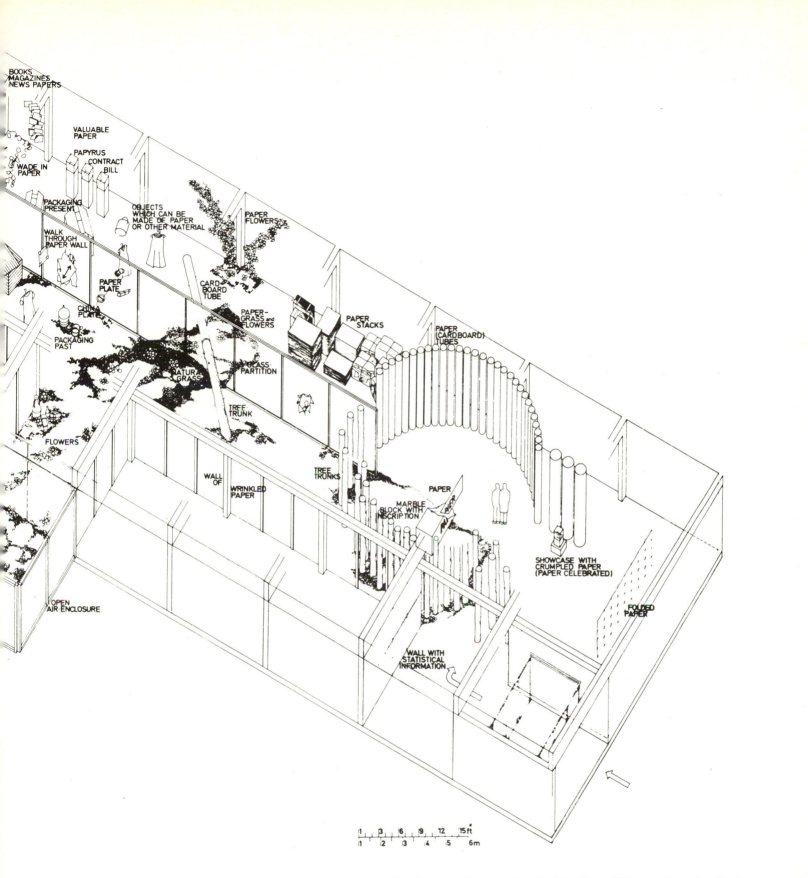

BOOKS
MAGAZINES
NEWS PAPERS

VALUABLE
PAPER

WADE IN
PAPER

PAPYRUS   CONTRACT
BILL

PACKAGING
PRESENT

OBJECTS
WHICH CAN BE
MADE OF PAPER
OR OTHER MATERIAL

PAPER
FLOWERS

WALK
THROUGH
PAPER WALL

PAPER
PLATE

CARD
BOARD
TUBE

PAPER-
GRASS and
FLOWERS

PAPER
STACKS

PAPER
(CARDBOARD)
TUBES

CHINA
PLATE

PACKAGING
PAST

NATURAL
GRASS

GLASS
PARTITION

TREE
TRUNK

FLOWERS

WALL
OF
WRINKLED
PAPER

TREE
TRUNKS

PAPER

MARBLE
BLOCK WITH
INSCRIPTION

SHOWCASE WITH
CRUMPLED PAPER
(PAPER CELEBRATED)

OPEN
AIR ENCLOSURE

FOLDED
PAPER

WALL WITH
STATISTICAL
INFORMATION

1 3 6 9 12 15 ft
1 2 3 4 5 6m

stance "a work which has to be interpreted at four different levels; first, as an art gallery designed by a man who reveres art; second, as a city in miniature; third, as a disconnected series of oniric tableaux and fourth as a ruined castle land-scape"[47].

Mönchengladbach

In 1963, at the height of a period of research, Hollein was writing that "...architecture dominates spaces, it soars upwards, it penetrates the earth, it stands out against landscapes, it spreads in all directions, it dominates space with its mass and void, it dominates space through space itself"[48]. About twenty years later in Mönchengladbach we find a complex of buildings placed on a height overlooking the town, with a tower and various buildings grouped around a large platform which is used as a public ruote and also as a roofing for spaces which have been "dug" inside the hill. This is the idea of the "walk-on building" which in fact implies a complex internal volume over which one can walk as in a town park, the same "walk-on building" that Hollein had already suggested in the sixties for the Florisdorf Bank and the St. Louis City Art Museum.

"In the Museum of Modern Art at Mönchengladbach he has realised the idea and extended it. The complexity of the interior volume is real enough. The variety of exhibition spaces, whose fixity is compensated by that complexity of plan and section, is concealed behind undulating walls: when seen from the urban garden which lies in the plain below them, they seem as if they were retaining walls of a hill"[49].

On the other hand, Hollein justifies[50] the partially subterranean positioning of the building with a particular reason concerning urban planning, as he wanted to avoid the contrast between the monumental scale of a public building and the reduced scale of the buildings of the town. Hollein however, refuses the idea of an institutional monument, because he has no particular interest in a space of public use, but on the contrary he believes in diversified spaces having their own meaning, not to diminish the importance of the works on show but to exalt them. "What is most attractive about museums placed in old palaces is that their spaces are interesting anyhow... One of the museums which I don't like particularly is Wright's Guggenheim Museum in New York; it's too simple to think that in a museum one should only look at the works of art... We didn't want to build a museum whose development was only linear, spatial or chronological"[51].

Even Frampton, who in 1970 had complained about an exaggerated connotation of the spaces in the Feigen Gallery which interfered with the works on show, talks about the Mönchengladbach Museum as "...an art gallery designed by a man who reveres art... the brilliance of Hollein's design resides in the compromise he has achieved between the 'en suite' planning of the traditional gallery (with one room leading to the next) and the open-ended gallery space of the modern free plan. The same infrastructural approach has in fact been applied to both kinds of gallery space, so that his 'cloverleaf' system of enclosed gallery volumes, is subtly interwoven with intersticial spaces which separate the square galleries and provide for various forms of service access... As far as the hanging and the viewing of art is concerned Mönchengladbach is virtually a textbook case with over a third of its gallery space being top-lit... By varying the mode of illumination in relation to the specific volume Hollein has succeded in creating a sequence of quite distinct 'places', from the monumental oblong of the temporary exhibition room to the labyrinthic half-cubic volumes housing the permanent collection"[52].

The complexity and the articulation of the museum which derive from a simple spatial concept, and basically recall the foundation of the Roman Castrum, seem to originate from the inside and nearly emerge towards the outside in a complexity of plans and sections. The external retaining walls "naturalize" the artifice of human manufacture with no precise boundaries, like in a seascape, where there's no real division between land and sea, but just an area where this changing takes place. Once across this filter, the top of the hill becomes "...an assortment of separate buildings, a variegated colony: the tall administration tower in stone and curtainwall, the white marble and chrome entrance pavilion; the zinc coated gallery-tents on one side, the sand-stone box of roof-light on the

other"[53]. Rykwert goes on saying that Hollein has played dangerously with the concept of disintegration of this organism, but also admits that he has won the challenge, especially because the tension expressed by the co-existence of such different elements renders their assembly perfectly natural. Even Frampton says that the disjunctive approach "...is the only principle of unity which pervades the entire scheme, made up as it is by episodic 'set-pieces' which are barely established in the mind before they are transformed into the next scene"[54]. The top of the hill is organized in such a way as to be included in a civic centre with views, coffee-house and entertainments. No cars are allowed on the upper part of the hill. Therefore the entrance to the museum is the entrance leading inside the hill,

Municipal Museum Abteiberg Mönchengladbach, 1972-82: lecture hall, approach from the bridge and axonometric.
Pages 56-57: general view.

APARTMENT BLDGS

ABTEISTRASSE

OST'S

CULTURAL C

SPATZENBERGSTRASSE

OLD CITY WALL

OLD CITY WALL

OLD GARDEN

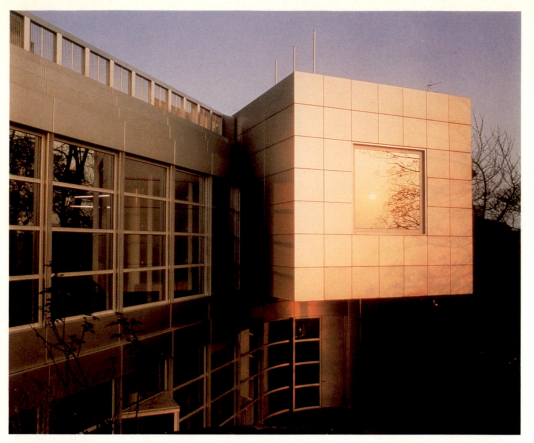

Mönchengladbach Museum: exterior of the cafeteria (left), lighting system (top) and detail of roof (below).

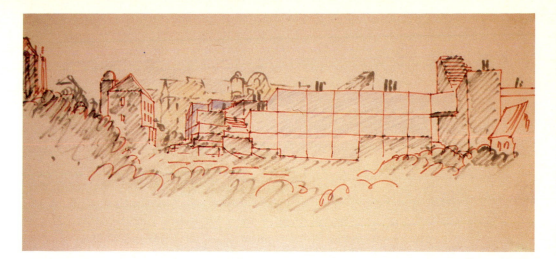

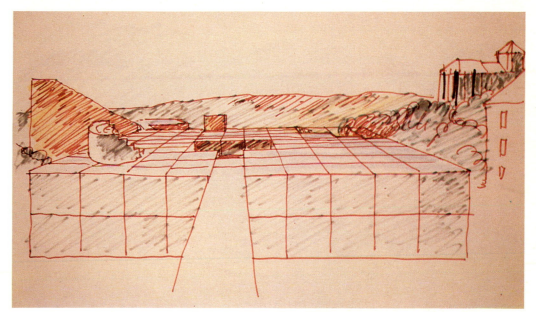

Mönchengladbach Museum: preliminary sketches by
Hans Hollein.

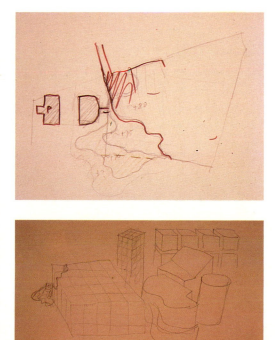

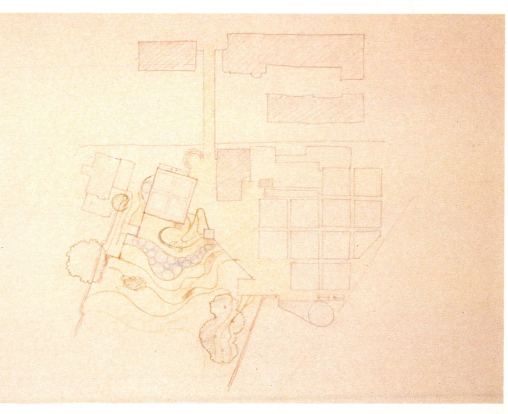

an articulation of exciting, magical and complicated routes, having their own pre-established rules which however, may be modified along the way like an ant-hill, whose labyrinthine courses seem to have no sense: a termitarium guarding treasures and having other openings, besides the one at the top. They are apparently transgressive compared to a guided tour: a series of surprises, a sequence of enchantments. The museum may also be interpreted "...as a city-in-miniature, wherein, as in the traditional city, one may enter the labyrinth at more than one point and discover for oneself a different sequence... In this way the interior of the museum is rendered not as a didactic repository of artifacts, but rather as a civic place, where among other pleasures one may also encounter art"[55].

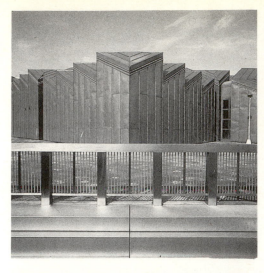

The outside on the contrary, even maintaining its quality of episodic labyrinth, puzzles the visitor, and even more the art historian, used as he is to finding himself in front of a monument, a diagram of absolute axioms, a "black stone" reflecting the culture and the historical period of which it is an expression. This is exactly what cannot be found in Mönchengladbach, and the comments of some critics contain an ill-concealed disappointment. Frampton himself says that Mönchengladbach, even in its complexity and sequence of thoughts and emotions, of its specular and immaterial double images, is not architecture; and perhaps, by architecture he means the diagram, something absolute, monumental, the complete reliability of simplification. To this Hollein opposes the total "insecurity" of complexity, a magic and vertiginous equilibrium of ambiguous elements, the apparent co-existence of assertions and denials; an apparent, only apparent babble of languages, the absence of the reassuring and reductive presence of unchangeable principles. Hollein suggests accepting the dialogue, the dualism, not between the different opinions in the mosaics of contemporary architecture, but as the vitality of those co-existences which may seem contrasting and not yet worked out. Therefore, the top of this hill repeats and amplifies vital themes of debate, being at the same time an archeological site, a subterranean structure, a lava flow in which the obsidian materializes forms of

Mönchengladbach Museum: details of roofs and view of the entrance and administration building from below.

Mönchengladbach Museum: exhibition rooms.

plain crystal, a lunar appearance, a base on the moon or an antarctic observatory.

The presence of nature, almost reconquering its place and prevailing over manufacture, has to be considered as history, emotional perception, the magic of archeology, a proof of hidden civilization. Hollein seems to say that nowadays we sum up all these elements, but he also talks about the obscure charm of nature and its materials, and of how nature "must" be interpreted in order to understand artiface and how natural materials, used and worked by the skilful hands of man, may change so as to become a mirror-like surface.

Earth-work makes sense only if produced by somebody coming from town, and Hollein's earth-work has all the qualities that are lacking in most earth-works of other artists. In Mönchengladbach Hollein quotes all the experience of land art as well as a great part of the conceptual art which analyzes physical space, but using a physical expression which in art is unthinkable; it is difficult, in fact, to find further examples of a work of *such* complexity, articulated as it is on *such* levels.

We may well understand the caution of contemporary criticism of architecture: when Hollein modifies the boundaries, the parameters of discussion inside which it is possible to talk about architecture, this vertiginous widening of prospects is bewildering, because it is always very difficult to abandon all convictions in favour of exciting but precarious uncertainties. What's more, one can't even say that Hollein denies the monument its role in contemporary architecture: certainly he doesn't make it a protagonist of all works of architecture. Perhaps only nowadays can one assert that the most significant sites of a town have to be the "monuments" or totally formal diagrams, isolated and venerated like the only existing God of reference and salvation[56].

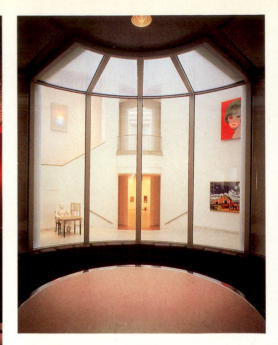

Mönchengladbach Museum: audio-visual room (top left), exhibition room, view from outside (top right); hall, garden level; garden (left).

Notes on contemporary eclecticism

The ten years between the commission and the opening of the Mönchengladbach Museum testify to the further specification, by means of very accurate details, of Hans Hollein's articulated and complex work, as well as to competitions and commissions still in the process of realization. Even Hollein's work as a critic "specializes": after his last general theorization at the exhibition MANtransFORMS in New York (1974-76), he limits his writings to presentations-introductions of his work concerning planning, to essays on artists exhibiting at the Venice Biennial in the Austrian Pavilion, and historical essays, like the one on Otto Wagner, of 1978[57].

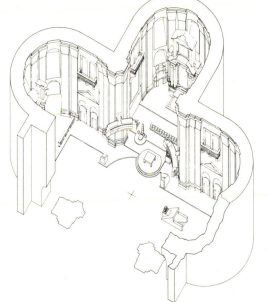

Salzburg Cathedral Competition, 1973: axonometric and sketch for the throne.

However, Hollein's criticism isn't only carried out by means of written essays; on the contrary it would be more correct, extrapolating from it his projects, to examine his fundamental course as a critic, regarding it from the point of view of his activity as an artist and an architect. His work constantly perceives and criticizes every element, every aspect of the architectural debate, totally participating, as it does, in the contemporary outline of architecture. With Mönchengladbach Hollein hasn't missed the chance of expressing in every possible way his personal views on architecture. If this is the project which visualizes every aspect of his theorizations, there are also other works and projects which have been carried on, till now, as a further opportunity to make a comment, by means of visual instruments, on architectural debate.

The development of all kinds of "specializations" in Hollein's work grows rapidly from the beginning of the seventies onwards in projects of great richness and vigour. Every aspect of his work, as it has been here subdivided, is highly integrated, so much that sometimes this subdivision might appear unnatural. On the other hand a subdivision is necessary in order to interpret such a rich and complex work which, once it has been analyzed, shows an autonomous continuity of development in each group, an attention towards the scale of intervention and the conceptual elements of a planning that, even if specialized, never gives up its global articulation. In every work there are elements which stand out in the foreground and others which serve as foundations or sequences, like in the wings of a theatre or in a stage-set where the "scene" changes continuously.

Architectures 1972-1987

Nowadays even more than yesterday, to follow in detail the activity of an architect means to examine critically competitions and projects that are very different in scale and importance, unrealized projects together with beautiful buildings which, however, stand up almost isolated from a tremendous organizing and creative effort of which unfortunately too seldom it is possible to see the results. This effort may apparently finish up as a heap of useless drawing paper; objectively, it's necessary to verify the continuum of the planning, of the "unbuilt" which is probably the most important part of the work of an architect. Even Hollein finds himself in this typical situation.

The competition for the rearrangement of Salzburg Cathedral, taking place at the same time as the beginning of the project for the Mönchengladbach Museum, introduces a planning activity which will have its most significant results during the second half of the seventies. The 1973 Salzburg Competition concerned particularly the inside of the cathedral, the main sites and "focuses" of liturgy together with a few spatial modifications in order to improve the acoustics in the choir. Hollein's work in this baroque context is accomplished by means of a platform on which the liturgical objects slide, together with the functional equipment, characterized by very simple geometrical forms, and suitable for a "neutral" dialogue with the over-decorated context. Again in 1973, for the Press and Culture Department of the United States Embassy in Moscow, Hollein uses supergraphics to create a continuity between the rooms while the original interior decoration is mostly reutilized, so as to show that even with a very small budget it is possible not to give up one's own convictions, and that any commission can be used as an occasion of verification and comparison. Still in 1973, Hollein adopts a brilliant solution for the reconversion project for the stables of the Villa Strozzi in Florence. To the historical building Hollein adds a structure of routes integrating the functions of the whole complex. Unfortunately, Hollein's project for the Villa Strozzi hasn't been realized, and like several other projects, it may still be considered one of the most brilliant planning proposals of contemporary architecture which Florence didn't want to encourage and carry out. Another important project, first prize at the 1974 competition, was the one for the Ecumenical Church on the Turracher Höhe, one of the first examples of architecture intended for the rituals of various religions. The site, on the high ground of a peninsula overlooking a mountain lake, is truly spectacular and stimulating for a project which had to emphasize more the courses than the volumes. As a matter of fact the church and its equipment stand at a crossing of a pedestrian street as in all country villages. The kind of architecture used on this occasion still remains a brilliant example of what can be achieved in these country sites, which are strictly related to their physical environment.

Villa Strozzi Museum of Modern Art Competition, Florence, 1973 (top) and Turracher Höhe Ecumenical Center Competition, 1974. Bottom: Competition Pedestrian Area Salzburg, 1975: Residentzplatz, perspective sketch.

Also the competition for the pedestrian area in the centre of Salzburg, an area where even now Hollein is working for the reconversion of a theatre, is very significant. By means of a few simple interventions, space has been more clearly defined. The very large surface of the pedestrian area (more than 400.000 sq. m.) required a superimposition, a continuum between elements of a diverse urban texture. The key structure of the project is a new paving formed by a wide range of materials; a conglomerate of asphalt of various colours, marble, granite, and gravel. The use of these materials depends on the particular functions which Hollein wants to underline, and also on the characteristics of the environment and the "history" of the urban texture.

Another competition, the one for the Nordrhein-Westfalen Collection in Dusseldorf (a town where Hollein opened a branch of his office in order to follow the works at Mönchengladbach), deals, even if on different terms and in a different context, with problems similar to the ones found in the Salzburg competition. In the case of the Nordrhein-Westfalen Collection, the task is one of giving formal and spatial continuity to a big square by means of a new building suitable for the collection. The building, being a museum, has several elements in common with Mönchengladbach, elements which in this case have more compact forms, without, however, giving up those spatial solutions and those theoretical propositions which characterize Hollein's particular way of dealing with museums. In 1976 Hollein works on the reconversion of the conference rooms and the board room of the Town Hall in Perchtoldsorf, where he adds further valences to the ones already used in the reconversion of the Siemens main office in Munich, Bavaria[58].

In the ancient medieval building, rebuilt at the end of the seventeenth century after a fire, Hollein has concentrated his work on the board room, with a conference table surrounding a marble mosaic with an inlaid bunch of grapes and vine shoots. The simplicity of the interior decoration is underlined by the original touch of the wall panels, while the air-conditioning system is set into the structure of the table and disguised by the wall panels. "Function follows decoration: even more offensive than a simple inversion 'function follows form'..."[59]. Also the sequence of chairs is visually very impressive.

Between 1976 and 1979 Hollein realizes four agencies for the Austrian Tourist and Travel Office. The first of the four was a peripheral branch, inside an extensive commercial area. "...for the interiors of the Travel Agencies, and especially the smaller ones, we have used a combination of straight lines and curves which exploits the space in the most efficient way possible"[60].

This basic principle of composite design, which Hollein had studied thoroughly for the commission concerning the travel agencies (of which the Austrian Tourist and Travel Office wanted about fifty to be built), is clearly exemplified in the realization of the Shopping City South Branch, where space is subdivided into different functional areas (offices and sales) by means of a serpentine counter.

Perchtoldsdorf Town Hall, 1975-76: table, armchairs, plan and council room.

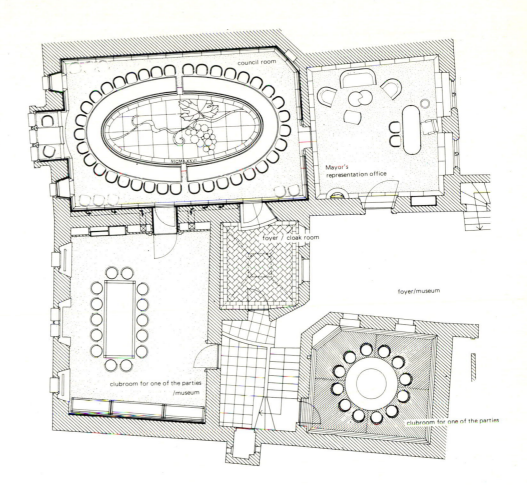

Also the waiting-room is made out of a little circular "temple", having its own particular function and simplifying the routes inside the small space of the Agency. Undoubtedly Hollein's intention is to underline the combination of straight and circular elements: this is proved by the "sky" of neon circles crossed diagonally by a tube, a lighting system which seems to reaffirm and verify Hollein's ideas and principles which on all occasions deal successfully with reality. The realization of the main office of the Austrian Tourist and Travel Office gives Hollein the opportunity of producing a highly dramatic scene, characterized by cultured quotations of unusual and ambiguous elegance. Together with the usual spatial subdivisions into episodes and events clearly characterized by the association of function, and quotations referring to various movements of architectural experience, together with a general strategy of planning which divides and isolates the central vaulted hall from the most technical service structures, Hollein concentrates on the hall which he interprets as a stage on which the various moments of utilization express themselves in further episodes.

But these "Wagnerian echoes" realized with an "obsessive attention to the object"[61], have to be interpreted differently. The production of this scene suggests an evocation balancing itself between quotations of exotic music and elements of a visual hyperrealism which serve as instruments of a mental and emotional escapism. All this is performed in a relaxed and ironic manner within the freedom allowed by the functionality and organizing strategy of all the elements. This is also the background for "unusual" quotations of works of visual art and architecture. The palms and the small temple "...quote John Nash's Royal Pavilion in Brighton. In the middle of this artificial oasis a shining steel support frees itself from a plaster fragment of an ancient column. The special final effect of the environment reaches its peak on a wall painted with a cloudy sky over it, which is also reflected on a canvas standing on an easel, in the style of Magritte"[62]. ·

Fisher von Erlach's catafalques and triumphal doors with Roman columns and obelisks are mentioned by Hollein himself as quotations of the Viennese tradition referring to the ephemeral; the counter of the Opera House is a cultured quotation of Serlio's principles for the stage of his '*Teatro Olimpico*' represented by a metal drapery which is itself a quotation of a popular baroque sculpture of a deposition. The eagles, the starry sky, and even the ceiling quoting Wagner, are all elements of a composition of mass culture which never becomes a serial. The windows of the counter in the form of a Rolls-Royce radiator grid even quote

Bottom left: Austrian Travel Agency, Shopping City Süd Branch Office, Vosendörf, 1976. Bottom right: Austrian Travel Agency Central Offices, Opernringhof, Vienna, 1976-78: details. Next page: Austrian Travel Agency Central Offices: general plan.

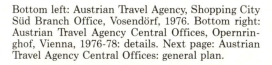

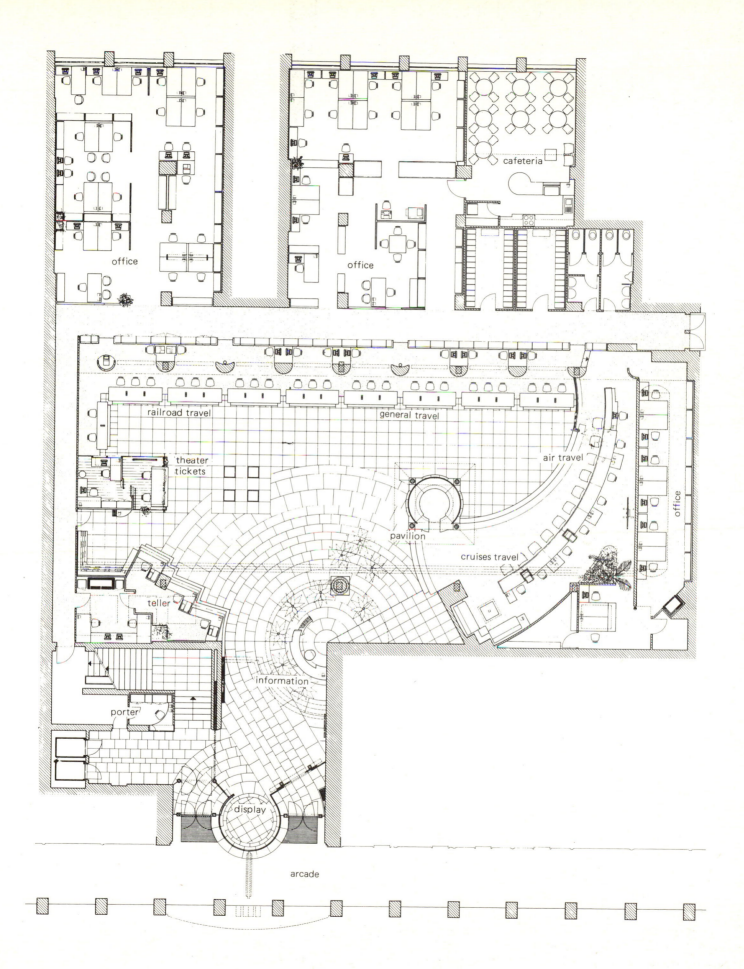

office

office

cafeteria

railroad travel

general travel

theater
tickets

air travel

pavilion

cruises travel

office

teller

information

porter

display

arcade

Hollein himself: everything is brought back to a level of a light game which is articulated in equilibria of great delicacy, the magic of the luminescent and translucent materials giving the strange effect of a scene-installation in which the visitor, being introduced in the foyer of dream, takes his first steps towards the illusion of desire. In this work Hollein focused some elements and strategy which however would allow further use and combinations: a kind of corporate image whose characteristic signs should have been repeated also in the other branches of the Austrian Tourist and Travel Office.

In the Ringturm Branch we find again, in a simpler and smaller version, most of the characteristics of the Opernringhof: the functional subdivision is realized by means of a screen with palms serving also as "scenery", which dissolves in the trompe-l'oeil of the closing wall; a link between reality and imagination, a "possible" opening, indeed a "real" one towards escapism.

The Stephansplatz Branch is carried out with the same method. Its rectangular space is divided by a wall, a ruin, which is at the same time a gate towards imagination, an escape towards mythical worlds, a quotation of other memorable walls; a wall which however should be interpreted as a symbol of nature and artifice, of the transformation of nature through the action of man. The space beyond the wall is totally symbolic, the game is less realistic, the metaphor is carried out by means of a rigorous allegory. The play of reflexes dissolves in the water of the "oasis" in the unreal, milky light of the transparent vault.

In his essay on Wagner published in 1978 Hollein says about Fischer von Erlach, considered the forefather of a "tradition which is typically Viennese": "Fischer's buildings... show an approach to architecture based on the complex arrangement of disparate, even conflicting elements of different origin and meaning to a seemingly heterogeneous whole (of plastic homogeneity however) whose message consciously draws upon the semiotic and iconographic capacity of the various components"[63].

Hollein however, besides quoting, not only from a conceptual point of view, Fisher von Erlach and certain elements of Wagner's architecture, overcomes "...in a spectacular way the traditional boundaries of modern architecture..."[64], interpreting the quotations of architecture with the various aspects of art work, thus extending the boundaries of architectural projects which he transforms into a sophisticated series of metaphorical remarks, allusions, considerations,

Austrian Travel Agency Central Offices: view from the theater tickets counter and details of the interior.
Next page: Austrian Travel Agency Ringturm Branch Office, Vienna, 1978-79 (top). Austrian Travel Agency City Branch Office, Vienna, 1978-79: "oasis" and axonometric.

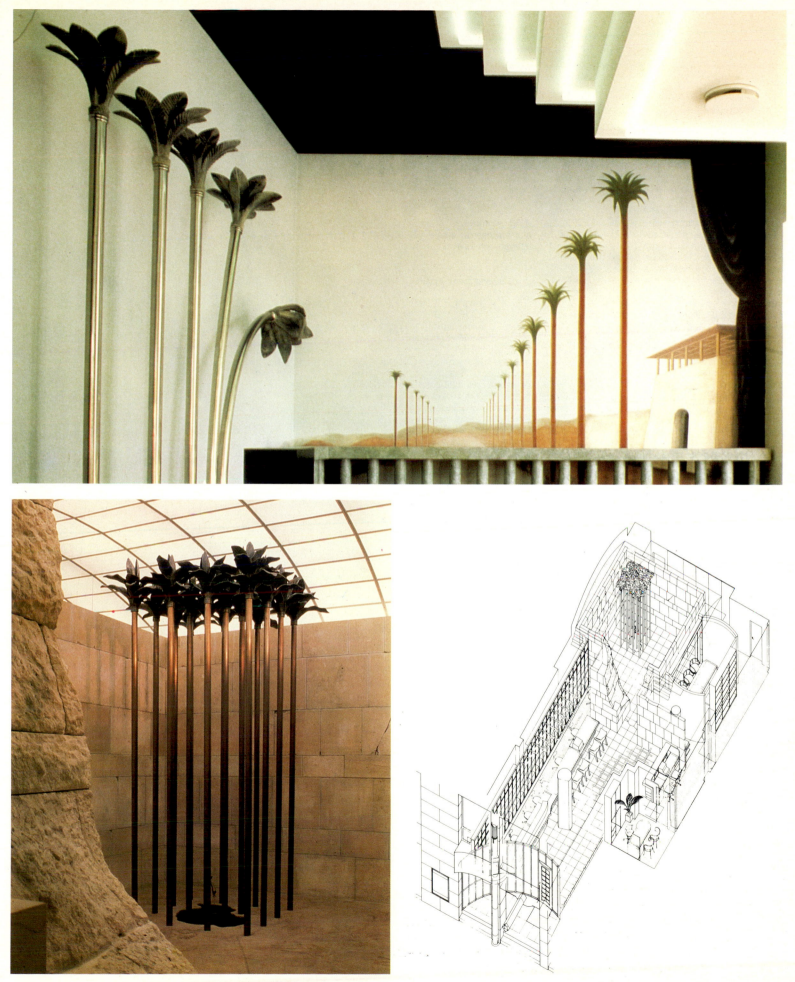

associations and illusions.

In 1978, shortly before the last branch of the Austrian Tourist and Travel Office, the Teheran Museum of Glass and Ceramics was completed, articulated like "...'a museum of showcases' in which the objects on display assume an importance rivalling that of the spaces they inhabit"[(65)]. This time Hollein deals with the theme of the museum, not so much facing a pre-existing space, but creating neutral surfaces, opposing the pre-existence by carring out his own architecture in the interiors, an architecture which is a sequence of episodes, forms and spaces that express (apart from exhibiting beautifully the objects on show) his idea on how a museum could and should be articulated, and also on how the museum could offer an interpretation of architecture apart from the objects on show. This is a technique which reminds us of Antonioni's films, where long descriptive passages start with a series of interior shots and end outside, thus comprehending the whole of the exterior. It's like the many integrated comments that Hollein introduces and that are easily interpreted, but that continuously, as in a game of Chinese boxes, suggest other autonomous descriptive sequences. Hollein extends enormously the boundaries of architecture, but at the same time he presents us with an exciting and endless variety of quotations and allegories. On the ground floor, the stronger presence of historical memory introduces the dialogue by means of combined or isolated showcases: a forest of perfectly cylindrical columns, ending however with forms that are themselves an historical memory, opposed to a square volume, a "black stone" offering its mysteries. On the upper floor, where the presence of history is less conditioning, the creation of a sequence of "classical" spaces underlines, with their perfection, the clear and perfeclty organized display of objects. This interior is autonomous, as are all absolute works of architecture. It almost seems that history gains quality from the interpretation produced by this contemporary moment.

Molag House, of 1977, is instead a small monument to architecture, a work that finds its place in the vast outline of theories concerning a typology which is to be found in all the history of architecture, not just in modern architecture. Molag House represents for Hollein the possibility to play this old game, deeply

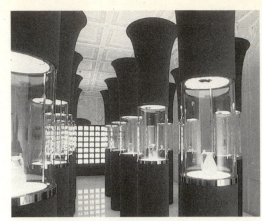

Museum of Glass and Ceramics, Teheran, 1977-78: showcases for pre-islamic glass objects (top) and for islamic glass object (center); bottom: hall, second floor.

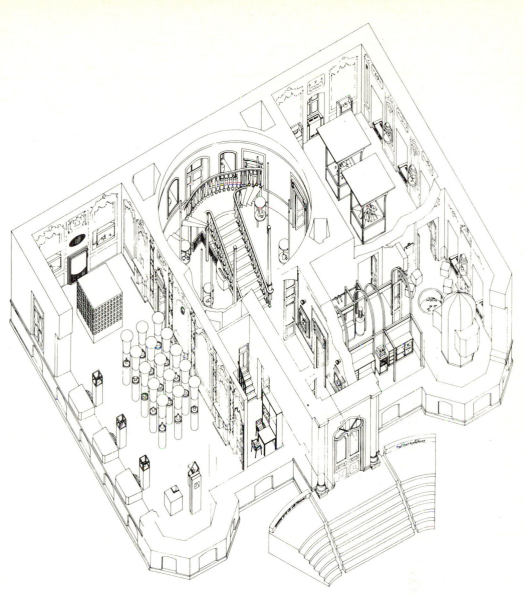

Top: Teheran Museum of Glass and Ceramics: show-cases for pre-historic ceramics and axonometric. Bottom: House Lagler-Molag, Vienna, 1977: sketch and model.

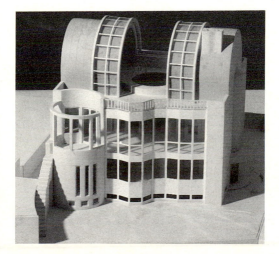

believing in it, which readmits him in the more official context of rationalism after he has provoked so many ill-feelings in those who, examining his work, observed "strange" developments and anticipations. Although this building is strongly influenced by its quotation from Loos, its rigorously organized plans and volumes introduce differentiating if not contradictory valences for the sake of purely functionalist organization, while maintaining ample references to Hollein's architecture of interiors, and also integrating the classical planimetry with broken and curved lines which recall a more mature way of planning that has freed itself from rigorously linear schemes.

The Berlin Museum of Applied Arts is a 1978 project. It's a proposal for the rearrangment of a nineteenth-century building of Martin Gropius which had been severely damaged during the Second World War. As a result of the aftermath of the war, the building stands pratically next to the Berlin Wall, so near to it that Hollein, in one of his solutions for the outside, suggests that a wall of mirrors should be placed very near to the Wall itself which would reflect towards the west side the façade that looks east. There are altogether nine variations of this idea in which interiors and exteriors interpret various roles, suggesting different solutions, but dependant on decisions which have still to be taken. For example, the new urban context imposes a choice between the old entrance and a new one, between a partial and a total reconstruction, a utilization of the interiors partially preserving the original structure on which Hollein intervenes with some autonomous volumes.

The most important aspect of the 1978 project for the Stephanplatz concerns the redefinition of the "wing" between the square and the Graben. The columns, eighteen metres high, are placed on the imaginary border which runs between the Karntnerstrasse, the Seilergasse and the Graben, and stand as a filter and a reference point, establishing a dialogue not only with the various elements of their surroundings, but even with the pavilion facing the Riesentor (one of the gates of the town). This project reveals how Hollein, through the development of his professional experience, may limit himself to elements which are minimal, but nonetheless essential and sufficient to define a space that is deduced, comprehended and "signaled" by means of simple and abstract forms.

The Primary School on the Kohlergasse, planned in 1978, is now nearly completed. It stands on a fairly small site on an incline (like a space resulting from demolition of other buildings, with trees to be preserved), and the school had to be built in two distinct phases of execution in order not to stop the teaching activities. The clever arrangement of volumes, the placing of the entrance on the Kohlergasse, the disposition on various levels and routes which also include the roofing, are decisive elements of a highly skilled intervention which seems to sum up in just one building the quotation of a fragment of urban texture.

The game of compositions is performed through the identification of autonomous volumetries which draw attention to their own functional destination and utilize broken curved lines in order to underline connecting spaces, openings, entrances, changings of tendency even in the planning process: "...the curve has a different quality from the straight line and the lines used must take into account

Top: Museum of the Applied Arts, West Berlin 1978: view of the existing building and example of restoration proposal. Left and bottom: Competition for a new design of the Stephansplatz area, Vienna, 1978.

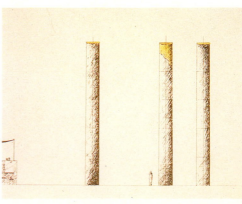

this difference in quality... for instance in the entrance of the school in Vienna the curve is used and its intention is to invite, to welcome the children when they enter and leave the school. A curve is used to achieve what F.L. Wright called 'the destruction of the box'. Certainly for Wright it was different and much more complex... Anyway the important point is the wish to destroy the box. What I mean is that one can use straight lines and cubic elements if there is a choice, a particular wish to do so. In architecture today, however, cubic elements are used in that way because they occur of their own accord, not because there is a particular intention to use them"[67].

The Frankfurt Museum of Arts and Crafts, a 1979 project which Hollein used as his entry to a competition (won by Richard Meier, whose plan has now been built) was awarded the second prize, together with the project of Venturi, Rauch & Scott Brown. Hollein's project suggests a "small town": inside precise spatial boundaries, the actual walls of a town, are gathered buildings, frragments and historical quotations. Also in this case one finds a contraposition of geometries apparently in contrast to each other, a risk, a challenge which Hollein loves to face as he gains more and more certainty, and solves, once again in a magic equilibrium of apparent unbalances and formal contrasts. A game in which Hollein starts to identify himself and that he will often suggest again in his later works. Following chronologically the development of Hollein's works classified as architecture, one then meets with two proposals of "second homes": Marsoner House and Sokol House, which however don't go much further than the first sensitive sketches.

Also the project for the Catholic Centre and the Church of St. Francis at Mainz-Lerchenberg in Germany proposes once more a clear division between

"Kohlergasse 9" Public School, Vienna, 1979: sketches by Hans Hollein, model and axonometric.

spaces and routes. As in several previous proposals, significant spaces alternate with routes, as one moves away from the main "focus", which in this case is the altar of the church.

The now very famous second Schullin jewellery shop, introduces Hollein, at least as far as the sign on the façade is concerned, to an ironical dialogue-contrast with generically post-modern themes. The years 1981-82, the ones during which the jeweller's shop was built, are in fact also those of a rather irresponsible celebration of a post-modern fashion, in which Hollein had little interest. It's also true that the realization of a work of architecture like the second Schullin shop inside a nineteenth-century building almost in front of the Retti on the Kohlmarkt, must have produced a certain bewilderment not only among the Viennese, but also on the whole architectural scene. Colleagues and critics certainly "suffered" this provocation rather than accepting it enthusiastically as a step ahead. With this project Hollein not only compares his last work with another one realized fifteen years before (the Retti), but also "destroys" mental and perceptive habits, obliging us to reconstruct the levels of conceptual and linguistic comparison. The façade now, more than expressing the shop's interior, or rather than being the only façade of an architecture which Hollein has set in the void of another building, reduces itself to a sign-filter in which the formalized elements of composition fluctuate on their own, gathering together again almost casually in abstract supergraphics. The process of composition is certainly played on the absences served by provocative and bare presences. Those who interpret this process as a *décor à la mode* have understood very little of how Hollein in this case acts more as a critic than as an architect. His architecture is a criticism of architecture produced by means of images, as we have learnt from examining his work, but at the same time he realizes a real project with formal inventions which only apparently quote a current fashion that is instead led back towards a planned architecture of which the fashion of post-modern decoration was losing track. One may talk about generosity distributed through the project, about a rescue, but at the same time about an umpteenth challenge. Hollein's experience calls back to order Post-Modernism (whatever it may be) from the rathes absurd libertarianism into which it had ventured, leading back superdecoration to a more objective role of support-integration to composition. Behind the "wings" of the façade, the interior is no longer characterized by protective walls which indicate the introduction of one architecture in to another, but by the more mature and usual "stage" preceded by the functional structures for exhibition and sale. The filter between the two spaces is double and narrow, and the ceremonial play is simple and rarified. The materials are interpreted and utilized for their richness, but also for their double technological reproduction: plastic stands next to gold. "The interior is as sumptuous as anything which Hollein has designed: marble, hardwood, brass, mirror play allusive games with the segmental curve, their juxtaposition deliberately risqué, yet never passing over the brink"[68].

The Ludwig Beck New York store, on the fifth floor of the Trump Tower, ends the period of criticism started with Schullin II, especially as far as the choice of materials and the creation of a very rich and exciting interior environment is concerned. This time the project, having a larger surface available, utilizes the most typical elements of Hollein's compositions: niches, small temples, columns, objects of design and quotations of architecture, all take part in the articulation, and perhaps in the conclusion, of this group of proposals dealing with widely different scales. One looses the dimension of the interior and one takes part instead in a treatment of the contemporary debate where there's obviously no sense of guilt. The liberation from the strict and ascetic rules of pre-war rationalism is by now accomplished. Now its's a matter of playing a complex game, the elements of which are of a different nature and origin, but which can achieve great results, as Hollein has proved.

"To my mind, Hans Hollein is the best interior designer anywhere and I don't mean this in any snide way and certainly not related to the British/American school of decorators. His facility with electrics, pop, Sturm und Drang, Sezession, humour, surrealism, graphics, kitsch, death, history, furniture, archaeology etc., is enviable. He is quite simply like a 20th-century Robert Adam and it is a symptom of our release from the purity of Modern architecture that we can now think of the interior as a separate entirely important entity not necessarily related to an

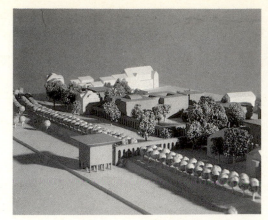

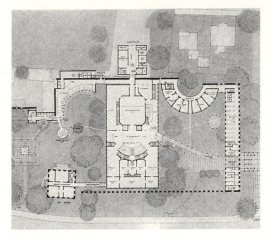

Competition Frankfurt Museum of Arts and Crafts, 1979-80: first floor plan and model (top). Below: House Marsoner, Innsbruck, 1980. Bottom: House Sokol, Baden, 1980.

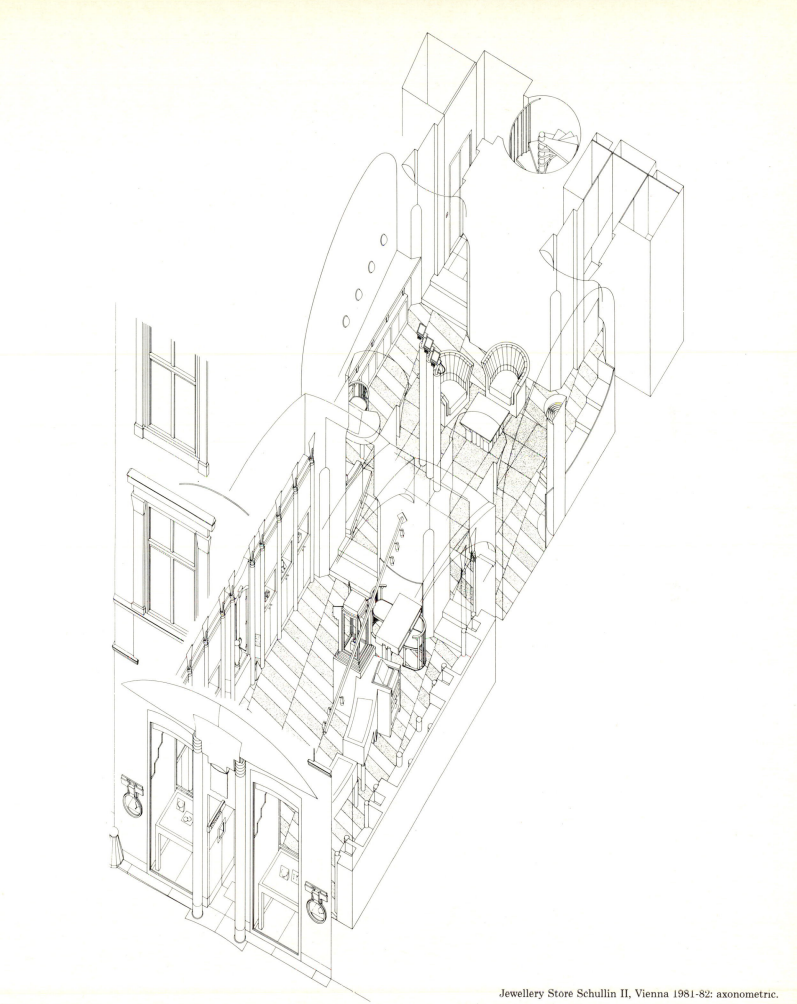

Jewellery Store Schullin II, Vienna 1981-82: axonometric.

Jewellery Store Schullin II: façade and view towards the entrance from the display room. Right: Ludwig Beck shop at Trump Tower, New York City, 1981-83: interior.

Left: Ludwig Beck shop at Trump Tower: view of the entrance from the passage. Below: Expansion project Museum of the Applied Arts, Vienna, 1981. Bottom: "Centrotavola", Cleto Munari production, 1980.

exterior"[69]. Stirling's enthusiasm should perhaps be extended to the other professional activities of Hollein, for example to his architecture; but this article was published in 1980, and the opening of Mönchengladbach took place only in 1982.

The project for the Museum of Energy in Essen refers to a very large area, that of Carl's old coal mine. Planimetrically it develops as an urban context with various buildings emerging as volumetrically autonomous points. The complex is organized around a centre from which various courses depart, and which are planned according to the visitor's need of information and the time available for the visit. The project embraces several periods of execution, with the possibility of its completion after the museum is open to the public. Hollein's intention is gradually to introduce to the public, half of which will be young people, knowledge and information concerning the evolution of technology, from the old windmills and watermills rebuilt as monuments, to the most modern equipment, such as solar panels, pylons, and so on; and then to stimulate the visitor to use the machinery in other sections of the museum according to concepts which are practically the same as those that Oppenheimer had put into practice in the first museum-laboratory of this kind, that is, the Exploratorium which was built in San Francisco just after the war. The diagrams, programs and expositive solutions suggested by Hollein are expressed by means of a complex and yet clear planning articulation which is facilitated by the design of the area itself. Solutions for a more compact and highly intergrated architecture are expressed here in new articulations, as we will see more and more from now on, as for instance in the Berlin Kulturforum. Still in 1980, Hollein planned the extension of the Jugendstil Museum in Vienna (to be placed between two buildings belonging to two different historical periods), in the area of the Hochschule fur Angewand und Kunst, where he teaches in the Department of Architecture.

The building is placed in a rather anonymous context, "in open contrast" with it, and with no desire for integration. Although the integration between the build-

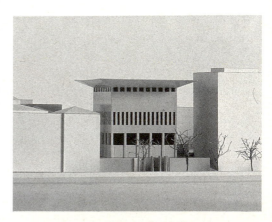

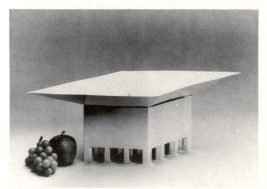

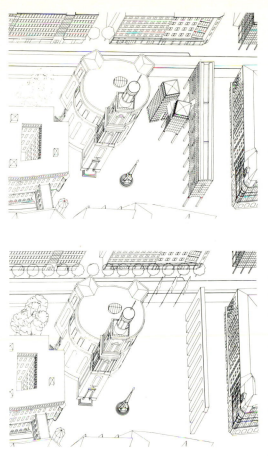

Competition for the Paulskirche area, Frankfurt, 1982-83: project A and B, model.

ing and its context takes place all the same from a functional and distributive point of view, the main purpose is certainly that of revaluing an aesthetic-conceptual "profile" of poor quality and of evident heterogeneity. The strong connotation of the volume and roofing is not only out of line along the façade overlooking the avenue, but it's also slightly out of axis. Therefore, it's obvious that the intention is that of rebuilding a fragmented texture which in this way regains energy and the valences of a volumetrical and spatial link.

The 1982 competition for the Church of St. Paul in Frankfurt concerns the town-planning resetting of the square in which the church is placed. The problem was that of spatially defining an area lacking any real formal and conceptual unity. Hollein confronts the problem by suggesting a "wall" meant to delimit the space of the square and to isolate and identify the Newekreme as a distinct street.

There are two proposals for the "wall". One is of extreme lightness, in which this "screen" has a mainly symbolic role and takes the form of an "aqueduct" whose proportions derive from those of the church of which the aqueduct becomes the "unrolling". In the other proposal the "screen" turns into an independent building on *pilotis* where the entrance is supplied by two towers of which the first one dialogues with one of the angular towers at the back of the church. This is a project that finds its place, in accordance with the other two similar proposals (the Stephansplaz in Vienna and the pedestrian area in Salzburg), in that part of Hollein's architectural planning dealing with the problem of the utilization of historically defined spaces and the contemporary "finish" of architectural-spatial problems which have been forgotten or left unsolved. Concentrating on the interpretation of an ancient context from which he gathers suggestions, Hollein gives a lesson on planning which limits itself to minimal interventions that only serve to achieve a spatial and conceptual "completion".

In 1982 Hollein won the competition for the Frankfurt Museum of Modern Art, now being built. This project represents one of the "monumental" propositions of Hollein's planning activity. It is this museum which completes the great cultural project of Frankfurt, articulated in the construction of several new museums among which we can find that of Richard Meier and that of O.M. Ungers. Also this project interprets and solves the historically defined context, saturating it this time with a compact volume which only on the smaller side of

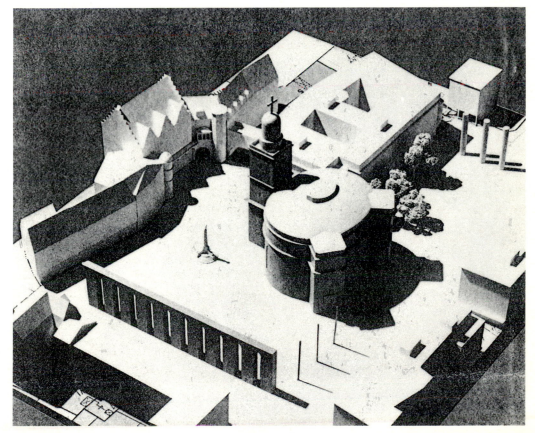

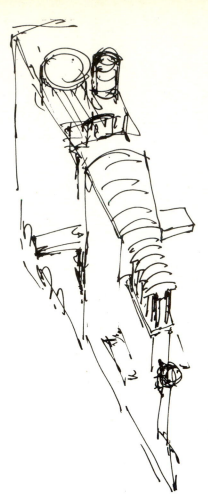

the triangular site breaks up into fragments, establishing in this way a dialogue with the street and the crossings. This museum planned by Hollein (it's impossible not to refer to Mönchengladbach) is an occasion to define and complete a proposition which had been introduced in its time in a not particularly "strong" urban context. Here, however, it finds a way of perfecting itself in a texture characterized by compact volumetries of which the museum itself should become the cornerstone. This project absorbs all those problems related to the planning of a museum, expressing them by means of a volume which, apart from its pedestrian area and only near the Domstrasse, refrains from connections and dialogues.

"Hollein establishes an incisive dialogue with the work of art; a 'neutral' caution (like the one to be met within most contemporary museums) for him is not possible. In Hollein's spaces the works of art seem to be set in an environment characterized by the same unchanging design expressing its need of perfection"[70].

The entrance on the corner between the Domstrasse and the Braubachstrasse leads through several different routes on various levels into a great central hall which receives light from an enormous skylight.

It seems that Hollein's conceptual formulation refers, not to the Viennese masters, who are however always quoted, but to sixteenth-century palaces, to a classicism revisited from a contemporary point of view, that is a classicism which is still present but interpreted in a less rigorous and conceptual way, with an introduction of the metaphor of the town, a town which is recalled for its narrow streets in the south-west of the United States, leading to the main square that symbolically recalls the pueblo.

Frankfurt Museum of Modern Art, 1982-83: sketches by Hans Hollein and axonometric.

These memories of old critical interests which characterize Hollein's full maturity are to be found also in Mönchengladbach where the hill, in the articulation of its internal routes, and in the symbolic rigour of its simple and abstract volumes, may certainly recall, apart from all the above references, the articulation of the pueblo which in Mönchengladbach is being quoted for its organic structure (even if the quotation is very controlled), and also for the symbolic spaces of its main square, which in this case are presented on the positive side, from the outside, while in Frankfurt they are to be found again in the great hall-gallery where the series of routes end.

In the same year there was a third competition in Frankfurt, this time concerning the project for the Post Museum, which is organized around a central hall leading to areas for exhibitions, to projection rooms, services and equipment. In an urban context lacking virtually any historical characteristic, the volume of the hall and the design of the façade almost seem to answer to this responsibility. The alternation, even if fragmented, of white and green stripes is an historical quotation of buildings which reflect certain characteristics of the Tuscan Romanesque. However, all this becomes a "sign" and an introduction, in a building which as usual expresses its continuity and spatial organization particularly inside, but which on the outside splits into highly characterized and diversified volumes, represented by means of different colours on the scale model.

Hollein's project for the Lingotto building in Turin wasn't exactly a competition. In fact, several famous architects had been invited to submit proposals for the reconversion of the beautiful industrial building planned and built by Mattè

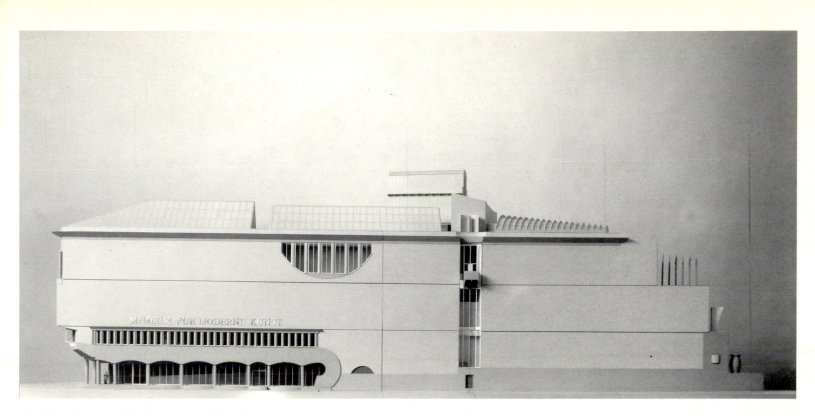

Frankfurt Museum of Modern Art: models and perspective of the exhibition hall.

Trucco between 1914 and 1920, a reconversion concerning also the surrounding area and buildings. In his project which was presented, together with all the others in an exhibition in 1984, Hollein suggests a Research Centre and a Museum of the History of Industrialization and of the Working Class which necessarily implied the preservation of the monumental building, and the demolition of only a few buildings of minor importance. Hollein organized his work in the usual way; that is, by means of commenting on the historical context, in which the architectural integrations answer to functional needs of reconversion and the new propositions assume symbolic, sculptural forms to express and underline a particular method of interpretation: that is, the one concerning the preservation of the Lingotto's main structure (which has a roof formed by a test track for cars that were produced in the building underneath) which is particularly significant for its documentary, artistic, structural and architectural meaning. Hollein's project for the reconversion of the Lingotto building takes into account all these basic priciples. The few alterations only partially involve the façades, but "changes and additions are realized so that one still may see the 'Gestalt' of the complex and of its parts..."[71]. Hollein's reconversion proposes an auditorium, a great external stairway, an entrance forming a secondary axis, transverse compared to the main one, and the image that mostly clearly characterizes the project: three towers which represent arms lifting hammers, an intense and definite interpretation of the whole reconversion.

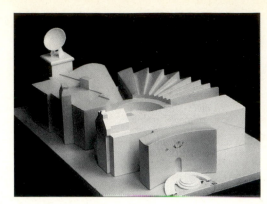

As a matter of fact Hollein's project also shows three poles holding the Fiat emblem. And this is something that counterbalances the image of a monument which is therefore not only the symbol of the working class, but also of an industrial enterprise that is acquiring even greater maturity. These two entities together have turned Turin into the capital of the Italian automobile industry.

A far-reaching project is the one for the Berlin Kulturforum, certainly one of Hollein's most important projects and one which concerns the largest area he has ever dealt with. The site is objectively West Berlin's cultural centre, even if it still cannot be considered so in terms of urban texture and spatial unity.

The realization of a cultural centre is in fact the main purpose of Hollein's project which only marginally, at least from a conceptual point of view, also suggests the creation of a parish centre for the Church of St. Matthew, one of the major elements of this organism which should be re-invented, together with the Scharoun Philharmonic, the National Library, the National Gallery built by Mies van der Rohe, and Gutbrod's 'Premssischer Kulturbesitz' Museums. Hollein "discovers" the presence of a square in a context which already suggests its creation, pointing out and connecting the strong existing architectural presences in accordance with a texture which gives back quality and general representativeness to those elements that have been left isolated until now. What before was intended virtually as a contraposition is now articulated as a whole around which Hollein discovers and invents the structures and the articulations. It's an important project, and so it should be, because it also represented one of the most importan events in the competition for the Berlin celebrations which both the east and west sections of the town wanted to win. Apart from these comments, this project (which however is characterized by a great technical and architectural skill, for example the realization of the channel created in order to define and connect the buildings of Mies and Scharoun, and the slightly curved portico on the opposite side which is also a connecting element) is still nowadays in a

PERSPECTIVE DRAWING

Competition Frankfurt Museum of the Postal Services, 1982-83: model.
Below: Consultation for the Fiat Lingotto Factory, Turin (Italy), 1983: perspective and aerial view of the existing buildings.

phase of evolution, even if its main concepts will certainly be respected.

Another project, which was realized in 1985, is the one concerning a commission from the IBA in Berlin for the construction of a tenement-house with twenty-four flats on a plot planimetrically organized by Rob Krier. For the realization of the flats the IBA had invited several world-famous architects. Most of these flats are now being completed, and they represent, together with other interventions promoted by the IBA, one of the typical German experiences of these last few years: that of producing a dictionary of architecture by inviting the most interesting architects of the contemporary scene to contribute to it. Very seldom, as in this period in Germany has one seen so many opportunities of this kind in which the debate turns into real building; and this has occured not only in Berlin and Frankfurt, but at least in twenty other smaller towns. It's a reaction of maturity to a long period following the Second World War in which one talked only in terms of "built architecture" and of technologies. Nowadays instead we may talk of several episodes in which we see the "adventure" of ideas, but also their realization. For the IBA commission concerning the tenement-house, Hollein expresses

Berlin "Kulturforum", 1983: sketches by Hans Hollein and details of the model.

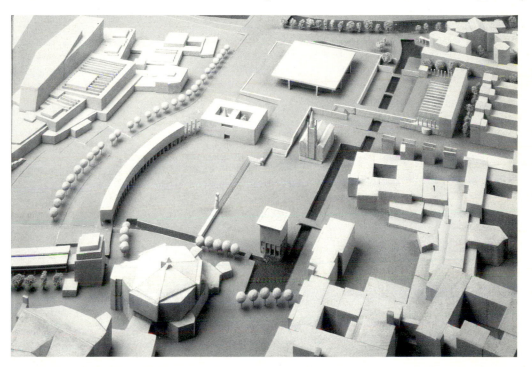

his architecture by means of a compact volume in which the solutions for the interiors and the surfaces of the façades visualize concepts and theories which he had already expressed in other ways. The building code of tenement-houses (twenty-four flats on five floors placed on a plot of 21.45×21.45) induced Hollein to create a structure which is articulated around several central hall-porticos from which lead the entrances to the various flats. The solution of the entrances placed diagonally in relation to the main axes of the building, allows the widest concept possible of spaces set in sequence, particularly for the very small dimensions allowed to the project. Thus, the distributive and formal inventions create unexpected valences offering a way out from the usually strict and repetitive scheme of construction. Every flat, every solution for the façades offers many different chances of avoiding this rigidity.

The possibility of recognizing, during this outline of Hollein's work, basic themes, theories and concepts, experiences of the past filtered and transformed in various occasions of architecture, is certainly reassuring. For instance, in Hollein's project for the IBA commission, one may easily recognize his quotation of Wright's "destruction of the box"[72]. And it's also reassuring to observe how much more important projects, spatial inventions of exceptional quality, may succeed in adapting themselves to a minor scale, having to rely on a limited budget, and to observe the building code of tenement-houses.

Hollein's participation in the competition for the Museum of Egyptian Civilization in Cairo confirms his theories on the concept of the museum as a citadel of art and culture having well defined boundaries, a project of a town which recovers its meaning of existence through the connotation of its volumes and spaces.

"Rauchstrasse, House 8", IBA Apartment Building, West Berlin, 1983: sketch by Hans Hollein, isometric, second floor and first floor plan (next page).

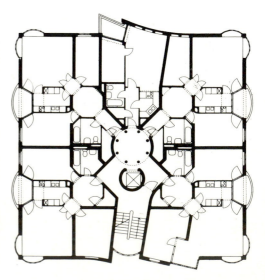

The main expositive structure is organized on a "generating" grid (deriving from Mönchengladbach) which holds a dialogue with other buildings and "main points", like the routes and the "descriptive" elements of Egyptian civilization, as for example the Mosque, the Statue of Ramsete, the Tombs of the Kings.

The restoration of J. Hoffmann's Pavilion in the Gardens of the Biennale in Venice shows another component of Hollein's planning: that of a delicate restoration executed with great attention, an intervention very well documented from a philological point of view on the Pavilion built in 1934. "Early on in his work, Hoffmann recognized the freedom of architectonic statement allowed by buildings for exhibition and for art..."[73]. Hollein recognizes himself in this statement, as he also believes in carrying on a Viennese tradition which is represented by Hoffmann. From this follows a rigorous concern for the preservation, the reconstruction and the restoration of the original structures, even with a barely sufficient archival documentation which, however, he examined closely. For example, the great portals of the entrance to the Pavillion, which are as high as the whole building, thus being a real filter-gallery, are restored as sliding portals which dissapear into the wall, re-establishing in this way the idea of the "airy open pavilion bathed in sunlight"[74] along the channel wich flows through the Gardens.

There are many projects on which Hollein is working nowadays: the Frankfurt Museum of Modern Art which is in advanced stage of realization, the Vienna Neues Haas Haus and the Berlin Kulturforum. Of these works, probably the most controversial one is the Haas Haus on the Stephanplatz, just in front of the cathedral. On the square which had been bombed and then rebuilt, mostly with anonymous buildings, Hollein's new work replaces one of these buildings. In Vienna, as in Berlin and in Frankfurt everything happens in a public debate and through confrontation. The discussions alternate with variations of the projects, as a consequence of these contrasts. The Frankfurt Museum and the Haas Haus are set in a highly defined historical context, and Hollein's intervention cannot but provoke a strong debate. Among Hollein's latest projects, the one for the National Theatre of Japan stands out, together with the one for the extension of the Thyssen-Bornemisza Gallery in Lugano: both are works characterized by an expressive maturity which is beyond dispute but they are not being realized because of local political disagreements, even though Hollein has devoted to them a great deal of time and effort, not only in putting down the projects on paper. So, the real problem of operating in architecture is the one related to the enormous work of continuous modification and adaptation. In this regard Hollein says: "The architect cannot be seen in general as an independent artist, free to realize his dreams and the ideas he has conceived. Professional engagements and commitments should be less individualistic and less restricted, and must be channeled towards more common ends. The relationship between theory and practice has changed and now a continuous and active presence is demanded of the architect, whether in the professional studio, in a public planning office or in the life of the city. It seems important to me that the young understand how vital and gratifying this task can be"[75].

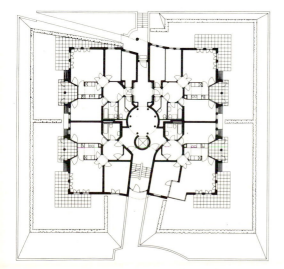

Exhibition and stage design (1973-1987)

This group of works is probably the most difficult one to "examine", because the level of intervention of language expressed by means of metaphor varies a great deal, ranging from simple installations and settings for exhibitions of objects and furniture to scenography, in which symbologies are obviously more substantial. Thus, the interventions may range from simple operations of service and functional organization to the purest theorizations visualizing entire allegories. So, one may regain continuity in the varying range of the elements of communication, from the minimal one in which the functional "service" is preferred, to that of pure metaphor in which the mental "service" is preferred and functional structures are "drowned" in the communicating form.

The designs for the Wittmann-Hoffmann exhibitions in Koln and Milan belong to functional structure, like the stand for the display of furniture or china objets-d'art for the Rosenthal Gallery in Dusseldorf and the display "system" produced for the 1974 Art Fair in Dusseldorf. But it's particularly on the occasion of the MANtransFORMS Exhibition held in New York (1974-76) at the Cooper-Hewitt Museum that theories and formal exemplifications, inventions and conceptual organizations of great quality happily integrate. The task was that of supplying the Cooper-Hewitt Museum with the new role of National Museum of Design, with the help of several famous designers, from Sottsass to Fuller, from Isozaki to Meier, under the auspices of the Washington Smithsonian Institute.

The main risk, which was, however, carefully identified and avoided on the occasion of this opening exhibition, was that of producing a retrospective exhibition of selected products. Instead, the very concept of design comes into the picture as an omnipresent, original, irrational, unconsciuous element in man's life. The exhibition presents simple materials and forms of which the endless possibility of transformation is pointed out, from the original needs of bare survival to the contemporary most sophisticated processes of industrial production. The exhibition also shows the various uses of such elements as cloth, which becomes pure energy when it's a sail, or a house when it's a tent, or a garment when it's shaped in various forms, or art itself when it's preciously embroidered or painted, thus expressing by means of infinite valences man's cultural diversity.

"MANtransFORMS" Exhibition, Cooper-Hewitt Museum, New York City, 1974-76.

So, the visitor is offered by means of objects, environments and installations, a "knowledge" of the many articulations concerning these problems, on which one may identify a grid of comprehension which the visitor himself should complete. As on other similar occasions, Hollein insists on the absence of historically defining educational intentions, or on that of the myth of man's progress through industrialization. On the contrary the exhibition encourages an autonomous experience, which is explained by means of simulations, transformations, allegories and metaphors with which are shown the subjects, the materials and the development of the objects.

The ritual aspects, the exemplifications of concepts, like the one of design which materializes the creative process, the product and every aspect of life, allow to state that apart from life one also talks of "... death, because that is why we all undertake the endeavours we call design – to live and to die, and possibly to live beyond death"[76]. On this occasion, once more one of the key elements of Hollein's poetics and culture emerges very clearly: life beyond death, the feeling of being part of a process in which the memory, for example of other architects and intellectuals, encourages him to follow a route, to connect his own work with previous languages and theories, thus linking his work to his own time through facts and occasions interpreted and formalized with inspired awareness. The characteristics of *mise-en-scène* are to be found constantly in most of Hollein's works. Architecture and, on a different scale, design produce in fact an implosive array of scenery which is itself a series of diagrams and visualizations of conceptual and emotional articulations that expect a way of behaving and a use from the consumer which the architect imagines, just like in an anticipated production. The settings, in the wide subdivision and distinction already produced, from one side tend to provoke an "active" and autonomous behaviour of perception and knowledge, while from the other, like in the scenography of "The Play of Seduction" by A. Schnitzler in which the consumer is an actor, the behaviour has a programming suitable for representing a text. And this is an unusual situation for an architect, certainly similar to the one in which he finds himself when he deals with artistic installations.

In Hollein's work there are very clear analogies between the work of art, the installations mainly expressed by means of metaphor and the scenography of "The Play of Seduction". The public is physically motionless; a perceptive and deductive activity is preferred. One may always consider architecture as an element of "cold" theatre, a *mise-en scène* from which man sometimes withdraws, letting forms act on their own, or (as in this case) "ritualizing" a behaviour. To think of architecture means thinking of its use, that is, the presence of man which is organized according to the architect's intentions. An installation is still architecture, but as its utilization is totally cerebral or meant to favour an idea, the physical presence of man is removed or, if it's still there, it's ritualized, thus turn-

Stage design for "The Comedy of Seduction" by A. Schnitzler, Burgtheater, Vienna, 1979-80.

ing into a ceremony. In this way one has also to see the appearance of the "image" of the architect as a performer. This doesn't happen to Hollein, but it happens and it has happened to many of his contemporaries, thus contradicting this axiom. And this helps to understand how this generation has investigated the discipline from the inside, breaking rules, extending boundaries or forcing an opening in order to keep alive the relations with the other disciplines. Hollein, on other occasions, as for the stage design for "The Play of Seduction' (which was performed at the Vienna Burgtheatre in 1980) doesn't personally take part in the play. Apart from the metaphor of architecture and the *mise-en-scène*, Hollein is represented by the actors, taking the place of the producer or availing himself of his advice. Therefore the architect is always a producer who talks about himself through a "performance", never mind if the actors are not physically present on the stage.

Chronologically, one should now quote the setting for the Alessi at the 1979 Triennial in Milan. It's a classic proposition of an "aqueduct" on whose pillars is represented in sequence the evolution of the centenarian firm, while the arches of the aqueduct are slits of light which are reflected on the opposite round wall. And this is another typical element of Hollein's language, that of opposing the straight line to the curve by "sectioning" the pre-existing space, a circular ring, thus underlining the critical temporary presence of the setting.

The façade realized for the "Strada Novissima", in the exhibition 'The Presence of the Past' at the 1980 Biennale in Venice, may well belong to one of the two subdivisions into which the group of settings have been divided, favouring the metaphorical narration. Concerning what Frampton defines a "curiously didactic exercise" (a definition of which Hollein doesn't approve, as he has always denied his work any didactic characteristic) one should perhaps say first of all that the choice of symbologies which are based on the transformation of a column is not a special "invention", a way of representing the metaphor of architecture by means of this element, even if Hollein himself defines it as "...a structural element which has become absolute architecture"[78], but rather a "deduction". It's from the interpretation of the context of the *Corderie*, from the sequence of columns of the nave of this industrial building that Hollein derives his comments. It's not a superimposition then, as for many other façades set in the space between one column and the other, but a rhythmical intensification which, through its own transformations, exemplifies the evolution of Hollein's concept of architecture: "...the metamorphosis of a column, starting from the reality of one of the actual stone columns of the 'arsenale' passes through a series of transformations. Thus the column in question was first rendered as itself, then as a crudely trimmed tree, then as an entire building (since its "place" was occupied by a large model of Adolf Loos's Chicago Tribune competition entry of 1922) and then as a ruined denial of itself, made explicit through the aerial suspension of a broken column so as to provide an entrance. Finally it appeared as an ambiguous sign of both nature and culture. This was made manifest through a piece of fake topiary; the vertical bush being trimmed so as to conform to the profile of the original column"[79].

Therefore, in the atypical situation of a direct comparison between architects of very different origin and commitment who also confront each other on the matter of the metaphor in real scale, Hollein behaves as if he had to deal with a professional commission: he analyzes the context and faces the problem as an architect, or rather, as an artist-architect. He realizes a functional and "real" façade, which is reliable in its physical definition and could even be accepted as architecture. It's not a manifesto of intentions, but still an occasion, among the others which have already occured to him, for defining the relations between thought and language, and maybe of adding something he hasn't yet said. What a difference on the whole from so many unskilled enlargements of sketches, which are the only usual form of expression, or from the clumsy quotations of Beaux-Arts! "Like in a small world exhibition which realizes in falsehood the dreams of reality, this show has the merit, compared with the usual heliocopies pinned on walls, of slamming in people's faces, in 'natural' dimensions, the virtues and miseries of theory, thus obliging it to come down on the major scales of architectural fake so as to take upon itself at least the responsability and the risks of a direct visual test"[80].

The last two most important exhibition designs in which the artist-architect

"The Turks in Vienna", Commemorative Exhibition of the Turkish siege of Vienna, Kunstlerhaus, Vienna, 1982-83: details of interior.

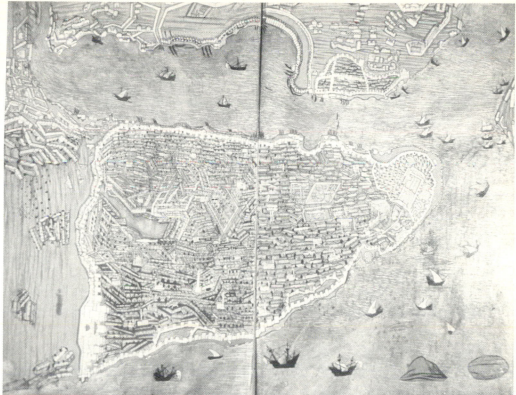

"The Turks in Vienna" Exhibition: map, detail and general view of the front side.

expresses himself with the skill of a great producer concern the *mise-en-scène* of two episodes of Vienna's history, both on show in the Kunstlerhaus. The 1982-83 exhibition is the one concerning the three-hundredth anniversary of Vienna's siege by the Turks. On this occasion Hollein replaces the façade of the building with an enormous 'signal' which transforms it into a Turkish tent. This represents another possibility for Hollein of proposing his work by means of languages of contraposition and integration, in a compact, allegorical structure. In Hollein's intervention there's also a certain consonance with the enamelled sheeting and decoration of Otto Wagner's underground station in the Karlsplatz, where the Kunsterhaus is also set. "He had the idea of covering the classical portico of the Kunstlerhaus in a Turkish campaign tent, which appeared with great effect in two parts and at two different scales, the first being the full tent with attendant figures on top of the portico, the second being the wall panels of a much larger tent arranged symmetrically on either side of the classical entrance. One is astonished by the proliferation of metaphors and metonyms which this juxtaposition engendered. On the other hand, the Turks are represented as having returned mysteriously to conquer classical Vienna, and in so doing they seem to reverse history and to challenge once again the supposed preminence of occidental over oriental values; on the other hand, an internal play is set up between the tent panels and the light enamelled steel cladding of Otto Wagner's nearby Karlsplatz station, so that the mind is bounced back and forth between the tent and the building, between stressed skin and classical stereotomy"[81].

"Dream and Reality-Vienna 1870/1930" Exhibition, Kunstlerhaus, Vienna, 1984-85: sketch by Hans Hollein and details of interior.

Therefore on this occasion the building is hidden and used as a pedestal, in order to underline the scene on top, and the cornice is re-interpreted as a balustrade from which some characters of the 'scene' itself appear. The building can be perceived again, beyond the ephemeral superdecoration, and be conceptually revisited in this new role.

For the 1983 exhibition "Dream and Reality – Vienna 1870-1930", the Kunstlerhaus is "adopted" as an element of the scenography of the façade: the main front expresses itself, that is, in the conceptual diagram of its time. Of the two façades of the side wings, the left one is completely covered by a gold film (the dream), while the right one is painted completely grey (reality). Above, a gigantic statue holds a dialogue, through the neon sign "Traum und Wirklichkeit", with a great model of the Carl Marx Hof. Therefore the building is included, as the main signal in a sequence of secondary signals, in a theatricality formed by

quotations which also point out the complexity and the articulation by means of 'stations', of the exhibition's organizing structure.

If the *mise-en-scène* of the show on the Turks' siege reconstructed spectacularly the atmosphere of that period, "Dream and Reality" procedes instead by means of descriptions and quotations, whenever this is possible, of architectures, of art and of the most important moments in history which have characterized this period. The interiors are articulated according to these intentions. In the 1983 exhibition on the seige, the *mise-en scène*, the precise reconstruction of the battles, the elements and quotations of the period expressed by means of original materials, represent faithfully, from a historical but also from a popular point of view, the chosen theme, as in Madam Tussaud's Museum, where the groups of characters are intentionally placed in spots where they can mingle with the crowds of visitors. In "Dream and Reality", another exhibition which has been historically reconstructed in an impeccable way, this concept is in practice overcome: "Even if this exhibition is scientifically exact, it also has to be popular and capable of transmitting experiences"[82]. When it's possible, whole pieces of history of architecture, theatre, cinema, intellectual, political and scientific tendencies are literally reconstructed by means of original materials. "The charm of the original is displayed not only in order to respect the authenticity of confrontation, but also to provoke associations..."[83]. These two exhibitions represent for Hollein an opportunity of quoting and mixing together typical elements of his poetic expression. Superimpositions and integrations extend their "narrow" planning boundaries in order to take part in a wider communication, which however doesn't withdraw from the strategy of the project. Both inside and outside, this strategy is visualized by means of significant episodes, sequences and associative stimulations which all have, every single one, a definite identity, a specific language, a totally autonomous precision

"Dream and Reality-Vienna 1870/1930" Exhibition: "Die Zeit", detail of interior (top) and general view of the front side.

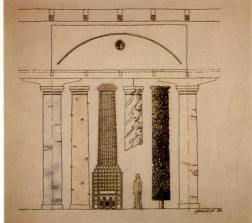

Left and top: "The Presence of the Past" Exhibition, façade project for the "Strada Novissima", Venice Biennale, 1980. Below: design for Bertelsmann Anniversary Celebration, Gütersloh, 1985.

of project and realization.

The 1983 setting for the celebration of the Fiftieth Anniversary of the Bertelsmann Publishing House, may almost be considered scenography. In the background, on the platform is an enormous set of shelves with golden books, but the scenography continues also in the hall, with three towers eight metres high which represent by means of a "monumental" metaphor the concepts concerning the evolution of books as a means of communication. The spatial definition of these objects-monuments is an element of continuity on various levels of interpretation. A game of references and quotations, exemplified through spatial suggestions, which finds another opportunity of expression in Hollein's exhibition on his own work for the Pompidou Centre in Paris, an exhibition which was then moved to Vienna and Berlin. For Hollein, this is a way of revisiting his own architecture, and in so doing, he finds a way of inventing a setting, a visit to "rooms" which are visualizations of the critical organization produced by my visit through his archival documents.

One should also say that the whole range of these experiences which go under the name of "exhibition and stage design" forms an important stage in Hollein's

"The Golden Eye" Exhibition, Cooper-Hewitt Museum, New York City, 1985. Bottom: "Perchtoldsdorf" chair, 1975-76.

planning and intellectual activity. This period, if on one side amplifies the possibilities of conceptual and expositive articulation supplied by the simple occasion of planned and built architecture, on the other side constitutes a clear sign for those who persist in considering architecture as a need for absolute monumentalization[84]. The objects of pure design which may be extrapolated from these settings are the absolute monuments-diagrams of a much more structured language. The extrapolation of his furniture and objects from the general context introduces a further autonomous critical valence which Hollein himself doesn't ignore even while working on projects of widely different scale and articulation.

Design (1972-1987)

This discourse in which one intentionally extrapolates from various contexts or one analyzes autonomous objects of Hollein's work could be entitled "Design as an occasion for architecture". It's an objective integration of Hollein's poetic expression as a whole, even if it's possible to analyze his design as separated from the rest of his work.

The sixties offered opportunities for many architects, including Italians, of the last generation to confront an apparently autonomous discipline rediscovered as a planning exercise, that is, a practically instantaneous way of planning and building, a verification in real scale of the "functioning" of one's own visual three-dimensional language. For the radical Florentine design of the middle of the sixties for example, this is an exciting discovery: the verification of metaphors, design submerged by intentions and revisitations. A piece of furniture brings within itself critical and often ironical intentions; form and function are reinvented and revisited. Often, as in the "Superonda"[85], the utilization of a piece of furniture is suggested, but never imposed: the freedom of the spectator is absolute.

Sottsass's work had pointed out in those years how design could be an opportunity to extend oneself through these experiences. Hollein, even if in contact with these situations, is already involved in more professional work. His design is absorbed in the general context of planning, of which it represents a synthesis, a formal and conceptual specification. The history of Vienna of the beginning of the century is already present, the references and relations are already integrated in a complex language.

The "Miller Relax Cell" produced in 1971 represents an element of connection between experimental experiences, since the time of the collaboration with Walter Pichler, and their transformation into a real environment: more than a cell, it's rather an extension of the idea of a relaxing armchair enclosed in a self-isolating shell. But it's particularly with the furniture which characterizes the Siemens AG interiors that Hollein seems to lay the basis of a different language of expression. The objects derive from minimal geometrical forms, almost a conceptual reconstruction, being then enriched with contructive and formal details and real research into colours, in sequence. A small vademecum, a designer's handbook, in which theory and practice mix together while also becoming more mature.

The 1973 production of sunglasses for the American Optical Corporation turns into a pyrotechnic representation of fantasies and formalizations which have freed themselves from the typical conventions concerning this kind of object. Already in the 1968 Austriennial, the glasses are a sign, an instrument of identification: in this case they even represent an escapism, a pleasure, an exciting moment of performance.

"Ensemble Diagonal" for the Wittmann (1974-75) is a series of armchairs, tables and screens, of identical formal design which recalls the concepts and ideas already put forward in the display system for the 1967 Retti exhibition systeme, continued in the furniture for the Siemens AG, and completing their life here in pieces of furniture intented for industrial production. The Ensemble Diagonal is a continuous game of references and variations of a diagonal which identifies boundary lines and intersecting surfaces.

The 1975-76 furniture for the Perchtoldsdorf town hall is not to be considered any more as part of a research, but on the contrary it expresses Hollein's maturity in this field. Tables, sofas and chairs recall instead built architecture, in particular a section of the "double" column at the entrance to the Feigen Gallery, or the curved profiles of volumes and surfaces of architectural projects which are now being realized. Hollein's syntax and visual alphabet are here being expressed through objects of design of real maturity, being themselves true models of architecture. The chair of steel tubes produced on this occasions is certainly an all-time classic. Equally defined in its form, and anyway impossible to relate to any previous examples, it is the "presence of the past".

Hollein's attention to the realization of an overall image, of a 'corporate image', for banks and travel agencies embraces even the details of design and furniture. Already in the visual design of corporate image for the Frankfurt Deutsche Bank (1973) one may recognize Hollein's almost schizophrenic ambivalence towards extreme functional detail, which visualizes itself in innumerable exemplifications of scale and role, a recognizable image being at the same time a memory and a theoretical statement. However, it's particularly in the travel agencies that eagles, palms and starry skies are used with greater autonomy, thus establishing a real novelty in the specialized context of the corporate image. These are the ideas which particularly show Hollein's introduction to a period of full maturity. Ideas significant in themselves and suggested almost with self-indulgence, but at the same time at the risk of becoming kitsch, which requires maximum control in the combinated use of all these elements: a dangerous path wich Hollein loves, and follows with great skill.

At the moment in which he seems to abandon the "intention" of stating something, his language expresses even more deeply, through these 'signals' and also through many others, the elements and articulations of his thought.

All that has been described in this section has been until now "extrapolated" from a complex planning context: installations, interior design and decoration in which the object is rendered autonomous. All those objects of interior design which could have been "removed" from their context have been overlooked. What is being analyzed here is that particular object which expresses right from the beginning an almost inconscious will of autonomous life. The commissions for Alessi, Munari, Memphis and M.I.D. between 1980 and 1981 probably represent the first really autonomous moment of this process: projects which synthesize a long process of development, formalizations which recall the main stages of Hollein's cultural and planning evolution, and at the same time carry out a role, that of relating a story which is also Hollein's story. For example, the Alessi tea-set quotes on the one hand, almost without letting it be recognized, the languages which belong to the origins of the Viennese modern design of the beginning of the century; on the other hand it also quotes the already historically defined aircraft-carrier of Hollein's theoretical statements. The tray represents the take-off and landing strip of an aircraft-carrier (as a matter of fact the trace of the landing fighters is carved on the tray), and the tea-pot and the other interlocking elements quote che control towers of the aircraft carrier.

The fruit dishes for Munari are real models of architecture, as well as quotations of Hollein's typical formal models which recall his original theories,

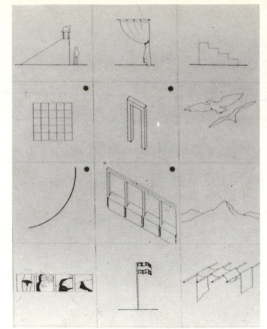

Top: Austrian Travel Agency, Corporate Image design, 1976. Below: Fruit Bowl, Cleto Munari production, 1980. Bottom: "Program 6" and "Melitta", tea and coffee sets for Alessi, 1980.

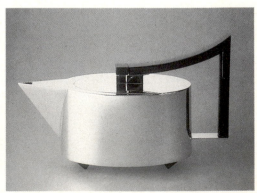

Top: Yamagiwa lamp, 1984. Bottom: "Kohlmarkt" lamps, Baleri Italia production, 1984.

his first articles on Bau. The Memphis table as well as the M.I.D. dressing table may be considered as rigorous and joyful visualizations of forms and thoughts which almost act by subtraction, essentializing and sometimes superdecorating basic concepts. "(P.) ...in the almost casual materialization of an object, like your table for Memphis, there are elements of the curve. Almost from a vacuum, it seems, the table was born. The lines enclose and embrace other situations and what remains, what one sees, is a piece of design. (H.) There are other reasons... even in the work for Memphis. First, there is a certain dialectic between hard and soft in my work and, naturally, the curved line stands for the soft and the straight line for the hard. In other cases this hard-soft dialectic is used without resorting to the curve but anyway, in a concise version, this is the case here. Then there are elements that are suspended, almost hanging, which I frequently use. As with suspension bridges, where one creates an accentuated curve that is entirely natural"[86].

The 1981-82 projects for Poltronova and Wittmann already follow a more integrated idea of industrial production. The Poltronova sofas recall and still quote quite accurately from Hollein's personal concepts, which are here expressed differently, however. With "Marilyn" Hollein allows himself a relaxing and liberating experience, while with "Mitzi" the experience seems more rigorous, referring as it does to more simplified planning schemes. The "City Bett" is a real altar, a site for ceremonies but not yet for sacrifices, however realized with the greatest attention towards materials and colours. The curves of these projects follow the idea of the "hanging curtain", but perhaps the more ironical element of the load diagram.

The display system first used for the Ludwig Beck store in New York, built in iron and perforated sheeting, is used again on other occasins in which the various elements that form the system assume their own functional autonomy. Also the lamps for Baleri and Yamagiwa are subject to this process, which extrapolates them from their original context. For example, the Baleri lamp is called "Kohlmarkt", because Schullin II is in this street, and the lamp is extracted from that particular interior. And even the tables and furniture designed for the exhibition "Dream and Reality", and for the one on the siege of the Turks, are still waiting to be produced. However, almost to underline the quality and the value of these projects of interior design objects, one may observe how Hollein, better than others, can carry out this process of extrapolation: after all he's quoting himself.

The exhibition "Le Affinità Elettive" (The Chosen Affinities) (1984-85) is one of Hollein's more recent opportunities for direct confrontation in time and space with other first-rate architects involved in the contemporary debate[87]. The installation is a quotation of his project for the Sigmund Freud Museum, and the sofa expresses, as for the other architects who have been invited to take part in the exhibition, his own chosen affinity, the process of inspiration materialized in an object, and underlines the unconscious processes by which every object is "interpreted" by the spectator through mental associations, memories and personal experiences.

The invitation to the exhibition "The Golden Eye" at the Cooper-Hewitt Museum for the Festival of India (1985-86) gives Hollein the chance of using different materials, those of Indian handcrafts, especially lacquers and precious materials, which stimulate him even more to enrich his already mature experience as an artist-architect, as with his designs for the jewels for Cleto Munari and for the Kochert Collection (1987). Here Hollein identifies the opportunity given by the project, especially the objects for Munari which may be considered as autonomous architecture, monuments realized in a scale appropriate to the level of celebrations and memories.

In 1987 Hollein successfully produced objects and installations for art exhibitions in which the object of design however played the main role. It is appropriate to discuss this because Hollein's participation in the exhibition "Nouvelles Tendances" in the middle of 1987 (together with A. Mendini, P. Starck etc.) as well as in the Documenta in Kassel during the summer of the same year, was an opportunity to present objects characterized by a strong symbolic significance, real moments of synthesis, intentional and ironical statements. The "Carillon-Turm", as well as, in a different scale, the glass tower for Swarovsky

International, are architectural projects whose models, or sketches, already have an identity of their own, and not only a conceptual use. Together with the jewels of the Kochert Collection, they may be considered objects whose beauty shows Hollein's full creative maturity.

"Designing furniture is basically a way of putting into practice your own architectural ideas, your own philosophy... In designing furniture... you ascribe to the piece a number of other intentions... I think that to design a chair is a great temptation for every architect; it is the ideal vehicle for transmitting simbolically your own ideas on fundamental issues in architecture. The specific characteristic of the chair as an object is that it can serve almost as a model for architecture. Not like a model that reproduces an architectural plan on a smaller scale than the real thing, but as an object that has its own dimensions and at the same time refers to something on a completely different scale. It is really this ambivalence that is so seductive for the architect because your relationship with the object is one to one and this is usually impossible"[88].

One couldn't find a better definition to describe the kind of evolution which has characterized experimental work in contemporary design. Even if expressed in a more implicit, if not unconscious way, these are the parameters inside which the young radical Florentine architects re-invented in the middle of the sixties a way of designing furniture as an opportunity of operating in architecture[89]. The second stage of this evolution took place in Milan, where Sottsass lives, and where at the beginning of the seventies Mendini, edited "Casabella", publishing in his review the new trends in design. Mendini, who in the next few years was to produce the "Tea and Coffee Piazza" (1980) for Alessi, inviting famous architects (including also Hollein) to draw trays and tea-pots. Carlo Guenzi, one of Mendini's former collaborators on "Casabella", produces in 1984 the set design for "Le Affinità Elettive" at the Triennial. The image of Italian design then goes beyond its national boundaries and starts to be exported worldwide. Hollein, from a critical and theoretical point of view, plays a part in Italian design particularly with regard to "elective affinity", and even nowadays he collaborates with several Italian firms. This concerns industries which have a limited production of the objects suggested by the architect, and which therefore only represent those theories and concepts to be developed in order to lead to industrial production. (Industrial design profits enormously by this, but officially insists on ignoring the origin of its own success.)

Top: "Mitzi" and "Marilyn" couches, Poltronova production, 1981. Bottom left: "Vanity", dressing table and mirror, M.I.D., 1981-82. Bottom right: "City Bett" and "Bio Bett", Wittman production, 1982-83.

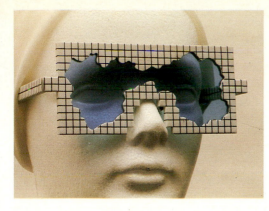

Artist's work (1975-1987)

To analyze the criticism on Hollein's work means to meet almost only with specialized analytical essays on his activity as an architect. On the contrary, his interventions as an artist are also part of his work, because of the many elements which integrate his professional work as a critic and an architect. However, there is no autonomous critical work on his activity as an artist, and no comparison between Hollein's work and the contemporary artistic debate. Hollein's interest in art cannot, however, be separated from the debate on contemporary art. His intellectual origins and his evolution establish a continuous comparison with the art disciplines which he never considers as separated from his activity as an architect and a critic. If in these recent years his artistic work has been expressed autonomously only on a few occasions, this only means that his general activity, in the various fields of intervention, is in any case converging with his architectural work.

One may analyze his planning activity as an artist and a designer, thus observing how he reflects every aspect of the evolution of the artistic debate in the same evolution of his projects, holding a continuous dialogue, characterized by vital and stimulating references, with Segal, Kienholz, Kosuth, Smithson, Oldenburg, Vito Acconci and many others.

One may start this chronological analysis with Hollein's participation in the 1975 competition "House for a Superstar" for the magazine "The Japan Architect", in which one may distinguish a conceptual theorization formally expressed by means of tombs and cenotaphs. Hollein takes the chance of defining the monument as a place of death and celebration of the image and memory of a superstar. The architecture of life is not the monument. "Every architect who designs a church, designs a house for a superstar..."[90]. For Hollein a superstar is a superstar because the memory of him lasts for centuries, therefore the most suitable house is a funeral monument. What he wants to say is that churches, banks and museums cannot be monumental.

The rigour of his analytical methodology has been recognized also in this case, and his work could have taken part in any kind of biennial, triennial or quadriennial...

For "Umanesimo-Disumanesimo" (Humanism-Inhumanism) held in 1980 in Florence, Hollein chooses the Pazzi-Quaratesi Palace, a Renaissance building probably designed by Brunelleschi, placing his installation in the classical inner courtyard: walls made of sandbags between the columns, and facing these, poles of natural wood, an obvious quotation from a place of execution. The disturbing

Top: Sunglasses, American Optical, 1973. Bottom left: "Ultima Scena" Exhibition, Venice Biennale, 1984. Bottom right: "The Gymnastics Lesson" Exhibition, Mönchengladbach, 1984.

presence of death redeems itself through a series of minimal interventions which establish another interpretation of life: bronze grafts spring up from the poles, in front of the door one catches a glimpse of a fire... Humanism and Inhumanism are therefore interpreted by Hollein with the maximum ambiguity through quotations and mental associations. Hollein's installation is still a project, an allegorical comment, a sequence of conceptual and visual metaphors, a reference to physically defined history expressed in the chosen architecture. Hollein is violent and provocative (where in this case is his famous irony?), but from life, which is also death, he draws continuous quotations, and Humanism and Inhumanism are considered as a whole, because one derives from the other and vice versa. When there is no presence of history, Hollein quotes it, and so it becomes part of memory, thus remaining a source of inspiration.

For the 1984 Biennale in Venice "Ultima Scena" ("Last Scene"), Hollein reconstructs the interiors of Leonardo's 'Last Supper' ("Ultima Cena"). Architecture is always a visual diagram of a culture, and here, through the absence of the characters, it represents the expectation of other table companions.

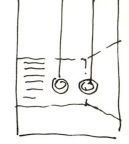

A few months away, the exhibition "The Gymnastics Lesson" inside the Mönchengladbach Museum, planned and built by Hollein himself, is certainly one of the most complex and complete examples of his activity as an artist. For the first time, also a real art critic, Johannes Cladders, the Museum's director, analyzes very accurately Hollein's artistic work. Cladders has been Hollein's companion for a long time, the person who has contributed most of all to the episodes concerning Hollein's activity at Mönchengladbach. "In 1970 Hollein held his first exhibition at Mönchengladbach, in the old museum on Bismarckstrasse. The theme was that of 'Death'. This exhibition was as complex as the present one in the new museum at Abteiberg. This building planned and built by Hollein, also represents one of the references, and not the last one, to this first exhibition devoted to concepts of relativity. In the new museum architecture itself undergoes a metamorphosis, becoming part of present life"[91]. The exhibition 'The Gymnastics Lesson' also includes "an unexpected transformation which takes place during the observation of the visualized conceptual articulation as well as in the reference to the spatial enclosure which, planned by the architect Hollein and meant for temporary exhibitions, is now revisited and re-proposed by the artist Hollein in a new aspect"[92].

In fact I think that from a historical point of view it is very difficult to quote another example of such a level of ambiguity which is employed here in order to destroy, at least from a conceptual point of view, a separation between disciplines which often justifies the existence of a well defined boundary that has only a strategical purpose. Hollein destroys this boundary operating in the same place, and almost foretelling, as an ironical actor and spectator, the critic's

"The Gymnastics Lesson" Exhibition, 1984: detail and sketches by Hans Hollein.

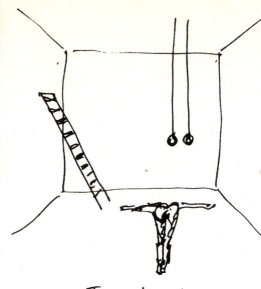

Tumshude

embarassment in front of this "impossible" co-existence. Even the division of the exhibition into environmental installation, watercolours exhibited in the Museum's Drawing Department and valuable catalogues numbered as a multiple, continues to express its ambiguity, in which none of these three elements comes second to another, but on the contrary each of them comprehends the others. Cladders goes on to say: "In the Graphics Department Hollein exhibited watercolours and drawings under the title 'Eros-ion', transforming the name of the God of Love into a geological term. Hollein's erotic drawings may also be interpretated as landscapes... His studies of the female body may certainly be considered autonomous drawings from the nude, but at the same time they contain a great number of principles and possibilities which may be interpreted retrospectively in the context of his whole work: in his buildings, in his interior architectures, in his design for domestic objects, in his environments and sculptures"[93].

Anyway, this way of interpreting Hollein's drawings, besides being quite legitimate, adds new elements of criticism and perceptive amplification, introducing us to the second 'station' of the exhibition: "The Gymnastics Lesson", the title of the great environment, doesn't try to change verbally the sense of the content, but what one sees in the exhibition justifies only superficially its title: objects similar to sports equipment... behind the eye however there's something which revolts at terms like horse, fixed bar, rings... which come so rapidly to our minds. Orders of magnitude which have been shifted, formal simplifications, different materials, impossibilities which point out the traps hidden beneath the ground. They are the traps of each metaphor which holds the prey of its statement in the 'tertium comparationis', that is, in a tangle which suggests ideas and stimulates imagination, unlikely, however, in a curious and eager direct perception"[94]. This pursuit of original perfection, which was still implicit in the first two 'stations', becomes explicit in the third one. The catalogue shows the ideal and historical references in the continuity of Hollein's whole work in which separations and disciplinary rules are overcome.

The search of the archetype as a model of perfection is exemplified in the quotation of the Horses of St. Mark, which were already present in the table-stands of the "Last Supper" and are here recalled in the horses' apparel. Mantegna, Piero della Francesca and Leonardo are regularly quoted, also as precise spatial and conceptual references. "In this context Hans Hollein resorts to his-

"The Gymnastics Lesson" Exhibition, 1984: drawings (1972, 1973) presented in the catalogue.

tory, to the emotional valences of materials, to the artistic disciplines of drawing, to the vulcanic energies of eroticism, to the coolness of observation and of intellectual dissection, to symbols and myth"[95]. So the catalogue is enriched also by these historical and conceptual references: the printing is realized with great care, some of the drawings are printed in gold, the pages are printed only on one side and bound together with an external cotton string, in order to suggest a final opportunity for active participation on the part of the owner, that is, that of finding again the only sheet of paper on which the catalogue has been printed.

This catalogue-integration, which is itself an element of the exhibition, is probably a perfect exemplification of how Hans Hollein intends to use his writings. From the original theorizations, as his work specializes in different fields, his writings also transform themselves and become more mature: they integrate the project by pointing out implicit elements of inspiration and assertion; they serve as introductions to the catalogues of exhibitions like "MANtransFORMS" or "Dream and Reality"; they are superimposed on the exhibition, as in "Death", or they reconnect memories as in the presentation of the artists chosen by Hollein for the Biennale as the Austrian Commissioner. Hollein also plays the role of architectural historian: on various occasions, as for Schindler, Hoffmann and Wagner, he has analyzed these architects' works with a thorough study which is the result of archival research and of a brilliant critical analysis.

"Humanism-Inhumanism" Exhibition, Palazzo Pazzi Quaratesi, Florence (Italy), 1980.

Vertigos and equilibriums: vitality of a dialectic

This is not the occasion, even from a critical point of view, to express a final opinion on Hollein's works, but on the contrary to add further elements of analysis to the study of a character who is very complex in his expressive articulations but, on the other hand, very clear in his intentions.

Hollein covers a region of visualized thoughts which starts from Vienna, and after many journeys, departures and verifications, goes back to Vienna, "...the big head-brain-city left over from an empire which is now, on a national level, wisely recalled more in irony than in impotent regret. The city itself and its inhabitants seem relatively immune from the frenzy of "progress", from the will to economic and consumer expansion, almost as though they had already been through it and, in a state of decelerated metabolism, looked on as others burnt themselves out in the lucid folly governing the mythology of the great metropolis"[96].

The origins of Hollein's work are to be found, even more than in the contemporary architects who have inspired him, in a research between art and architecture which has been lead for example by Terzic, Lesak, Peintner, Himmelblau and Missing Link. However, for Hollein the most important reference is certainly Walter Pichler, who chooses art, even if he doesn't abandon architecture, as the principal way of expressing his own evolution. Considering the conceptual rigour of the period, Hollein's choice of entering the field of planned and built architecture perhaps seemed questionable to his companions. For them, but also for Hollein, "...there is an attitude of ancient reflection, of children's wisdom, an archaic quest for the meaning of one's existence, of human action, of architecture, and of history"[97]. To the ascetic rigour which leads Pichler towards a progressive "reduction" in order to reach a "specification", perhaps Hollein opposes the first

Below: "Hollein Pichler Architektur" Exhibition, Vienna, 1963: drawing. Bottom left: Retti Candle Shop, initial sketch. Bottom right: Jewellery Store Schullin I, façade detail.

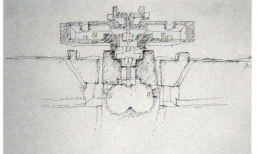

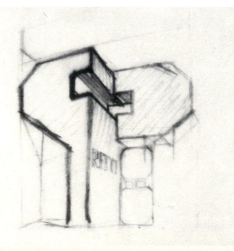

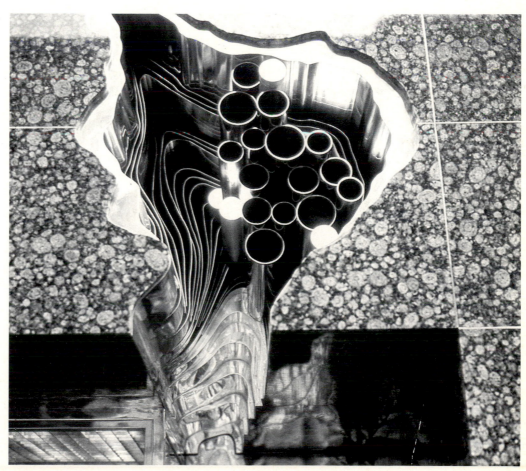

great risk of his life, that of not withdrawing from a context but of facing reality, even at the risk of endangering his original rigour.

His first trips and the consequent theorizations expressed by means of writings and images, almost seem as if they intended to balance, with the seriousness of analysis, the potential risks of dispersion caused by his initial, but apparently minimal and diversified, professional opportunities.

However, already with the Retti and with the positive reactions produced by this kind of architecture, Hollein recovers confidence about the possibility of producing rigorous diagrams, manifestos of absolute architecture, even as far as the realization of the volumes and the façade of a small shop are concerned. This possibility-necessity of expressing his evolution continuously, even if on occasions which may sometimes seem banal, produces more and more verifications: positive remarks together with bitter comments. Hollein seems to interpret them all positively: the critics come from those who, having woken up from lethargy, have to find new reasons for falling back to sleep, supposing that this is still possible.

Anyway, in this period Hollein finds himself alone among the other architects. The international scene in which the new tendencies take place is practically confined to Florence, where those architects who will later be called 'radical' or 'supersensualist' establish a dialogue at a distance on common theorizations and their consequent visualizations. Perhaps one should conduct an inquiry into the kind of activity which the fifty-year-old present stars of the international scene were leading in the middle of the sixties, and the results would probably be quite surprising.

The mid-European component in Hollein's work assumes, however, different aspects which cannot possibly be compared with those of other architects. His trips and studies in the USA give Hollein a detached way of looking at things which allows him to identify his origins in a better, more disenchanted way. The first emotional elements which were expressed through strong contrapositions turn into quotations that are clearer, while Hollein's experimental intentions become his first opportunities for professional activity. Although "...the experience of American stylistic pluralism and the shallow treatment of the phenomenon of architecture" has certainly been important for Hollein's evolution, "...nevertheless, without the semantic spectre of Viennese historicism and the Secession and without its aesthetic precision, his work would be quite unconceivable"[98]. As Achleitner rightly says, "A citizen of Vienna, in particular the architect living in this city, is continually being confronted with an architectural reality that in different forms stimulates and influences his thoughts and his choices. In this way, no matter how different his starting-point may be, there comes to be created a common basis of communication and implicit agreement on a number of points. Even though this basis is not – perhaps cannot be – analyzed (that is to say it does not play a direct role in his awareness) it nevertheless remains an evident reality for the subconscious, always taken for granted. It could be defined also a system of visual axioms, which need not be discussed openly"[99].

Hollein however, in the progression of his planning and intellectual experience, detaches himself from this context when, for example, in his 1978 essay on Otto Wagner published on "Global Architecture", he talks of "...a clear line of a development which is somewhat specifically Viennese and which had its first strong manifestation in Fischer von Erlach... an approach to architecture based on the complex arrangement of disparate, even conflicting elements of different origin and meaning to a seemingly heterogeneous whole (of plastic homogeneity, however) whose message consciously draws upon the semiotic and iconographic capacity of the various components. Contradictory elements, both in the objects and in the personality of architects who created them, inconsequential manner as part of an uncompromising attitude, relation to history as germinating impulse for innovation, for "modernity", cynical pragmatism as nucleus for florid emotions and sentiments, these are phenomena typical for the creative substance of this area through centuries and also very much apparent in the man Otto Wagner and his work"[100].

The same statements, without being modified, could be applied to Hollein, author of the writing. It seems almost that he utilizes the metaphor of the quotations of both Fischer von Erlach and Wagner to show a mature version of his

Below: "Work and Behaviour" Exhibition, Venice Biennale, 1972: detail of the "Everyday Situations" room. Bottom: Austrian Travel Agency Central Offices.

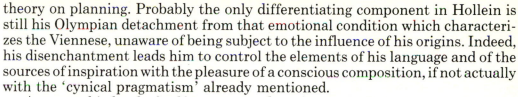

theory on planning. Probably the only differentiating component in Hollein is still his Olympian detachment from that emotional condition which characterizes the Viennese, unaware of being subject to the influence of his origins. Indeed, his disenchantment leads him to control the elements of his language and of the sources of inspiration with the pleasure of a conscious composition, if not actually with the 'cynical pragmatism' already mentioned.

Anyway, this level of self-awareness doesn't save Hollein from those influences originating from the most subtle elements of the Viennese culture of the beginning of the century. "Here, we can remember that Freud was from Vienna... all his research was done in that city. Wittgenstein was also born here... It is a city full of the image of death to such an extent that it is rather not necessary to talk about it. That may be related to the fact that the Baroque style as the expression of Catholicism covers the whole town"[101].

But even in this case Hollein expresses his strategy with the utmost ambiguity. He deals with the themes of death and eroticism; he deals with many combinations of these elements even from a psychoanalytical point of view, but once more he seems to practise exorcism, he seems to want to "solve" once and for all the problems concerning his origins. Perhaps, also in order to put an end to the continuous and often superficial criticisms which try to confine the disturbing presence of his architecture, so discomforting and destructive of many contemporary commonplaces, in a Vienna which is interpreted more like a ghetto than as the main source of the culture of this century. "It is very irritating to be told that any view you happen to be advancing, or design which you have made is 'typical' of what you are – or worse, of your environment: that your arguments or design are 'typical' of your being Japanese or East coast or French – or Viennese. Hollein must be fairly exasperated at being told how 'typically' Viennese he is: as if any artist of distinction could be sensibly be taken as being 'typical' of any place or time... the irritation is firstly due to having an argument parried and not

Below: Jewellery Store Schullin II, 1982-83, view of the display room. Bottom left: Earring, Cleto Munari Collection, 1985-86. Bottom right: "Ludwig Beck" Exposition system, 1983.

answered, the design belittled by a refusal to acknowledge that it may be right or good or even just interesting: by a refusal to see it for what it is; an secondly, by an element of truth"[102].

On the contrary, Hollein represents an atypical example in the context of contemporary Vienna, both as an architect and as a man of culture. "But what many may find disturbing is that the aesthetic handling of the subject does not illustrate the content in a reductive fashion but the subject itself in all its facets"[103]. Hollein's ties with the past are expressed as *one* of the elements, *one* of the components of his language, in contrast to many protagonists of the Viennese but also international architectural debate, who instead are still engaged nowadays in relating themselves dialectically to history as well as to the history of architecture. Hollein is already beyond all this: having solved these problems, he devotes himself to more abstract arguments, to more specialized conceptual structures and to their transformation into a language of architecture.

The different combinations of the elements relating to history, and to the contemporary architectural debate, and especially the many valences composing these elements, constitute the true interest of Hollein's work in this period. What mostly distinguishes Hollein from any other contemporary architect is his skill in expressing himself, whether taking linguistic risks, or inventing new theories and conceptual schemes, in his relation with the past and with the present debate. He uses the fact that he is Viennese in his favour. Only those who have resolved, as Hollein has, their relationship with their origins and have exorcized the ghost of the past, are able to control with such skilful awareness the many contradictory elements which form the eclectic and complex contemporary scene. The complexity of juxtaposition and integration, the evolution of original themes which develop autonomously into more and more diversified languages, the memory of history, the fascination of techniques and materials, the relationship with the art world and with the whole architectural debate, suggest to the critic just one possibility: that of analyzing Hollein's work while keeping well in mind that none of these elements can be separated from one another, and that one should consider their evolution, from their experimental origins until today's development into a "classical" language, in a balance where perhaps one can still point out the single elements of inspiration which, however, cannot and don't have to be considered separately. Every statement or comment concerning the relationship with the original Viennese historical context, the irony which is often considered as part of his work[104], the theme of death, the interest in technologies, the concept of 'transformation', the symbologies which run the risk of becoming décor – the flirt with kitsch –[105], or even the exaggerated attention towards art which is expressed in a too literal quotation, or his celebration as the greatest existing interior designer[106], etc., all this seems insufficient to describe the figure of Hollein as architect.

What should be underlined in the total analysis of his work is the co-existence of all these elements, and probably of others too, and also the constancy of such co-existence, from the overall comprehending and original experimental propositions, to their full and detailed formulation in the specific and typical expressions of his maturity. Probably only Achleitner[107] points out how disconcerting it is that Hollein's language is expressed not only through an aesthetical formulation of the chosen theme, thus explaining its contents impartially, but also in all its possible expressive and conceptual valences. The world of references and allusions suggested by Hollein is strange: nothing is ever what it is or what it really appears to be. Instead, everything is always an instrument of knowledge. "This 'metamorphosis' is one of Hollein's characteristic: architecture may change into figurative elements, so as on the opposite symbolic images are always led back to tectonics"[108].

Inside this definition one may recognize the main elements of Hollein's language. Every professional opportunity is an occasion for criticism and for overcoming conceptual conventions related both to function and to its formal expression. In the Retti, as in the Schullin, in the Opernringhof Agency as in Mönchengladbach, that is to say, whether he's dealing with the context of a town or of a single building into which to fit his own architecture, Hollein criticizes and meticulously rehearses every element of his analytic and operating process. The walls are never a neutral surface, but an occasion for "breaking through", which

Below: "The Turks in Vienna" Exhibition, 1982-83. Bottom: "Sigmund Freud" couch (prototype), "Le Affinità Elettive" Exhibition, Milan Triennale, 1984-85.

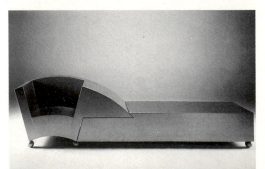

goes from the simple *trompe-l'oeil*, in which one finds again the painted palms that before were physically defined, to the more classic and abstract diagram of the Retti, characterized by an extremely pure geometrical theorization expressed in the form of absolute architecture.

Hollein's monuments, those which some would want to be expressed in gigantic forms, suitable for memorizing an idea of architecture as the monument of reason, are instead always very small: a ring, a piece of furniture or, at the most, the Retti itself, which may be interpreted as a furniture-container. Mönchengladbach instead is an organism, a combination of diversified elements, an integration of conceptual and physical forms which put up for discussion apparently stable ideas and conventions considered to be beyond dispute. Contrapositions like nature and artifice, rationality and intuition, etc., are in this case almost didactically emphasized, the results of an intricate alliance intentionally composed so as not to dissolve. But also descending from the level of global considerations to that concerning the evolution of Hollein's formal language, the structure of "juxtaposition" still holds, together with the elements of criticism and "breaking through". This may be found again in the detailed analysis of his architectural design, in the projects, in the plans, in the perspectives, as well as in all materializations, in the detailed choices of materials and forms which, defining themselves, instead of becoming definitive and unequivocal, introduce the subject of total and absolute ambiguity once again.

Below: Frankfurt Museum of Modern Art, elevation. Right: Mönchengladbach Museum, exterior wall of exhibition hall, gallery and administration wing.

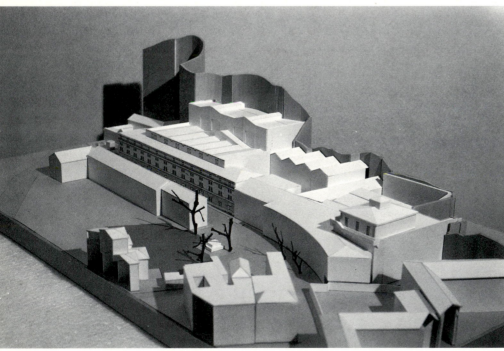

"Neues Haas Haus", Vienna, 1985 (in course): models (general view, interior, site). Bottom left: "Kleinen Festspielhauses" restoration project, Salzburg, 1985-86, model.

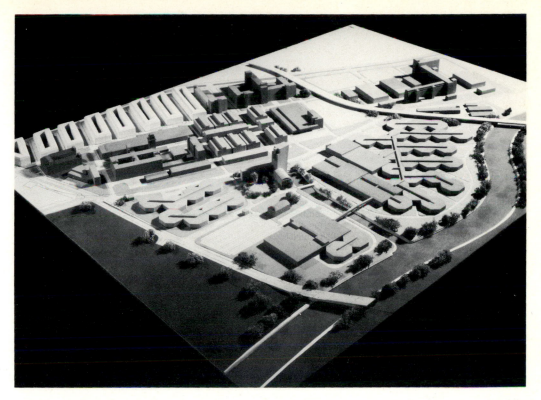

Right: "Siemens City", West Berlin, 1986, model.
Below: New National Theatre of Japan, sketches by
Hans Hollein and general view of the front side.

Left: New National Theater of Japan, model. Below: Thyssen-Bornemisza Gallery expansion project, Lugano: model and sketches by Hans Hollein.

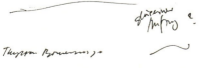

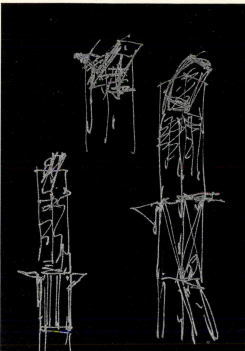

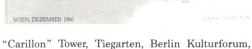

GUTACHTEN CARILLONTURM
BERLIN-TIERGARTEN
ISOMETRIE M.1:100

WIEN, DEZEMBER 1986   HANS HOLLEIN

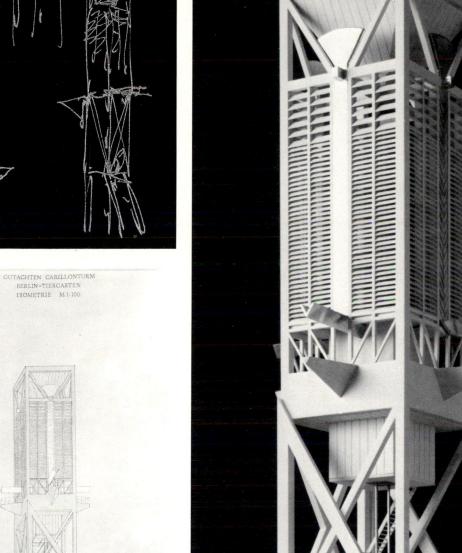

"Carillon" Tower, Tiegarten, Berlin Kulturforum,
1986: initial sketches, axonometric and model.

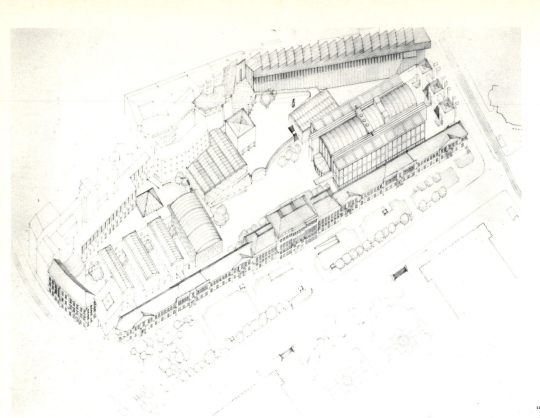

"Messepalast" International Competition, Vienna, 1987: axonometric and model.

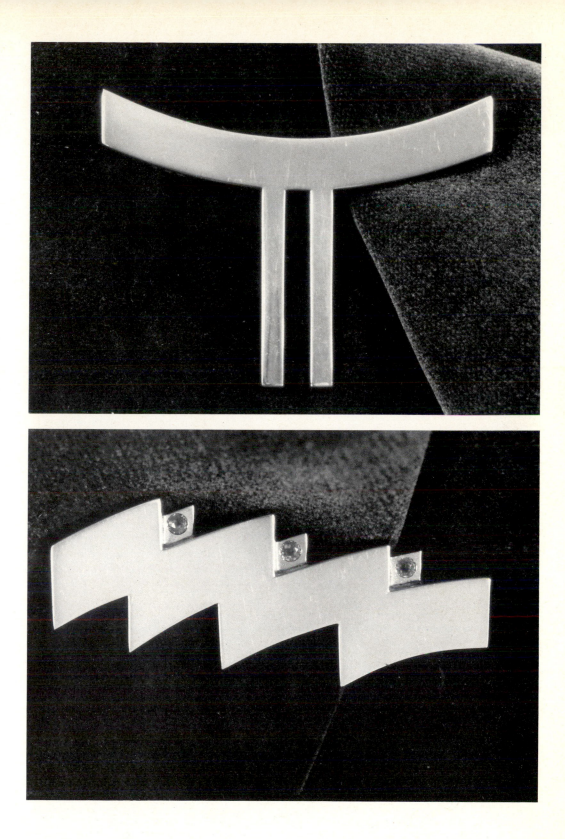

Brooches, "Kochert Collection", 1987.

Notes

1. F. Hundertwasser, "Verschimmellungsmanifest gegen den Rationalismus in der Architektur" (Manifesto of Mouldering against Rationalism in Architecture), Sechau, 4 July 1958, published in *Hundertwasser*, Haus der Kunst, Munchen, 1975, p. 346 and ff.

2. M. Prachensky and A. Rainer, "Architektur mit den Händen" (Architecture by hand), Sechau, 3 July 1958, published in *Markus Prachensky. Arbeiten*, Ulysses Gallery, Vienna, 1978.

3. H. Hollein, "What is architecture?", Chicago 1957-58, published in *protokolle '66*, Vienna, 1966, p. 105.

4. H. Hollein and Y. Futagawa (ed.), "Otto Wagner", *Global Architecture* 47, Tokyo, 1978.

5. H. Hollein, "Zurück zur Architektur" (Return to Architecture), lecture held at the nächst St. Stephan Gallery, Vienna, 1962; published in *protokolle '66*, Vienna, 1966, p. 105 and ff.

6. "Hollein Pichler Architektur", catalogue of the exhibition at the nächst St. Stephan Gallery, Vienna, 1963.

7. U. Conrads, "Programme und Manifeste zur Architektur des 20. Jahrhunderts" (Programs and Manifestos for Twentieth-Century Architecture), Gütersloch-Berlin-Munchen, 1971, p. 147 and ff.

8. M. Brix, "Hans Hollein", in *IDEA III*, Jahrbuch der Hamburg Kunsthalle, Prestel, 1984, p. 169.

9. Cf. Brix, op. cit., p. 169.

10. Cf. "Hollein Pichler Architektur", cat. cit.

11. Archizoom, "La distruzione degli oggetti" (The destruction of objects), *IN* 2-3, 1971;
A. Branzi, "Il ruolo dell'avanguardia 1: la Gioconda sbarbata" (The role of avant-garde 1: the shaven Gioconda), *Casabella* 364/1972;
Archizoom, "Distruzione e riappropriazione della città" (Destruction and re-appropriation of the town), *IN* 5, 1972.

12. K. Frampton, "Meditations on an Aircraft Carrier: Hollein's Mönchengladbach", in *A+U*, E 8502, 1985, pp. 142-144.

13. Cf. Brix, op. cit., pp. 169-170: "Later on the sculptor Pichler has turned away from his text. His once pitiless urban worlds have changed into houses and cages in which human beings follow tormenting rituals, or else try to restore life. Hollein instead acknowledges his provocative theses of 1963, even if with his last works, like for example the fashionable shops and museums, he seems to have turned away from them. However, one wonders if there's still something in common between his attitude of that time and his present one.
"I don't think there are sufficient elements to justify these statements: each work doesn't necessarily have to be a summary of the previous ones (as it happens however in Hollein's work, for example in the Mönchengladbach museum), as emotional and creative tension must not necessarily have the same intensity. It's also wrong to compare a phase of an artist's theorical development (while, in the pursuit of his own identity, he expresses rigorously and through axioms the characteristics of his poetics) with projects and realizations produced twenty years later, that is, when his maturity and possibility of operating in real scale, or rather in accordance with it, allow him a less tense way of expressing himself and a more serene analysis of his intentions and language. There is a continuity in Hollein's work, which may be expressed in a different way at different moments: at first it is highly critical, and later on it turns into a conversation conducted with himself or even expressed in didactic terms.

14. H. Hollein, "Pueblos", in *der aufbau* 9, Vienna, sept. 1974, pp. 369-377.

15. A. Loos, "Architektur" (1909), published in A. Loos *Trotzdem, Schriften II*, Innsbruck, 1931, p. 107.

16. In this case, the comparison with Oldenburg's over-dimensioned objects is dutiful: both Hollein and Oldenburg produce in 1963 this kind of projects but, while Oldenburg designs objects that are almost limp, Hollein juxtaposes them in their original physical context, modifing only their scale.

17. H. Hollein, "Technik", in *Bau* 2, Vienna, 1965, pp. 40-45.

18. A. Isozaki, "The Feast of Death" (Hollein of Vienna), in *Space Design*, May 1975.

19. H. Hollein, "Rudolph Schindler-ein Wiener Architekt in Kalifornien", in *der afbau*, Vienna, March-April 1961, pp. 102-108.

20. Cf. H. Hollein, ibid.

21. H. Hollein, "Städte-Brennpunkte des Lebens" (Cities - Crucial points of Life), in *der afbau* 3-4, Vienna, March-April 1963, pp. 115-117.

22. Cf. lecture "Return to Architecture", op. cit.

23. Cf. H. Hollein, "Pueblos", op. cit.

24. H. Hollein, "Zukunft der Architektur" (The Future of Architecture), in *Bau* 1, Vienna, 1965, pp. 8-11 and cover.

25. Cf. M. Brix, op. cit., p. 174.

26. H. Hollein, "Negozio a Vienna: la sigla è la facciata" (A shop in Vienna: the store-front as a symbol, the symbol as a store-front), in *Domus* 456, Nov. 1967.

27. K. Frampton, "Richard L. Feigen & Co.", in *Architectural Design*, March 1970.

28. Like Adolf Loos Hollein too would have had the equivocal opportunity of serving the needs of an élite consumerism: "...a pattern of exploitation of a major talent which surely reflects the priorities of our society", cf. K. Frampton, "Richard L. Feigen & Co.", op. cit.

28.bis. H. Hollein, "Alles ist Architecktur", *Bau* 1/2, Vienna 1968, pp. 1-28.

28.tris. J. Rykwert, "Irony: Hollein's General Approach", in *A+U*, E 8502, 1985, pp. 194-196.

29. These years see the theoretical propositions of the Florentine groups Archizoom and Superstudio with "Non-Stop City" and "Monumento Continuo" respectively, as well as further propositions of other 'radicals', like Lapo Binazzi and Gianni Pettena who point out, through their writings and projects, the connection with the contemporary experiments in the visual arts.

30. Cf. J. Rykwert, "Irony: Hollein's General Approach", op. cit.

31. Cf. H. Hollein, "Alles ist Architektur", op. cit.

32. H. Hollein, in catalogue of the Austriennal exhibition, June 1968.

33. The "Z" light-sign is one of Hollein's first projects of Corporate Image, in this case for the Zentralsparkasse. It is not only a signal of identification for the bank's offices, but also an object which is itself an element of urban fittings.

34. "HH Interview", cf. in this text Pettena-Hollein Interview, Vienna, March 1986. This is how Hollein explains (in this case for the oval table in the board room of the Perchtoldsdorf Town Hall) the functional motivations of this formal choice: "...I chose the curve instead of the rectangle because it creates a situation in which everybody is almost equal. It's functional because everyone, can see everyone else perfectly; if the table had been circular, the equality would have been absolute."

35. Cf. "HH Interview", op. cit.

36. Cf. M. Brix, op. cit., p. 184.

37. F. Correa, "Hans Hollein: Una entrevista biografica", in *Arquitecturas bis*, Nov. 1975, pp. 1-13 and cover.

38. Cf. F. Correa, op. cit., p. 13.

39. Cf. J. Rykwert, "Irony...", op. cit.

40. Cf. M. Brix, op. cit., p. 186.

41. See, for an example of Loos as a figure of reference, Hollein's 1958 drawings which paraphrase the famous project by Loos for a Chicago skyscraper as a clenched fist-phallus. For the images of Hollein's drawings, cf. "Vita e Morte - Opera e Comportamento - Situazioni quotidiane" (Life and Death - Work and Behaviour - Everyday Situations), catalogue of the exhibition at the 1972 Venice Biennale.

42. H. Hollein, catalogue of the exhibition "Death", Mönchengladbach, 1970.

43. On the work of artists like Gunter Brus, Otto Muehl, Hermann Nitsch, Rudolf Schwarzkogler and others, cf. L. Vergine, *Il corpo come linguaggio* (The Body as a Language), Milano, 1974.

44. Cf. A. Isozaki, "The Feast of Death", op. cit.

45. For example, in Rykwert's quoted article, irony is seen as a 'leitmotiv' which is present in all Hollein's work. Rykwert talks about the meaning of irony in the classic retoric and of the presence (or not) of this meaning in Hollein's work. He also compares this component of Hollein's work with that of other Viennese contemporary architects.

46. Cf. M. Brix, op, cit., p. 178.

47. Cf. K. Frampton, "Meditations...", op. cit.

48. Cf. lecture "Return to Architecture", op. cit.

49. Cf. J. Rykwert, "Irony...", op. cit.

50. Cf. F. Correa, "Una entrevista biografica", op. cit., p. 6.

51. Cf. F. Correa, op. cit., ibidem.

52. Cf. K. Frampton, "Meditations...", op. cit.

53. Cf. J. Rykwert, "Irony...", op. cit.

54. Cf. K. Frampton, "Meditations...", op. cit.

55. Cf. K. Frampton, ibidem.

56. This is for example Frampton's opinion in his already quoted article: "Thus the very success of the Mönchengladbach Museum is linked paradoxically to its partial failure, for the fact remains that despite the dressed stone facing of the administration tower and the primary entrances, the museum is not really perceivable as a civic institution in this indifferently organized 'Wirtshaftwunder' town... This being so, we are brought to conclude that, consciously or otherwise, the urban monument has been eschewed... In this respect, it could be claimed that the Mönchengladbach Museum has been, in some way, compromised by the modern welfare strategy of presenting culture as though it were another form of popular entertainment. And although there are no doubt many different criteria for the evaluation of architecture in a pluralistic age, the critical challenge of the Italian Neo-Rationalist movement still has to be answered."

57. H. Hollein, "Otto Wagner", op. cit.

58. Cf. in this text, the part concerning the Siemens projects.

59. A. Natalini, "Stanze e stili nei più recenti arredi di Hans Hollein" (Rooms and styles in Hans Hollein's most recent furnishing), in *Modo*, Sept-Oct. 1977, pp. 21-26.

60. Cf. "HH Interview".

61. R. Pedio, "Hans Hollein", in *Venti Progetti per il futuro del Lingotto* (Twenty projects for the future of the Lingotto), Milano, 1984.

62. Cf. M. Brix, op. cit., p. 188.

63. Cf. H. Hollein, "Otto Wagner", op. cit.

64. Cf. M. Brix, op. cit., p. 189.

65. "Western Artifice celebrates Eastern Art", in *Architectural Record* 5/1981, pp. 88-95.

66. This aspect has been underlined several times, especially for Hollein's famous shops (Retti, Christa Metek, Schullin), but also for other interiors-integrations of ancient buildings.

67. Cf. "HH Interview".

68. Cf. J. Rykwert, "Irony...", op. cit.

69. J. Stirling, "Hans Hollein: Vetrine di un'esposizione" (Hans Hollein: Show-cases of an exposition), in *Domus* 607, June 1980, pp. 8-13.

70. Cf. M. Brix, op. cit.

71. Cf. R. Pedio, op. cit.

72. Cf. "HH Interview".

73. H. Hollein, "Il Padiglione di Josef Hoffmann alla Biennale di Venezia" (Josef Hoffmanns' Pavilion at the Venice Biennale), in "Josef Hoffmann-I 50 anni del Padiglione Austriaco alla Biennale di Venezia", Venezia, 1984, pp. 16-17.

74. Cf. H. Hollein, ibidem.

75. Cf. "HH Interview".

76. H. Hollein, "Concepts for an exhibition", in the catalogue of the exhibition MANtransFORMS, New York, 1976.

77. Cf. K. Frampton, "Meditations...", op. cit. In many texts which go with his exhibited works, Hollein has expressly denied any didactic component. Since the catalogue of the Austriennal (1968), he has rather underlined the need of a personal and autonomous effort of transformation and mental association.

78. "Hans Hollein" (by H. Hollein), in "La Presenza del Passato" (The Presence of the Past), Catalogue Prima Mostra Internazionale di Architettura, Venezia, 1980.

79. Cf. K. Frampton, "Meditations...", op. cit.

80. A. Branzi, "I post romani a Venezia", in Modo 34, Nov. 1980, pp. 41-45. However, with regard to the exhibition and to the post-modern phenomenon, Branzi goes on saying: "In fact, the difference between the book on post-modern language written by Charles Jencks ("The Language of Post-Modern Architecture", London, 1977) and the exhibition at the Biennale (apart from the revealing title), consists in the fact that Jencks has written a book on the 'language' of post-modern architecture, while Portoghesi has organized an exhibition of post-modern architects. This is to say that, while the former, through a series of single works, has tried to give the phenomenon the dignity of a specific linguistic area, contradictory but, however, identifiable, Portoghesi has instead brought together anyone who was just a bit eccentric in comparison with an orthodoxy which is so difficult to identify as to be practically hypothetical. So, we see one next to the other, an ironic Hans Hollein and a reactionary like Leon Krier, a great architect like Arata Isozaki and an inventor of images such as Massimo Scolari. That is to say, planners which have really gone beyond the Modern Movement, together with many others who still have to get there, i.e. the pre-moderns. The feeling... is that of a difficult crisis of a system of certainties which for the moment doesn't follow a new outline of values, and in this void one can sense a great risk of involution of the debate and project."

81. Cf. K. Frampton, "Meditations...", op. cit.

82. H. Hollein "Das Konzept zur Präsentation der Austellung 'Traum und Wirklichkeit', Wien 1870-1930", in the catalogue of the exhibition, Vienna, 1985, pp. 36-37.

83. H. Hollein, ibidem.

84. Cf. for example Frampton's already quoted article ("Meditations..."): "...the critical challenge of the Italian Neo-Rationalist movement still has to be answered. If we take our line from the discourse of Giorgio Grassi and concede that the autonomous charge of architecture is to create the civic monument and to establish the space of public appearance then we can easily see that this critical position would not accept the Mönchengladbach Museum into the canon of architecture. It would find it wanting on almost every count; it would surely deem it experimental, avant-gardist, figurative and literary; in a word, it would claim that its discourse lies outside the limits of architecture as such. Neither typologically based nor urbanistically grounded..."

85. "Superonda" sofa, Archizoom, 1968.

86. Cf. "HH Interview".

87. Opportunities like, for example, the ephemeral façades in the intercolumnations of the Corderie of the Arsenale for the "Strada Novissima" at the 1980 Biennale, or "Tea and Coffee Piazza" for Alessi, which compare architects 'builders' or designers on themes mainly expressed by means of metaphor or in an atypical scale of project.

88. Cf. "HH Interview".

89. With regard to the furniture of the Florentine radicals, like Archizoom, Superstudio, Ufo and Pettena, designed or produced as prototypes, for settings or even for a limited production, one should also point out that, unlike the furniture designed by Hollein or Sottsass or by the second experimental generation (Mendini, De Lucchi, etc.), it was also an instrument of functional revisitation, of re-invention, of participation. Its ironic dimension was undoubtly an essential component.

90. H. Hollein, "House for a Superstar", in 'Winners in the Shinkenchiku Residential Design Competition 1975', The Japan Architect, Tokyo, Feb. 1976, pp. 24-25.

91. J. Cladders, in "Die Turnstunde – eine Rauminstallation von Hans Hollein", catalogue of the exhibition, Mönchengladbach, Sept. 1984. To Hollein the monument always and only means celebration and myth, connected as it is with the idea of death and memory. Instead, anything that concerns life is an organism, a diagram of thought, a complex of metaphors, an anti-monument of vital compenetrations.

92. Cf. J. Cladders, "Die Turnstunde...", op. cit.

93. Ibidem.

94. Ibidem.

95. Ibidem.

96. F. Raggi, "Vienna Orchestra", in Casabella 392/393, 1974, pp. 41-60.

97. Ibidem.

98. F. Achleitner, "Viennese Positions", Lotus International 29, Milano, 1981, pp. 5-17.

99. Cf. F. Achleitner, op. cit., p. 5.

100. Cf. H. Hollein, "Otto Wagner...", op. cit.

101. Cf. A. Isozaki, "The Feast of Death", op. cit.

102. J. Rykwert, "Irony...", op. cit.

103. Cf. F. Achleitner, "Viennese Positions", op. cit., "Hans Hollein", p. 9.

104. See for example Rykwert's already quoted article "Irony: Hollein's general approach", or Andrea Branzi as regards the Strada Novissima, where he calls Hollein 'ironic' (cf. note 80).

105. Cf. J. Rykwert, "Irony...", op. cit.

106. Cf. J. Stirling, "Hans Hollein: vetrine di un'esposizione", op. cit.

107. Cf. F. Achleitner, "Viennese Positions", op. cit.

108. Cf. M. Brix, "Hollein Beitrag zur Gegenwartsarchitektur", in Idea III, op. cit., p. 103.

Born in Vienna, Austria, on March 30, 1934.
Studies: Bundesgewerbeschule, Vienna, Department of Civil Engineering; Academy of Fine Arts, Vienna, School of Architecture, Diploma 1956.
Graduate Studies: Illinois Institute of Technology, Chicago, 1958-59, Architecture and Planning; University of California, Berkeley, College of Environmental Design, 1959-60, Master of Architecture (M. Arch.) 1960.
His wide range of activities, besides Architecture, include Product Design, Exhibition and Stage Design, Personal Shows and Exhibitions.
Prizes and awards, a.o.:
Reynolds Memorial Award, USA, 1966; Prize of the City of Vienna for Architecture, Vienna, 1974; Grand Austrian State Award for Fine Arts, 1983; German Architecture Award, 1983, for the Municipal Museum Abteiber Mönchengladbach, FRG; Reynolds Memorial Award, USA, 1984 (awarded for the second time); The Pritzker Architecture Prize, USA, 1985.
Other professional and public positions a.o.:
Member of various Boards, Panels, Commissions and Juries of Professional and Governmental Institutions in Austria, Germany, USA, Japan, etc.; Austrian State Commissary for the Venice Biennale, 1978, 1980, 1982, 1984, 1986 and 1988; Member of the Austrian Chamber of Architects (licensed architect since 1963); Member of the German Chamber of Architects (AKNW licensed since 1967 and AKH licensed since 1986); Member of the League of German Architects (BDA); Vice-President of the Austrian Architects Association (ZV); Honorary Fellow of the AIA; Member of the Royal Swedish Academy of Fine Arts; Honorary Member of the Royal Academy Den Haag; Member of the Jury of the Award of the City of Vienna, 1986; Member of the Advisory Council "Kunst + Bau", Ministry of Education, Art and Sport since 1986; Member, steering committe Gallery of the State Opera, Vienna, 1982-1985; Master Juror of the Aga Khan Award, 1980, 1986; Member of the Club of Rome/Austrian Chapter; Honorary Chairman of the R.M. Schindler Centennial, Los Angeles, 1987.
Jury member of a.o.:
Federal Arts Museum, Bonn; Staedel Museum Extension, Frankfurt; Art Museum, St. Gallen, Switzerland; The Nationalgalerie, Berlin, FRG; Station square, Salzburg; AIA Award, New York, Progressive Architecture, New York; Reynolds Memorial Award, Washington; Yamagiwa Foundation, Tokyo.
Teaching, Lectures:
1963-1964 and 1966 visiting professor at Washington University; since 1967 full professor at the Academy of Fine Arts, School of Architecture, Düsseldorf; since 1976 Head of the School and Institute of Design at the Academy of Applied Arts, Vienna; since 1979 leading one of the two masterclasses in architecture at the Academy of Applied Arts, Vienna; visiting professor at Yale University, New Haven; various activities in the past years as visiting lecturer at numerous European and overseas universities and schools.
Architectural History comprehensive studies and research concerning a.o.: R.M. Schindler; The Pueblos of the North-American Indians; Miners Housing Reitwinkelkolonie; Otto Wagner.
Publications: 1965-1970, editor of "Bau", Vienna, a magazine for architecture and planning; contributions to numerous professional magazines, anthologies, books; correspondent and advisor for various international architectural magazines.

Synthetic illustration of the works

House Lintschinger I, Wels (Austria), 1960.
The structure is based on a series of units, potentially repeatable. The units or "houses", are joined by routes and spaces. House as city and city as house: the project reflects Hollein's interest in the spatial themes of the urban structure in the early sixties.

House Lintschinger II, Wels (Austria), 1960.
See house Lintschinger I. In this second project the house is a two-storey building of raw reinforced concrete.

Jewellery Store Dorotheergasse, Vienna, 1961, (Sketches).

"Hollein Pichler Architektur" Exhibition, Vienna, 1963.
The exhibit graphically presented the ideas of Hollein and Pichler on the situation in architecture by means of plastics and models/sculptures, and proposed a visionary conception of megastructural buildings/cities. The urban macrostructures (metal models) presented in this exhibit already reveal the complexity and technical perfection of many future works, but also have the characteristics of design objects.

"Transformations", 1963-64.
These collages and photomontages are "not far from reality": so, a train car put on a pedestal with a change of scale, can become a temple. The "Transformations" have multiple meanings since they prompt various stages of comprehension in the mental process. The figurative gesture, the irony, the monumental and sacral aspects, the ambivalence of the signs, and the violent collision between the 'transformed' object and its environment are all elements already present in these works; elements that Hollein will continue to refer to in the course of his following work.

Experimental Theatre for the Washington University, St. Louis (Missouri), USA, 1963-64.
The project provided the possibility of various scenic displays based on the concept of a different relationship between the actors and the public. The differentiated use of space created a plurality of choices; the people moved, not the stage sets or the objects.

Retti Candle Shop, Vienna, 1964-65. Project realized.
This work was awarded the Reynolds Prize for the use of aluminum and established Hollein's celebrity through numerous reviews and publications. In an area of just 16 sq. meters, two environments, functionally distinct but united by the use of materials and the global conception of the design, have been obtained. The aluminum is used as a covering for the façade and entrance, and continues without interruption in the interior which has a diamond-shaped floor plan. The façade, flat except for the two small lateral window niches, is interrupted by a tall and narrow portal which culminates in an enlarged window. From this opening it is possible to see the four-sphered lights inside which, even though artificial, determine the suggestion and idea of a lighted candle.

Compact alternative of a competition for an orphanage, Hinterbrühl (Austria), 1964. Prize-winning competition entry.
The building is spacious, articulated, and well-integrated with the surrounding greenery. The distribution of the internal spaces is meant to reflect criteria of individuality: the independent living units (2 or 4 beds) are joined at the center in the communal space of the dining area.

"Existenz minimum", Paris Biennal, 1965.
Since the space available for each participant was very limited, the project consisted in a model of a human figure with all the necessary accessories needed for survival and for communication with the outside world, like in a space capsule.

House Wippel I, Strobl/Wolfgangsee (Austria), 1966. (Sketches).

Study for prefabricated housing for Bauring, Vienna, 1966-67.
The study was elaborated by Hollein and other architects for "Bauring". The request was for proposals of prefabricated buildings based on new architectural criteria which however should be based on the construction requirements of this technique. No project was ever realized.

"Roto-Desk Miller", 1966.
Steel and formica turntable. It is an object with various functions obtained through its movement while allowing the user to remain seated, thus upsetting the traditional idea of "table".

"Svoboda", Project for the restoration of new premises and showroom for the Svoboda company, Vienna, 1966.
The most interesting element of the project was that the façade had to be realized using the name of the company in gigantic letters. The project was never realized but holds a certain importance because it anticipated by many years similar projects proposed by other architects.

"CM", Christa Metek Boutique, Vienna 1966-67. Project realized.
By definition of Hollein himself, in this work "the mark is the façade". The entire storefront is a signal. The façade is recognizable from afar and detached by its own proportions from the rest of the building. The interior, articulated by fiberglass elements that permit to brighten up the rigid rectangular space, corresponds to the painted aluminum exterior.

Landstrasser Club – Haupstrasse 18, Competition, Vienna, 1966.
Initial study for a recreation and meeting club.

Savings Bank of the City of Vienna, Project I, Florisdorf, 1966-68.
The project proposed the expansion of a pre-existing building using a new structure "to be walked on", consisting of a surface for public use "above" the entire area of the bank. Hollein interprets the relationship between the interior and the exterior as a vertical connection, thus creating a building whose roof is at the same time a public street or green. The "walk-on building" idea is one which Hollein will come back to with more clarity in numerous projects (cf. Mönchengladbach Museum).

Austrian Embassy in Brasilia, Competition, 1966. (Sketches).

"Selection '66" Exhibition, Museum für Angewandte Kunst, Vienna, 1965-66.
Exhibition design for the Svoboda furniture company. The stand drew its inspiration from classic works of modern furniture design, using simple devices to transform them into oversized sculptures.

Study for the Burgtheater, Vienna, 1966.
Project of some theatre workshops equipped for a small audience. Hollein proposed a subterranean environment in which only the entrance would be visible from the outside, since the building's function required neither natural lighting nor direct communication with the activity at street level.

Wiedner-Haupstrasse, Competition, Vienna, 1966.
An unfinished project for a building that was to take the place of a baroque church demolished by the City of Vienna because it was considered an obstruction to traffic. Since the new construction was to be placed in the space of the old one, the entire operation seemed absurd to Hollein.

Experimental Gallery, City Art Museum, St. Louis (Missouri), USA, 1966.
In this project, Hollein repeats and stresses the idea already proposed for the Florisdorf Bank. Since the building was for the most part subterranean and was used almost exclusively during the evening, the roof area was opened to the public during the day for use other than that of the specific intent of the theater.

Richard L. Feigen & Co. Gallery, New York City, 1967-69. Project realized.
Restoration of the façade and interiors of a New York townhouse to be converted into an art gallery. Part of the original structures are maintained in order to obtain a space on two levels in which the exposition surfaces make up an uninterrupted whole. A string of lighting runs along the ceiling of both floors and acts as an outline for connecting audiovisual devices and lamps. The use of reflective materials contributes to the idea of continuous movement and of multiple colors and objects. The sexual symbols are evident: the double rounded balcony with "nipples" of neon tube and the double steel column of the façade evoking the masculine principle, are unequivocal.

"Unipap", Stand for the Papier Treuhandges. Vienna Fair, 1967.

"Gustav Mahler Memorial", Vienna, 1967.
Project and models for a commemorative "monument" to Gustav Mahler. It was to be placed in the entranceway of the Vienna Concert Hall but, in the end, it was not realized.

"Schwarzenberg Table", 1967.

Stand Retti I, Vienna Fair, 1967.
Here is used for the first time a system of variable fiberglass elements for interior design or exposition. Each square element can be divided into four parts each of which can be used separately. The four parts screwed together form a square shelf on which a light or a metal cross that holds up levels of support in metalacrylic can be inserted at the center.

"Inflatable Structures", Kapfenberg Cultural Festival (Austria), 1967.

Restoration of Schattenberg Castle, 1967.
Sketches and collages for the project of a country residence for Prince Schwarzenberg. It was to be derived through the restoration of one part of a family property, the antique Schattenberg Castle, in Stiria.

"Austriennale", 14th Triennal of Milan, 1968.
As a contribution from Austria, Hollein proposed an environment intended to stimulate different forms of perception of space and to get a direct reaction from the user to sensory "provocations". Inside a series, that appeared infinite, of corridors closed at both ends, the visitor was submitted to situations of physical and psychological stress. At the end of this forced route, visitors received as a "prize" a pair of red and white plastic glasses that were very rigid and difficult to remove: the point of this was to force them to look at things through "Austrian" eyes.

"Interface-Space", Project for the restoration of the Olivetti offices and showrooms, Amsterdam, 1968.
As in other showrooms, Olivetti asked for an environment in which the public could participate more actively. Hollein presented several proposals for a very flexible use of the space on the three floors of the building. The design was meant to underline the idea of "interface", functional for the demands and habits of the Dutch clients, more than the formal aspects of the building.

Project for Z-Haupzollamt (Savings Bank of the City of Vienna), 1968. (Sketches).

Theme Pavilion "Towards Fuller Enjoyment of Life", Expo 70, Osaka (Japan), 1969-70.
Hollein cut out his own space structure in Kenzo Tange's big pavilion. On the inside was a series of enclosed circular stairways that allowed access (only with the head) to an environment where audiovisuals were shown.

House Wippel II, Vienna, 1969.

"Eternit" Exhibition, Vienna, 1969.
The setting was structured in several parts: other than the didactic-informative panels, the tubes and their accessories were exposed in illuminated "pits" enclosed by a fiberglass cover that also served as the public floor. A diametrically larger tube (2 meters) was used in one of the palace rooms to create a rest and meeting area. Outside, the tubes and other objects were presented according to their dimensions, either singularly or assembled into "artificial" constructions.

"Wiener Souvenir - Das Kleine Geschenk", Vienna, 1969.
The commission requested ideas for a more conceptually advanced Viennese souvenir. Hollein projected several. One of these was a sphere that provoked particular sensations at the touch, depending upon the diverse surface and temperature.

Dispenser for Hirsch, 1969.
Realized together with Ernst Graf, this object was intended for the presentation-exhibition-choice of watches and watch accessories. It was produced and is in use in many stores.

Restoration of IBM Offices, Vienna, 1969. (Sketches).

Svoboda Showrooms and Offices, Vienna, 1969. Project realized.
Restoration of Svoboda premises in a building on the Halbgasse. The project, which dealt with limited space, already reveals the presence of some fundamental elements of successive interiors: the long environment divided into three functionally different spaces by means of a studied geometrical contrast, the more "closed" offices, and some decorative elements that will be used again later on.

Project Art-Competition for the railroad Station square, Ludwigshafen, 1969.
The project confronts the theme of urban scale which Hollein will often face in his following work, suggesting solutions of great interest. Here, the structures designed for the square also serve as environmental conditioners. In this project the attention given to technological aspects is already clear; it will become even more evident in successive years, starting with the Munich Olimpic Village project.

IOS Handles, 1969.
The handles used in the IOS Hamburg branch were meant as the first element of the general "corporate image" of the company, and were to be used in all of the agencies.

Sigmund Freud Museum, Vienna, 1969.
The project was commissioned by the Sigmund Freud Foundation and concerned the restoration of the Bergasse 19 house where Freud had worked and lived for most of his life, which was to be converted into a museum. Hollein proposal did not intend to "reconstruct" the entire environment, but zeroed in on the famous studio and the couch, the only object in the all-white room.

"Z" Street Lamp and Sign, Vienna, 1969.
The lamp-sign is various colours for the Vienna Zentralsparkasse, is a "signal" that allows an immediate mental reference to this institution. It is an element of a group that he will later call "corporate image": a design containing characteristic features to be used in

various offices of the same company or institution.

Shop "Mylord", Vienna, 1970.
The project, for the design and realization of a new store for an important company, was worked out in detail with drawings and models (3 floors joined by balconies and mezzanines), but was never realized because the company modified its production line.

Carl Friedrich von Siemens Foundation, Nymphenbourg (Munich), 1970-72. Project realized.
Hollein's first job for Siemens AG was the restoration and expansion of the Carl Friedrich von Siemens scientific Foundation which was hosted in a small building inside the Nymphenburg baroque complex. Since the space was insufficient, there had already been some expansions but they had proved to be of little functional value. It was decided to eliminate them except for the conference room and to restore the inside of the building, adding some service areas and a wing for informal meetings and receptions. The project was to maintain intact the characteristics of the baroque "scenery", and new structures were allowed only if invisible from outside the semicircular walls of the complex. It was these requirements that suggested the placement of the new building and its connection to the pre-existing one, with an ideal reference to the Bavarian gardens of the 18th and 19th centuries and the use of wrought iron and wood. The proposed solution for the meeting/lounge room is of particular interest in that the supporting steel structures are removed 45° in respect to the central axle. The relaxed and "intimate" atmosphere is obtained through the interior decorating, with furniture arranged in a seemingly casual way, and through the lighting which is warmer and more concentrated in the various conversation corners.

Siemens Museum Consultancy, Munich, 1970.
Hollein, as an advisor for Siemens, participated in the realization of this technical museum which was planned and realized with Siemens objects and machinery.

Siemens AG Headquarters restoration (Siemens Casino I), Munich, 1970-75. Project realized.
In the Siemens headquarters premises (a building by Leo von Klenze), the internal spaces were partly conditioned by the necessity to preserve the façade. Attention was therefore given to areas considered at that time of minor importance, in order to partially eliminate the "heaviness" of the building. In the big meeting room, the spatial covering, which has a highly technoid look, is enriched with an accurate, quasi-perspective, decoration of joints. This finds a reference in the neoclassic symmetry of the square upon which the building faces. The foyer/reception area on the ground level took up about two thirds of the building's width, while the entrance, at the center of the façade, was off to one side in respect to the room. In order to remedy this apparent disadvantage, the glass cylinder of the entranceway was moved by half its diameter in respect to the entrance axle. This produced an internal wall segment of a quarter cylinder and a small space that at the same time is separated from the main room with a round fence on the side. The interesting aspect of this interior design lies in the ability to create different functional areas without sacrificing the open characteristics of the hall. The cylindrical spatial elements blend very clearly with the cubic and flat elements; this concept is also underlined by the ceiling and the lines of the floor.

"Death" Exhibition, ("TOD"), Mönchengladbach, 1970.
The exhibit deals with the symbolism, associations and transformations that are the composite base of Hollein's artistic work from the beginning of the sixties. Structures are used to determine a space and to create an architecture. Death is not presented through the body but through the disappearance of the body. It is the living who "dig" for traces of death

from a terrain that only in this operation acquires significance: the archeological excavations and the deceptive foundings that take on different meanings in different contexts, the rites / non-rites of daily death, the smells and colours of death in withering flowers and in candles that burn and melt in immaterial space.

Miller Relax Cell, 1970.
An object-environment intended as a remedy for neurosis and for the frustration of those who work in the offices of a big company. It is acoustically isolated and supplied with "relaxing" elements like music, television, air conditioning, etc.

PIZ BUIN Sun Boutique, Exposition stand, 1970. (Sketches).

"Tomb of a racing driver" Exhibition, ("Das Grab eines Rennfahrers"), Graz, 1970.
The theme of the quasi-contemporary "Death" exhibit is taken up again here. In the perfectly rectangular "Tomb of the racing driver" which is dug in a field, only the upper half of the wheels and a hat at the centre, which corresponds with the rear wheels, emerge. The excavation brings to life a memory and the associative mental process that conveys life images can only be stimulated by death images.

Siemens Employees' and Guests' Dining Facilities, (Siemens Casino II), Munich, 1971-72. Project realized.
The employees' and guests' dining facilities planned for Siemens were realized in a dépendence built in the fifties. Three floors were used, including the kitchens and service areas. While the space of the employees' facilities larger rooms and areas was "transformed" by maintaining the original structural covering, in the visitors' dining area new spacial coverings were created as a remedy to the uniformity imposed by the pre-existing structures. Hollein chose to design dining rooms different both in interior design and atmosphere, however avoiding the risk of too much heterogeneity. The idea of a "closed" spacial shell is dominant and in some rooms even the windows have been sacrificed since such a clearly artificial creation had to exclude daylight. For example, in a small room the walls and ceiling are covered in square panels on an aluminum framework. The covering is spray painted in deep blue, the ceiling is milk white, and the last strip of wall is covered with mirror panels, with direct lighting. Thus, the room is enlarged by an artificiality that explicitly brings to mind the famous Loos American Bar in Vienna. Hollein himself speaks of this and other small "historical" references as conscious quotations and not just moment of eclecticism. Finally, the hallway is not just a corridor but a meeting point for the environments, each having their different characteristics brought out on their hall doors.

"Paper" Exhibition, ("PAPIER"), Vienna, 1971-72.
In the presentation text, Hollein specifies that the exhibit doesn't have any didactic motivation; he doesn't intend to exemplify a production, but to illustrate a phenomenon. Paper is presented in the past (the inscription on marble) and in the present, in the raw material and in the finished product, in its value and in its extreme frailty, and as the only means of information and circulation of news in the past, now threatened by the impact of media technology. Even in the preparation and presentation of the objects or situations, Hollein intends to eliminate every idea of order and continuity, emphasizing in this way the need for an active intervention of the public; he does not want to inform them, but to stimulate their awareness, thus activating mental processes.

"Section N", Furniture and Design objects Showroom, Vienna, 1971. Project realized.
The project presents some fundamental differences in respect to other Hollein's interior restorations. The façade and structures were kept intact and only a few

elements were added instead of creating a new and independent interior shell. The original openings in the façade have been preserved and the big cylindric trademark designed by Hollein receives light only from the inside. The windows of the entrance are not connected directly with the street but through a brief "access" corridor placed behind the building's corner pillar. Internally, in order to expand the exposition area, a mezzanine has been added to which one accedes gradually, by means of short ramps that connect some of the intermediate levels; these spaces have been naturally derived from the already existing structures.

Urbanistic Study for the City of Vienna, Wollzeile-Landstrasse, 1971-73.
After an attentive analysis of the possible future consequences of traffic in its totality and in its individual aspects, some alternative solutions are proposed that favor pedestrian traffic; new possibilities are explored to better activate the area in question.

Competition Subway Entrance Area Olympic Village, Munich, 1971.

Competition Forum Olympic Village, Munich, 1971. First Prize.
Ten artists from different countries were invited to develop proposals for the activation and the artistic organization of the central area (forum) of the Munich Olympic Village. Among the jury's evaluating criteria was "...the consideration of visual, acoustic and tactile information, the conception of a multimedia system, and the organization of urban space (also for use after the Olympics) through colour, light and sound, with a possibility of modifications and adaptations according to specific requirements." Hollein's 'Media-Linien' project which won first prize, corresponded so well with the competition requirements that it was decided to use it for the entire Olympic Village.

"Media-Linien", Multimedia System of Information and Communication. Olympic Village Munich, 1971-72. Project realized.
The "Media-Linien" system, installed at a height of about three meters along a route of almost two kilometers, consists of tubular elements along which run a track for the electrical lines and luminescent tubes. The height of the steel supports is adjustable. The system consists of a variable and adaptable framework that corresponds with the demands of the particular urban situation of the Olympic Village. Some of the fundamental functions were: orientation (the differently coloured tubes lead to different places indicated respectively), illumination (other than the luminescent tubes, there were electrical sockets every two meters for reflectors and supplemental wiring), audiovisual communication and information, heating and airconditioning, information (mobile panels, projection screens), and protection from atmospheric condition (sunshades and fiberglass roofs). The "Media-Linien" represent an innovation in the field of urban design even though they were intended for a public space with special requirements. At the same time, it is an aesthetically valid architectural intervention whose presence lightens the massive architectures of the Olympic Village.

Competition for the reorganization and activation of the Vienna Town Hall Square and Ringstrasse area, 1971-72. Prize-winning competition entry.
It is a complex proposal and extremely accurate as for technical details. In order to better activate the area and convert it into a pedestrian zone, Hollein proposed paving the square in granite blocks and installing a modular lighting and conditioning system. The covering of the internal courtyard of the Town Hall palace was also suggested along with the expansion of the existing underground parking lot. There were also alternative proposals for the commercial activity of the area and for the installation and organization of ceremonies in the square.

"Work and Behaviour - Life and Death - Everyday Situations", XXXVI Venice Biennale, Austrian Pavilion, 1972.
The environment staged in the Austrian pavilion (with precise spatial references to its borders) synthetized the concepts theorized over and over by Hollein, once again proposed to the visual experience of the observer, to be interpreted in their ambivalence through mental processes of association and transformation. The theme was illustrated in all of its aspects. The "everyday situations" room presented white, tiled furniture-objects, rigidly cubic, according to a minimal uniformity criterion that eliminated every characteristic of form and surface. In only one of the objects, the grid of the tiles was marked by an incision of blood, while the coercion of this oppressive space was accentuated by a tall, narrow, almost impenetrable door. In this environment, even before observing the external objects and situations, one could already grasp the sense of Hollein's proposal: that every form is perceived in a mental, immaterial, space in which life and death alternate and slowly define themselves in symbolic implications that emerge from personal and collective memories. The breech in the wall opens a way towards myth and memory: a wooden runway leads to a canal where a modern "funeral monument" is displayed on a platform. The cubic chair of daily use floats nearby on a raft. Behind the pavilion, the geometric chair is set against a "throne" of twisted branches and a vehicle which is apparently ready for use. In his comment to the exhibit, Hollein explains the ambiguous metaphors of this environment with memories and peculiar impressions of his life, such as the crosses dripping with blood and the sacrificial altars seen in Mexico, the cemetery-parks of Chicago, death in a hospital bed, the raft of his childhood and the one in front of S. Maria della Salute, etc. If space becomes significant only in the awareness of past and present, of life and death, one also understands how forms constructed and materialized in this space may acquire a different significance.

"Roto-Desk with glass", 1972.
A glass version of the 1966 Roto-Desk Miller.

Expertise Haus Wittgenstein, Vienna, 1972.
More than a work, this is a battle sustained by Hollein in defence of the building planned and costructed by Wittgenstein that was to be demolished as part of a vast requalification plan for that area of the city. Backed up by accurate documentation, Hollein succeeded in disputing even the Supervisors' judgement and in obtaining the preservation of the building.

Jewellery Store Schullin I, Vienna, 1972-74. Project realized.
Once again the shop had to refer to the preceeding structures and to the fact that the space available was extremely reduced for both the façade and the interior. Hollein created a new spatial surface using diverse and precious materials. The attraction, as in previously realized stores, is the façade: done in granite slabs which are asymmetrically interrupted by a deep niche for the window and portal on which there is a split made of "layered" brass plates that continue as a decoration in the doorframe. Being a jewellery store the allusion to the "gold mine" is evident and Hollein also inserted a technical element: the air-conditioning ducts that emerge in sight. The interior is a precious and perfect shell in which the space has been utilized in every minimum detail. Set off against the longitudinal wall closet (result of the lowering in three different levels of the ceiling) covered in velvet, is a granite wall, while part of the ceiling is a mirror. The lighting has been given particular attention and is intended to stress the sensation of splendour and iridescence of the metals and precious stones.

"Kriemhild's Revenge" Exhibition, ("Sage und Gegenbenheit"), Folkwang Museum, Essen, 1972.
The associative mental process and the reflection on the co-existence and omnipresence of life and death are inevitably suggested in this narrow corridor that is obstructed by a body laid across it. The body must be climbed over and walked upon in order to arrive at the second obstacle that closes the space vertically; it is a garment (armour?) of metal tiles which has a disturbing geometry interrupted by one missing square and by the presence of a blood stain.

Municipal Museum Abteiberg Mönchengladbach, Urban and Architectural Conception, 1972-1982. Project realized.
The global architectural concept had to consider the integration of the entire complex to the surrounding urbanistic situation (the museum is situated on a hill near the city center), in addition to planning the exhibit spaces, the administration offices, and the restoration laboratories. The integration problem was solved by constructing the various parts of the complex around a big sand-paved platform that served both as a cover for the lower levels of the museum and as an area for pedestrian traffic leading towards the gardens and the side street. The museum's main entrance is through a small white marble pavilion in which the glass walls are cut by four steel chromed pillars. The internal staircase leads to the permanent collection areas which are characterized externally by seven big square volumes with shed coverings and zinc finishes. The office tower emerging in the west, has sand-finished walls that border on the ondulated glass and aluminum façade. Sand-finished, even on the sloped terraces that connect with the gardens (with winding smooth brick walls), is the big square space volume for the temporary exhibits. The permanent collection areas cover three floors, one above and two below the level of the entrance platform. The illumination comes from natural light (skylights and large windows) and artificial light (neon). All of the exposition areas are painted white while all the other areas are painted in different colours or have different coverings (wood, laminate, etc.). The variety of the spaces, obtained through the deliberate juxtaposition of such elements as the entrance ramps and stairways, is what dominates the museum interior. Wide spaces alternate with small isolated environments or with a series of small rooms based on a "cloverleaf" plan. Rigid circular or square symmetries contrast with winding forms. Balconies and small bridges offer unexpected views and large windows create a transparency between the interior and exterior.

Study for Zentralsparkasse (Savings Bank of the City of Vienna), Liesing (Austria), 1973. (Sketches).
Since it dealt with a very anonimous area, the building had to present characteristics that clearly distinguished and identified it. The idea, which goes back in part to the "walk-on building", is for a bunker building. It is almost completely covered by a hill which remains untouched, and only the entrance of the construction is visible.

Salzburg Cathedral Competition, Salzburg, 1973. Prize-winning competition entry.
Hollein's proposal particularly regarded certain specific points and objects of the liturgy: the altar, throne, pulpit, and the tabernacle. In addition, he suggested some minor spatial modifications in order to improve the choir's acoustics. The altar area is moved up in respect to the apse, with a reference to its spheric form both in the new altar's support platform and in the two jutting "matronei" that almost "close" the new space and define it as independent. The platform continues laterally in respect to the altar until it reaches the sacristies. There is a flexibility principle for the use of the new elements in accordance with the requirements of the liturgy. In fact, all objects are mounted on wheels and can easily be shifted or removed. In addition, they all have characteristics of

uniformity in both form and materials (light coloured stone finished in steel and marble panels).

U.S. Embassy in Moscow, internal restoration of the Press and Culture Office, 1973-74. Project realized. Most of the technical objects and equipment were re-utilized while the wall changes were kept to a minimum. A light, grated ceiling cover was added in order to soften the light and hide the old lamps. Above all, Hollein played with colour in order to liven up the environment and to accentuate some geometries. He used white clouds on the ceilings, stylized hedges in two tones of green on sky-blue walls, objects and fixtures in bright yellow, etc.

Corporate Image for the Deutsche Bank, Frankfurt, 1973.
The extremely accurate design of the interior and exterior was elaborated in drawings and models; it concerned the signs, walls, floors, furniture and several objects.

Austrian Cultural Institute in Budapest, 1973. (Sketches).

Competition Museum of Modern Art Villa Strozzi, Florence (Italy), 1973.
The competition concerned the restoration of the Villa Strozzi gardens and building complex and their utilization as a cultural center and a modern art museum. Among the architects invited to participate (Scarpa, Gardella, Aalto, Irvine, Michelucchi, Meier, Hollein), these last two were entrusted with the transformation of the stables and carriage houses, an elevated, independent complex that included a courtyard formed by those same buildings. Hollein's proposal was for a series of polifunctional rooms and an auditorium in an area of 650 sq. meters. It maintained, for the most part, the original structures, due to their historical value and to their quality in terms of space and environment. The original courtyard and façade, integrated with new glass and steel structures, were kept almost completely intact. The large windows and "bridge" at the back established a connection with the park, which was considered a fundamental part of the project.

Sunglasses for American Optical, 1973.
The design appears to be free from the typical conventions connected with the object's functions. If, as early as 1968 at the "Austriennale", the glasses were a "signal" and instrument of recognition, here they are an object of relax, fun and pleasure.

Stand Wittman I, Cologne, Furniture Fair, 1974.
Setting for presentation of Josef Hoffmann's furniture.

Competition "Turracher Höhe" Ecumenical Church, 1974. First prize.
The church is situated on an alpine pass in the Austrian mountains at an elevation of about 1800 meters. It is used for Catholic and Protestant religious ceremonies. The site, a peninsula on a mountain lake, is protected by environment and landscape laws. The square volume of the church is joined diagonally with the main entrance area which has the form of a spherical segment. At south and east, the church's roof inclines towards the volume's interior from which a smaller square is cut out that acts as an element of communication between the church and entranceway. The structure and surface area of the construction are in wood with some gold underlining. The church can accomodate up to 120 people and can be entered from the pass road or from the lake.

Gallery System Rosenthal, Dusseldorf, IKI Art Fair, 1974.
This was the first exhibition design realized using a new system based on metal panels and some fundamental lighting techniques. All of this was to be used in both the Rosenthal stores and in other premises of the company.

Rosenthal Gallery, Frankfurt, 1974.
The exposition system presented at the IKI in Dusseldorf was used here to display porcelain art objects.

Hotel in Lisbon, Project, 1974. Sketches and preparatory studies.

"MANtransFORMS" Opening Exhibition, Cooper-Hewitt Museum, New York City, 1974-76.
Hollein, with the contribution of a group of famous international designers (Sottsass, Fuller, Isozaki, Meier, etc.) was asked to conceive this project in occasion of the re-opening of the Cooper-Hewitt Museum and its transformation into the National Museum of Design. The show did not intend to be a retrospective of selected products. Instead, Hollein's proposal involved the concept of design itself, an original, non rational and subconscious element omnipresent in the life of man, tied to the world of physical survival and to the hope of survival in after life. To illustrate this concept, the exhibit presented simple materials and forms which demonstrated the almost infinite possibilities of transformation used to adjust to the various needs of man. In this manner, a piece of cloth that is initially a "live" flag in the wind, can harden into marble, demonstrating its eternal significance. Cloth is energy (sails, windmills), it is a home and defence from the elements, it is a garment, and it is art when it is worked, embroidered or painted. The same thing goes for bread, for any simple tool, and for any form or object conceived by man.

Stand Wittman II, Milan, Furniture Fair, 1974.
Setting for presentation of Josef Hoffmann's furniture.

"Ensemble Diagonal" for Wittman, 1974-75.
A line of mobile furniture (chairs, tables, screens) of identical formal planning. The design is based on a continuous play of reference and variations of a diagonal.

Offices and Storage Spaces for IIASA, Laxenburg, 1975.
General plan for spaces to be converted into offices and warehouses. The two types of space were in close contact, with very conditioning functional requirements.

Competition Pedestrian Area Salzburg, 1975. Prize-winning competition entry.
With the exclusion of vehicle traffic, the historical center was turned into a large pedestrian zone (about 400,000 sq. meters). Hollein's intervention intends to respect the spatial characteristics and "historical" atmosphere as much as possible by placing the attention more on the details of the new proposals than on the spatial modifications. The project's fundamental element is the paving system which is based on various materials (concrete, marble, granite, gravel) used according to a criterion of uniformity with the surrounding context and response to precise functional requirements. Also some small urban design interventions are suggested, both for touristic use and for the activation of the city life. Therefore, the proposal does not intend to alterate the formal and cultural spatial characteristics of the city, but to offer some "facilitations" by redefining some areas, simplifying routes, and making simple and enjoyable a visit, a commercial activity, and life in the historical center.

Competition Art Collection Nordrhein-Westfalen, Dusseldorf, 1975.
The museum which was to host the Nordrhein-Westfalen art collection, had to be built in a square with other historical buildings of extremely heterogeneous styles. The project for the new building takes its start from this contrast, in the scale, in the structure, and in the historical references.

Perchtoldsdorf Town Hall, internal renovation, 1975-76. Project realized.
In particular, Hollein's intervention concerned the City Council Hall, the two meeting rooms for the parties, and the Mayor's office, but furniture was designed purposely for all the other rooms, too. The Council Hall contains only a huge oval table (with chairs) that follows the outline of a marble mosaic on the floor with a cluster of grapes in relief (the zone is famous for wine). Such a simple interior decoration leaves no room for "disturbing" elements. For example, the air conditioning system is included in the table's structure and hidden in the wall panels.

"Perchtoldsdorf", furniture and interior design elements initially created for the interiors of the Perchtoldsorf Town Hall, 1975-76.

Wallraf-Richartz Museum, expansion proposal, Cologne, 1975.
The museum courtyard was to be used for a temporary expansion. In this manner, space is obtained for painting classes, conference rooms, video workshops and a restaurant.

"House for a Superstar", Competition. "The Japan Architect", Tokyo, 1975. Second prize.
Hollein refers once again to the theme of death and burial places with a much more ironic (apparently at least) project. "A superstar is only a true superstar if he remains one for centuries. Consequently, the true house for a superstar must be a tomb or a cenotaph...". On this premise, Hollein chooses Onassis from a given list of superstars. He designs a very simple tomb because, according to him, the ideal funeral house/monument for Onassis would have been the Taj Mahal which couldn't however be reconstructed with the funds allowed by the competition. It was evident (also to the jury who awarded him second prize) that Hollein was aiming his ironic comment at the proposed theme.

Austrian Travel Agency: Shopping City Süd Branch Office, Vösendorf (Vienna), 1975-76. Project realized.
The task regarded a branch office on the outskirts of town in a small building inside a large shopping center. In the room is a large winding counter that interrupts the horizontal space and separates the area for the public from the actual office. In front of the counter is the waiting room which is a small circular "temple" with columns, with a single divan running internally. The lighting is neon and in particular, above the counter, a sky of neon circles is crossed diagonally by a tube.

Austrian Travel Agency: Corporate Image, 1976.
The functional and decorative motifs that recur in the offices of this institution (and had to be used in the future as well): the palm-trees, temples, clouds, flags, eagles, etc.

Austrian Travel Agency Central Offices, Opernringhof, Vienna, 1976-78. Project realized.
The new offices had to be placed in a construction inside the courtyard surrounding the Opera which was rebuilt after the war with the integration of a transverse courtyard closed in by a skylight. Hollein's intervention takes its cue from three fundamental premises: the utilization of the existing structures, the functional and operative sequence of each single sector of work, and the creation of a "scene" composed of both single iconographic and metaphoric elements and of a few basic tipologies. The big room open to the public is divided into different functional zones in which the spaces are characterized by "scenic" elements in an almost didactic manner. For example, the "oriental" pavilion has the double function of waiting room and separation point between the entrance area and the two counters of the travel offices. In the functional distribution, the figurative elements are nevertheless only a part of all that contributes to the definition of this large area. In fact, various inter-

ventions already experimented in smaller areas, have been here further developed. These include the graduation of the ceilings, the floor lines and the corresponding neon tubes on the ceiling, and the use of colour which always harmonizes with the marble of the floor. However, the interest and popularity of this work derive from the formal novelty and from the game of "cultural" accessories. The intention is not just to create objects that suggest an idea or memory, but also to indicate precise cultural and historical references which coincide with the significance of this particular area where tickets are sold for a world of "illusions" (theatre, voyages).

House Lagler-Molag, Vienna, 1977.
A project of great maturity and interest, dominated by the clear Loosian reference and by a rigorously organized spatial and volumetric plant, which is nevertheless detached from criteria of absolute functionalism. The broken lines and the curves indicate, by their use, a language free from strictly orthogonal schemes.

Vaduz Art Museum Competition, 1977. (Sketches).

Museum of Glass and Ceramics, Teheran, 1977-78. Project realized.
The museum had to be created inside a 19th century small palace which belonged to a group of buildings surrounded by a park. The villa had to be preserved as much as possible in its original state, for the particular interior atmosphere caused by the extremely elaborate Rococo-Victorian stuccos on the walls and ceilings. This premise was not considered a hindrance but rather, a stimulant for the criteria of intervention. This included a system of showcases, exposition elements, and air-conditioning and control units that adapted to the pre-existing space, with the goal of underlining its qualities and particularities. Leaving aside some considerations of functional character, the structural changes were reduced to a minimum. The most considerable intervention was that of reopening the central staircase with the two curving ramps. Special showcases were studied for the rooms on ground level, either singularly or in groups, that had the double aim of showing the objects in optimal conditions and of highlighting the stuccos and the ceilings with a lighting system diffused upwards. This gives the exhibited pieces a warm light that at the same time is not too direct. On the upper floor, where the structural requirements were greater yet the areas to preserve were less, Hollein created real internal "shells", making easier once again the fruition of the objects, free from every "obligation" to the preexisting conditions. Even the surrounding park was considered an integral part of the museum's activity.

Expertise for the restoration of the Museum of Applied Arts, West Berlin, 1978.
The museum was designed by Martin Gropius in the last century and was extremely damaged during World War II. Situated right near the Berlin Wall, the original main entrance faces East Berlin while the front part of the stairs is cut by the east/west border. The fundamental problems to be faced were the urbanistic placement, a new entrance and the restoration of the interior which had to be almost completely reconstructed. Hollein proposed total restoration of the interior in only a few specific zones. For the other areas, he suggested the introduction of new environmental situations based on intentionally contrasting criteria. Nine different alternatives were worked out for the exterior. Each took into consideration both the position of the entranceway and the back façade, and the existence of the Wall and its physical and ideological "presence".

Competition for a new design of the Stephansplatz area, Vienna, 1978.
The most important aspect of the project consists in the definition of the two zones of the Stephansplatz and the Graben. A linear posting of three columns (18

meters high), at irregular intervals, is proposed in an imaginary meeting point in the Stephansplatz, between the Kärntnerstrasse, Seibergasse, and Graben. This structural intervention constitutes a common reference point between the Stephansplatz, the streets that face it, and the surrounding buildings. Another intervention occurs where the Graben opens onto the Stock-im-Eisenplatz. This consists of a pavilion that also acts as an access to the subway, a rectangular element and an urban sculpture, useful for pratical functions as well. The three columns were to be in grey granite, gilded at the top. One of the columns, meant as a fragment, could be completely gilded, in order to underline the "signal" effect.

Austrian Travel Agency: Ringturm Branch Office, Vienna, 1978-79. Project realized.
For the most part, the same themes of the Opernringhof are found here, though in a simpler version and in a smaller environment. The functional subdivision is realized through different geometries while the "scene" (the screen and line of palm-trees that go on in the infinite on the back wall's trompe-l'oeil) connects the space and evokes visions of different worlds. The curve of interior and exterior, which corresponds to the building's corner, is accentuated by a curved counter, by the corresponding line of neon lights on the ceiling, and by the asymmetrical "cage" that penetrates the façade with its waviness.

Austrian Travel Agency: City Branch Office, Vienna, 1978-79. Project realized.
In this branch office, where there was to be a department dedicated to Israel, the long rectangular space was deliberately interrupted and divided into two different semantic zones. In the front part, where the office activity was more intense and anonymous, the ceiling and the wall closets were unified by the "neutral" structure of an olive green trellis. The back area (waiting room and Israeli department) is introduced by a semi-ruined sand wall and by an artificial line on the floor on the point of passage which means to underline the change, not only functional. The second room in which the motif of the archaic walls continues, contains an "inmobile" oasis with sixteen palms set in a cube form. It is a perfect representation of the transformation into object of every idea evoked by the environment.

"Kohlergasse 9" Public School, Vienna, 1979 (still in course). Project already partly completed.
The site was not very extensive (2,332 sq. meters) and presented a difficult sloping topography. In addition, the construction had to be done in two phases so as not to completely interrupt the school's activity. The main entrance is on the Köhlergasse, from a small square created around a pre-existing tree. Through a covered access, one gets to a central point of rest and recreation from which it is possible to reach all sectors and levels of the school. On the north side, in respect to the entrance, are the offices and some classrooms. Most of the other classrooms are on the west side, while on the south side are more classrooms, the refectory, and the service areas. The gymnasium is a huge room in reinforced concrete, under which are foreseen parking areas which will also have other functions, and particular air circulation and conditioning systems. Since the limitations in space did not allow for the creation of playing fields, parts of the cover floors are used as courtyards and recreation areas. Considering the kind of building, of public service, the project sticks to traditional construction materials and methods. The walls, fixtures, and floors are nevertheless treated in different materials depending on the area's function.

"ERSTE", The First Austrian Savings Bank Head Office, Exterior Corporate Image, Vienna, 1979.
The 19th century building which housed the "First" Austrian Savings Bank, had been seriously damaged during the last war. Hollein suggested bringing the

façade (as much as possible) back to its original state and designed a new insignia that blended with the building's characteristics.

Stage Design for "The Comedy of Seduction" by Arthur Schnitzler, Burgtheater, Vienna, 1979-80.
The society which appears in this play perceives external events simply as disturbances of daily life while continuing to deal with its own meddling and petty problems. "Residues of this society – says Hollein – still live among us and they are the majority of the Burgtheater's public. This society... has a limited knowledge and opinion on Schnitzler and how he should be interpreted or presented through his plays..." The stage design was a result of these considerations and of the possibilities (or limits) offered by the space on stage. The different stage settings act not only as a "background" for the play but also as an interpretation of its content. The objects, lights and colours, always find a precise reference, by way of metaphor, in the unfolding of the plot.

Exhibition Design for Alessi, Milan Triennal, 1979.
On the pillars of an "acqueduc", the evolution of the company's production is presented in sequence. The arches are slits of light that reflect on the opposite round wall. The relationship/opposition between the straight line and the curve, by sectioning the pre-existent space, underlines the critical temporary presence of the setting.

Competition Museum of Arts and Crafts, Frankfurt, 1979-80. Second prize.
Seven internationally famous architects were invited to this competition, for a new arrangement of a complex of three neo-classic villas (Museum of Arts and Crafts, Anthropological Museum, and Museum of Musical Instruments) that were to be restored and enlarged inside a vast park. Hollein's project creates a small "city" in which a large number of buildings, fragments and historical quotations are gathered, inside precise spatial definitions. Even on such a vast scale, the purposely opposing and seemingly contrasting geometries, are recognizable on the blueprint. In his description of the project, Hollein underlines the importance of the complex's integration with the surrounding park. Without neglecting the functional requirements, architectural elements for gardens which at the same time are historical references and parts of the city, were inserted in the park. The central building seems very compact at sight, but opens up progressively to the upper floors in a series of loggias, terraces, and internal courtyards that establish the connection with the park.

"Humanism-Dishumanism" Exhibition ("Umanesimo-Disumanesimo"), Florence (Italy), 1980.
For his setting, Hollein chose the courtyard of the Renaissance Pazzi-Quaratesi palace and "transformed" it through symbolic interventions. The spaces between the columns are closed by sandbags, up to a height of two meters. Execution poles the columns are closed by sandbags, up to a height of two meters. Execution poles (clearly indicated by bloodstains and the rope at the bottom) are erected in front of the columns. Nevertheless, wheat sprouts from the blood and branches and bronze leaves emerge from the poles. Every element of this installation is ambivalent, and infact Hollein's idea is to express the polarity and the extreme dialectics of the theme. Dishumanism is not just the negation of humanism: the dishuman is part of the human, as one of its possible developments. The Renaissance was not exclusively 'human' as our times are not exclusively "dishuman".

House Marsoner, Innsbruck, 1980. (Sketches).

House Sokol, Baden, 1980. (Sketches).

Competition Catholic Center Mainz-Lerchenberg, 1980. Second prize.
The project corresponds to the specific social and urbanistic situation of a church situated in an urban context. The complex is characterized by a series of functionally distinct spaces. A small square, partially covered, that acts as a churchyard, extends towards the street. The church has also an atrium, a meeting area, and a corridor that curves around the central nave. The structure of the church is in reinforced concrete while all the external surfaces (the paving of the square and the façades that face it) are in yellow/red sandstone. The project constantly refers symbolically to Saint Francis d'Assisi, to whom the church is dedicated. The architectural typology is that of a large rectangular complex that distinguishes itself from the other buildings by its dimensions, its different materials, and its unusual curve.

"The Presence of the Past" ("La Presenza del Passato"), Venice Biennale, 1980.
Inside the "Corderie" of the Arsenal, the 'Strada Novissima', a new street made with ephemeral materials, was created, thus proposing to the visitors a direct verification of the fundamental terms of post modern research. Twenty architects were invited from all over the world to design a façade. For each façade there had to be a corresponding space in the back for a personal exhibit on the architect's work. In his project, Hollein goes back to the column motif, evidently taken from historical references and very often used in the course of his work. It is an interpretation of history in its totality: like history of architecture, like cultural heritage and personal history. The references to Bernini and Loos are "historical" memories, as are the references to "gardens" and to archaeology that are also an aspect of personal history.

"Program 6" and "Melitta", coffee and tea sets for Alessi, 1980.
The tea service openly recalls the by now "legendary" aircraft carrier. The tray is the runway and the insertable teapot and other objects suggest the aircraft control towers.

"Centrotavola I", "Centrotavola II", "Candeliere", Cleto Munari production, 1980.
These design objects are real models of architecture suggesting Holleinian motifs and recollections of his original theorizations.

"Schwarzenberg II", table for Memphis, 1980.

Jewellery Store Schullin II, Vienna, 1981-82. Project realized.
The jewellery shop, almost in front of the Retti store, was created inside a 19th century building where Hollein used the fundamental structures and covered them with a distinct "layer" of new functional and decorative elements. The internal space is ample but corresponds with an entranceway that is almost "flattened" between two high, narrow shop-windows. Two wooden tubular columns with gold-ringed capitals rise at the sides of the door. The columns support a bronze plated scythe which corresponds to a neon arch above the first floor windows. Inside, the first room is meant more for passing through than for stopping. Both the diagonal design of the marble floor and the symmetric showcases illuminated by light "poles", invite to continue towards the second room, which is almost a waiting area from which two doors lead to the safe and to the upstairs room where the route ends. The two rooms at ground level are purposely contrasting in their use of materials, in the lighting, and in the atmosphere as a whole. Even the passage from one to the other seems "difficult" because of the tall, narrow, round-edged openings. The most intriguing aspect of this interior is, without any doubt, the use of materials that suggest as a whole an impression of wealth, splendor and mistery, but that in reality are used by playing ironically on their "value" (real gold and marbles, but also fake ones in plastic or wood).

Ludwig Beck at Trump Tower, Fifth Avenue, New York City, 1981-83. Project realized.
The store is divided into four departments for a total area of 308 sq. meters. The main entrance, which is on the fifth floor of the Trump Tower, is characterized by a series of columns along the corridor and by a portal flanked on both sides by three golden columns that sustain the store sign. Inside, the relationship among the different areas is established by means of a rotunda (that is half outside and half inside space) in which a large blue and white ceramic star inlaid in the floor suggests the various directions. The most particular "scenes" are characterized mainly by different materials and colours. These include the large grey wooden shelving with set-in showcases and niches illuminated from the inside, the plate glass spray painted wall, the see-through metal panels, etc. The "historical" references are evident, like the "Homage à Philip Johnson" shelf-wardrobe which quotes the upper floor at the AT&T building, or the trompe-l'oeil of the Plaza Hotel. The extreme attention to details, and the use of different materials nevertheless give to the environment a general atmosphere of "neutral" uniformity.

Expertise Germany Energy Center (Museum of Energy), Essen, 1981.
Since the problems and techniques concerning energy can "scare" the un-initiated, Hollein suggested various possibilities. The complex is organized around a center from which different routes depart, according to the time available for the visit and to the level of information required. The buildings are isolated but integrated among them in a comprehensive structure to which other parts could be added in the future. Some of the buildings are partially underground and visitors can walk on their upper part. The quality of this project results from the great attention given to functional requirements (see the direct access from the subway, the administration area, the library and meeting rooms, etc.) and from its basic conceptual clearness.

Museum of the Applied Arts ("Jugendstilmuseum"), Expansion project, Vienna, 1981.
Constructions built at different times had already been added to the main building of the museum and also the surrounding context doesn't have specific characteristics. The basic issue in this case was whether the new building should be totally integrated to the context or it should maintain its own identity, also from a formal point of view. Hollein chose the second solution: the planned building does not just intend to "fill in" the space by creating a continuous façade on the streetside, but is a very distinct object. It is a cube that imposes its "diverse" presence in respect to the context with deliberately contrasting elements. On the other hand, both the windows and the large jutting roof frame contrast with the cube's geometry and almost try to establish a relationship with the other buildings.

"Vanity", dressing table and mirror for M.I.D., 1981-82.

"Mitzi" and "Marylin", couches for Poltronova, 1981.

Expertise-Competition for the Paulskirche area, Frankfurt, 1982-83.
For a more clear and adequate definition, both architectural and urbanistic, of the square where the church stands and of the surrounding streets, Hollein proposed to add a division element between the two areas (the square and the streets). Hollein himself calls this element "acqueduc", since it looks as a wall interrupted by regular arcades. The division "wall" has a different form in the two proposals. The first one intends to underline the historical and political importance of the site (the first German Parliament gathered in the Paulskirche in 1848): the ten arches refer to the ten länder (regions) of Germany and the last, interrupted, one, symbolizes Berlin. In the second proposal, which deals more closely with the city problems, the "wall" has the form of a building held up by an arcade and which is entered through two side towers. This permits the total opening and ability to move around in the space underneath the construction. Towards the Berlinerstrasse, three monumental flag poles should "close" the space while west of the church a pedestrian area is suggested in which the routes are defined by a different paving.

Competition Frankfurt Museum of Modern Art, 1982-83. First prize. (Under costruction).
The museum was to rise in a central site with a difficult triangular form which imposed, among other things, the connection with the nearby Römemberg/Cathedral area. Therefore, the project dealt with a new building in the city center that, other than valuable formal and functional characteristics, should have a notable urbanistic relevance. Hollein's project responded largely to these requirements, using the site's asymmetry for a compact triangular building. The edges are treated like sculpture elements while the main faces of the triangle are compact façades interrupted only by closed balconies or rows of encased windows. The function of the entrance façade (the lower face of the triangle) is expressed by a monumental plastic motif, but the real entrance is under the colonnaded south west corner. Inside, the rooms seem "closed" to the outside world behind the impenetrable walls. Nevertheless, the exhibit areas receive natural light from the large skylights. The whole interior is organized around a great trapezoidal hall several stories high, on which the balcony of the last floor opens.

Competition Frankfurt Museum of the Postal Services, 1982-83.
The façade-signal almost seem to take on itself the responsability of an urban context where the historical presence is absent. The entire organism is divided into strongly characterized and diversified volumes. The interior is organized around a central room from which, according to criteria of continuity and spatial distribution, exposition and service structures depart.

"The Turks in Vienna" ("Die Türken vor Wien. Europa und die Entscheidung and der Donau 1683-1983"), 300 Commemorative Exhibition of the Turkish siege of Vienna, Exhibition Design, Vienna, 1982-83.
The neoclassic portico of the Kunstlerhaus was covered by an enormous Turkish tent, in two parts and two different scales. At the top, an entire tent with "Turkish" figures on the balcony while two walls of fabric, symmetrical in respect to the entrance, covered a good part of the façade. Besides the metaphorical presentation, the real contrast between this ephemeral cloth architecture, the stone buildings of the historical context, and the light steel structure of the nearby Karlplatz Station by Otto Wagner, created a visual skirmish that could insinuate doubts in the mind of the observer. Inside, "scenes" of battles and historical episodes were reconstructed with accurate quotations and the utmost attention to details.

Contribution to Islamic Achitecture, Venice Biennale, 1982.
Images of the Teheran Museum of Glass and Ceramics, to demonstrate how a European can bring his own contribution to the architecture of those countries while at the same time respecting all their historical and social values.

Expertise Fiat Lingotto Factory, Turin (Italy), 1983.
Since the Fiat Lingotto factory was no longer used for production, a complex of buildings on a total area of

181,000 sq. meters, was available for a new use. Twenty architecture experts from all over the world were invited to propose new "architectural concepts" which should however respect the original characteristics of the complex. The Lingotto holds particular importance for the city, not only socially but also for its significant architectural dimensions and central placement in the metropolitan system. Hollein's project proposed a "Study Center and Museum of the History of Industrialization and of the Working Class". It is divided in nine distinct parts and intends to preserve the original structures for their historical, documentary, artistic and architectural importance. Only a few minor buildings are abolished. The courtyards are covered in order to obtain more space to accomodate the great products of industrial history, as well as to create a large auditorium. The central towers and large external staircase with the bridge and four poles with the Fiat emblem, have a strong iconographic value.

Expertise Berlin "Kulturforum", 1983.
The "Kulturforum" represents the cultural center of West Berlin with famous monuments (the Philarmonic, the Scharoun National Library, the Mies van der Rohe National Gallery, etc.) that nevertheless need a connection among them, so as to give the area a more correct urbanistic structure. Hollein's proposal suggests a new "square" that would highlight the relationship between the already existing buildings. In addition, since the dimensions of the area are so big, the project also foresees the construction of a large parochial center near the "Matthäikirche" and two pavilions at the other end of the square. As a connection element, but also a border to the entire area, a long slightly curved loggia, supported by columns and not as high as the other buildings, acts as a separation line between the urban zone and the Kulturforum area.

"Rauchstrasse, House 8", IBA Apartment Building, West Berlin, 1983-85. Project realized.
Several internationally famous architects were invited to design social housing buildings of 24 apartments each on a lot planimetrically organized by Rob Krier. The dimensions and the floor plan were for the most part decided according to the requirements of the entire complex. Therefore, the organization and the quality of the interiors became of fundamental importance. In realizing five apartments per floor as prescribed, Hollein makes use of a central corridor on each floor; in each of the four corners is an entrance to an apartment while the fifth is inserted in the side of the square floor plan. This diagonal disposition of the entrances allows a greater "opening" to the interior where irregular elements are inserted to lighten the scheme's rigidity. Also outside there is a great variety: openings and windows of different form and placement, establish a multiple relationship between the internal spaces and the surrounding environment. Even the colours, while underlining the building's structure, are meant to highlight those elements that purposely contrast with the static nature of the square volume.

Table for Knoll International, 1983.

Competition National Museum of Egyptian Civilization, Cairo, 1983.
As in previous proposals, the museum is interpreted as a small city, an entity in itself, enclosed by walls. Inside the walls one re-lives the fascination of a disappeared world, with the efficient and discrete support of equipments and techniques guaranteed by modern technology. The main entrance, inside a wall that runs parallel to the Nile, is monumental, with stairs and platforms (under which are parking lots). The project is open to a large choice of solutions, allowing visitors the possibility of access to the major interest areas without having to go through the entire museum. "Central points" that respond to functional require-

ments are suggested, both for the visit to the museum and for the maintenance and surveillance. These areas face the gardens and are fully illuminated by natural light, according to a criterion of affinity with Islamic and ancient Egyptian architecture.

"City Bett" and "Bio Bett" for Wittmann, 1982-83.

"Ludwig Beck" Exposition System, 1983.
Used for the first time in the Ludwig Beck New York store, the system is based on modular elements in pierced metal to be used singularly or in different compositions and dimensions for shelves, background or divisional panels.

Restoration of the Josef Hoffmann Pavilion, Biennale Gardens, Venice, 1983-84. Project realized.
In the fiftieth anniversary of its construction, it was decided to set up an exhibition inside the pavilion of original documents, studies and drawings, to illustrate the genesis of the building which, for the occasion, had to be restored to the original state after the heavy changes it had endured. Nevertheless, this was not totally possible due to the unsufficient documentation on such changes and to functional and economic necessities. The heavy glass entrance doors were removed to go back to the original large sliding doors. In addition, the "cassettoni" which can be seen in the original drawings, have been restored and also the outside colour (creme) which harmonizes with the "travertino", while the interior has remained white. Among other things, the original red benches have been reconstructed.

"Ultima Scena" Exhibition, Venice Biennale, 1984.
The work (whose motif will be seen again and more thoroughly examined in "The Gymnastic Lesson" exhibition) intends to deal with the two issues (art and scene) in the ideal reference to the work of art (in this case, Leonardo's "Ultima Cena") as the archetype of perfection and the spatial "scenery" of ritual communication.

"Yamagiwa Lamps", 10th International Lighting Design Competition, Tokyo, 1984.

"Köhlmarkt", lamp for Baleri Italia, 1984.

"Courtyard" ("Hofchen"), D.A.M., Frankfurt, 1984.
A permanent installation in a small courtyard inside the museum. Once more, in a "transformation" process, the plants and bushes sprouting between the stone slabs of the courtyard, are fixed into a permanent form.

"Dream and Reality, Vienna 1870-1930" ("Traum und Wirklichkeit, Wien 1870-1930"), Exhibition Design, Vienna, 1984-85.
The Kunstlerhaus, where the exhibition was hosted, is used as a scenic element of the façade, in which the main front tells its own story. One of the façades of the back side wings is covered with a layer of gold (the dream) while the other is painted completely grey (the reality). At the top, a gigantic statue dialogues, across the neon writing, with a big model of the Karl Marx Hof. The building is therefore used as the main signal in a sequence of accessory signals. The exhibit is divided into 24 "stations", each of which proposes a subject according to a chronological principle but without any disciplinary or stylistic limitations. Each "station" presents a starting point of ideas, events or characters; the effects are therefore shown beginning with their causes. The exhibition was organized and designed according to both rational and emotional criteria since it was not supposed to provide just information, but also create an atmosphere that would communicate something about the spirit of those years.

"Kaleidoscope" and "Festival", table services for Swid-Powell, 1984.

"The Gymnastics Lesson" Exhibition ("Die Turnstunde"), Mönchengladbach, 1984.
The exhibition, set up in the museum planned by Hollein himself, includes a large environment, drawings and water-colours, and (not last) the catalogue. The large installation represents the scene of multiple relationships between man and object in which the body is an instrument of "ritual" communication. It is an intervention inside a space created by the author himself, where the play of metaphors is established by the use of materials, the formal simplification and the shifting in scale and size. The studies on the feminine body, a theme repeated in the exhibited drawings and water-colours, contain principles and possibilities that can be recognized in Hollein's entire work. Erotic nudes together with landscapes are exhibited under the title "eros-ion". The catalogue is a fundamental part of the exhibition since it illustrates the historical and ideal "references" in the continuity of the author's work.

"Le Affinità Elettive" - "Sigmund Freud" Couch, Milan Triennale, 1984.
In the occasion of the exhibition "Le Affinità Elettive", 21 Italian and foreign designers were invited to present a proposal on furnishing according to the most congenial motifs of their poetics. The couch designed by Hollein was inspired (also with a photographical reference) by the famous couch in Freud's studio. The object "designed" even used the original decoration motifs that where however abandoned when the couch was realized. The object "realized" shows a particular functional elegance.

Social Housing on Meierstrasse, Vienna, 1985 - (in course).
The project, still at the stage of introductory studies and general planning, deals with a complex of social housing living units of 140 apartments on the banks of the Danube, at the outskirts of the city area next to the Prater. The conception takes its start from urbanistic considerations since Hollein interprets the area as a "corner" of the city.

"Neues Haas Haus", Commercial Building, Vienna, 1985 - (under construction).
The new building is situated in the center of Vienna, almost directly in front of the Cathedral. It represents both a meeting and a distinction point of three different zones of the city center. The curved façade finds its inspiration in the "historical" evolution (from the Roman monuments to the bow-windows of the buildings that face on the Graben). The traditional motifs of the "perforated" façade are realized in forms and materials more appropriate to the times. Inside, the four sale floors face onto a glassed in "courtyard" with several entrances at street level. Above this are three office floors and a "panoramic" restaurant. Besides the functions, even the building materials reflect the characteristics of the context: stone towards the Graben and the Goldschiedgasse and glass surfaces where the view is more open.

Laboratory and Office Building for Neusiedler AG, Umersfeld-Hausmening, 1985. (Sketches).

House Wetscher, Lans (Innsbruck), 1985. (Sketches).

Design for Bertelsmann Anniversary Celebration, Gütersloh, 1985.
The project for the 150th anniversary of the Bertelsmann publishing house was to be completed in a short time. Hollein therefore decided not to create a new spatial shell but rather a "background", by covering the central walls with blue and grey fabric. On the "stage", a symbolic scenery was created: a curtain that opened on a large shelf in which books, submitted to a transformation process, appear both real and set in gold. Nevertheless, the fundamental elements of this interior design are the "towers" (about 8 meters high) that have the double function of highlighting

the space in an architectural sense and of metaphorically representing the concepts tied to the evolution of press and of communication media. The towers were red, gold and white, and multi-coloured flower arrangements were placed in front of them on tall bases, in order to underline the character of the celebration.

"The Golden Eye" Exhibition, Cooper-Hewitt Museum, New York City, 1985.
Design objects in vivid colours and precious materials realized for the Festival of India.

"AUDI", Design of façade and sign for the Audi distribution Center, Ingolstadt, 1985-86. (Sketches).

"Rauchstrasse" Streetlamp, Berlin, 1985.

"Mayor's Room", table and interior decorating for the Vienna Town Hall, 1985.
"Kleinen Festspielhauses", Study and restoration project, Salzburg, 1985-86.
The "Kleinen Festspielhauses" auditorium (theatre complex and performing arts center) was to be restored to be used by a larger public according to criteria of better acoustics and visibility in every seat. The restoration project was then expanded to some of the office and stage service areas. After an initial phase of analysis and consultancy on the present conditions of the Festspielhauses and on the possibility of restoration (1985), Hollein presented a first project (1986) for a new, small theater (Festival Hall) to be realized either as a separate structure or integrated to the pre-existing complex. The project is still in course.

FSB Handles, Brakel, 1985-86.

"Siemens City" ("Vision Siemensstadt"), Berlin, 1986.
Introductory study, sketches and model for a new organization of the Siemens Center.

Stand SCITEX, Dusseldorf, DRUPA Trade Fair, 1985-86.

Jewels "Cleto Munari Collection", 1985-86.

Competition New National Theatre of Japan, Tokyo, 1985-86. Second prize.
Hollein's project was chosen (first prize was awarded to Takenaka-Komuten, the most important architecture studio in Japan) out of more than 200 participants due to its extreme functional possibilities and its total adherence to the program that regarded a complex of three theatres (distinct in their dimensions and functions), areas for experimental activities (one of which outside), and office and service areas. From a formal point of view, the projects shows some of Hollein's by now typical elements, such as that of the intentional contrast of volumes and geometries, and of the curve that in this case acts as the "backbone" of the entire complex.

Thyssen-Bornemisza Gallery, Expansion project, Lugano, 1986.
A competition, by invitation, for a proposal of expansion of the Gallery headquarters (Villa Favorita at Castagnola) that would permit a better accomodation of the temporary exhibits. As in previous occasions, Hollein gets its start from the question with the most difficult solution: in this case, the relationship between old and new and the integration to a context (even physical) which already had its own history. It's infact for an idea of "historical" continuity and at the same time of the utmost functionalism, that Hollein chooses a building with characteristics similar to that of the pre-existing construction. Leaning against the mountain slope, it uses of an already existing containment wall and leaves intact the large back garden. In addition, it connects with the old building with minimal interventions. The internal distribution distinguishes the temporary exhibits rooms (with side lighting and openings on the view) from the permanent collection areas with lighting from above and a "grand" entrance from a staircase that leads to an atrium-foyer.

"Hans Hollein - Métaphores et Métamporphoses", Paris Pompidou Center, 1986. Exhibition design.

"Nouvelles Téndences", Centre de Création Industrielle , Paris 1986-87.
Intervention-comment on design in the occasion of the 10 years celebration of the Pompidou Center.

"Centerpiece" for Swarovski International, 1986-87.

Vassar College Art Facilities, Expansion and Renovation Project, Poughkeepsie (USA), 1986-87. (Sketches).

"Piscinas y Deportes", Recreational and Cultural Center, Barcelona, 1986. Introductory study, sketches and model.

"Carillon Tower", Tiegarten, Berlin Kulturforum, 1986.

"Hans Hollein - Metaphern, Metamorphosen", Museum des 20. Jahrhunderts, Vienna, 1987. Exhibition design.

"Messepalast", International Competition for the area of the former Imperial Stables, Vienna, 1987.
Hollein's project, along with six others, was chosen to proceed to a further planning stage. The program foresees the restoration of Fischer von Erlach's baroque Royal Stables and the construction of a new complex and exposition center including the Museum of Modern Art, an expansion of the Kunsthistorisches Museum, and the Museum of Cinema.

"Idealmuseum", intervention at "documenta 8", Kassel, 1987.

Jewels "Köchert Collection", 1987.

Hans Hollein's writings

Photographic Documentation for the Dutch publication: J.B. Bakema, "Schindlers spel med de riumte", *Forum,* vol. 16, no. 8, Amsterdam 1961, pp. 253-263.
"Rudolph M. Schindler-ein Wiener Architekt in Kalifornien", *der aufbau* 3, Vienna, March 1961, pp. 102-108.
"Städte-Brennpunkte des Lebens", *der aufbau* 3-4, Vienna, March/April 1963, pp. 115-117.
"Pueblos", *der aufbau* 9, Vienna, September 1964, pp. 369-377.
"Zukunft der Architektur", pp. 8-11 + cover. "Steinbüschel u.A.", p. 31, *Bau* 1, Vienna, 1965.
"Teknik", *Bau* 2, Vienna 1965, pp. 40-45.
"Canaletto", *Bau* 3, Vienna 1965, p. 91.
"Biegen oder Brechen", *Bau* 4, Vienna 1965, p. 122.
"On Architecture in the Future", *Arkitekten* 12, Stockholm, December 1965, pp. 217-218.
"Background USA", *Bau* 5/6, Vienna 1965, pp. 127-135.
"Transformations", *Arts & Architecture,* Los Angeles/Ca., May 1966, pp. 24-25.
"Idea" – International Dialogue of Experimental Architecture, *Bau* 3, Vienna, 1966.
"Architecture", p. 54; "Technique", p. 55; "Les Cités. centres où converge la vie", p. 55; "L'avenir de l'architecture", p. 55-61; *L'Architecture d'aujourd'hui* 53, numéro spécial art et architecture, Paris, May/June 1966.
"Rudolph M. Schindler", *Bau* 4, Vienna 1966, pp. 67-82.
"Team X Urbino", *Bau* 5/6, Vienna 1966, p. 132.
"André Bloc 1896-1977", *Bau* 1, Vienna 1967, p. 28.
"Edifices publics. L'architecture: image et enveloppe de la communauté?", *L'Architecture d'aujourd'hui,* Paris, December 1967/January 1968.
"Alles ist Architektur", *Bau* 1/2, Vienna 1968, pp. 1-28.
"Neue Medien der Architektur", *Wort und Wahrheit* 2, Vienna, March/April 1968, pp. 174-176.
"18th Aspen Design Conference", *Domus* 466, Milan, September 1968.
"Die schlaffen Austellungen", p. 67; "Die grosse Zahl", p. 68; "18th International Design Conference in Aspen", pp. 68-78; "50 Jahre Bauhaus"; *Bau* 4, Vienna, 1968.
"Ludwig Wittgenstein" (Documentation), pp. 4-10; "Die vergessene Wagnerschule-Vorbemerkung", p. 11; "Osterreichische Architektur 1960-1970", pp. 16-17; "Hochschule - Planen - Bauen", p. 21; *Bau* 1, Vienna, 1969.
"Neue Konzeptionen aus Wien"; "Fragmentarische Anmerkungen eines Beteiligten"; "Vortrag vom 1.2.1962 in der Galerie St. Stephan, Wien"; *Bau* 2/3, Vienna 1969, pp. 1-31.
"Map Guides 14, Vienna", *Architectural Design* 10, London, October 1969, p. 576.
"Rudolph M. Schindler", *Schweizerische bauzeitung* 46, Zurich, November 1969, pp. 906-912.
"Zu Diesem Heft", *Bau* 4/5, Vienna 1969, p. 25.
"Haus Wiener, USA, by Josef Hoffmann", *Bau* 1, Vienna 1970, pp. 22-27.
"Alles ist Architecture", *Architectural Design* 2, London, February 1970, pp. 60-61.
"Karlsplatz", *Architectural Design* 5, London, May 1970, p. 218.
"Geld im Grünen", pp. 8-9; "Wo liegt die Zukunft der Architektur?", p. 10; *Wochenpresse* no. 22, illustrated supplement, Vienna, June 1970.
"Das Bankett", *Transparent* 8/9, Vienna 1970, pp. 12+41.
"Artikel über Architekt-Beruf", *Prolegomena,* Vienna, January 1973, p. 21.
"The Three Worlds of Los Angeles", Architecture Exhibit (organized by Beat Inaya), Hans Hollein – Introduction, p. 8, Los Angeles 1974.
"Antworten", *kunst und kirche,* Linz, 1/1975.
"Kolumne: Architekt und Tagespresse", *Deutsche Bauzeitung* 4/75, Stuttgart, April 1975.
"Position and Move", "The Architect as a Work of Art

or Mr. Isozaki Marries the Happy Widow", *SD Space Design*, Tokyo, April 1976.

"Messages", *The Japan Architect*, Tokyo, June 1973, p. 13.

Témoignages "Une évocation personelle", *L'Architecture d'aujourd'hui* 191, June 1977, p. 119.

"Erotische Architektur - wie könnte sie aussehen?", *Der Architekt* no. 6, Bonn, June 1977, pp. 231-233.

"Otto Wagner: Post Office Savings Bank, Vienna, Austria, 1904-06, Church of St. Leopold, Am Steinhof, Vienna, Austria, 1905-07", *Global Architecture*, Tokyo 1978.

"Introduzione - Austria", Venice Biennal, General Catalog-Visual Arts, p. 78.

"Introduzione - Maria Lassnig", Venice Biennal 1980, Austria Catalog.

"Introduzione - Varie Export", Venice Biennal 1980, Austria Catalog.

"La Presenza del Passato", Contribution to the Catalog - First International Architecture Exhibit, Venice Biennal, Editions 1980, pp. 43+189.

"Osterreischeichisches Verkehrsbüro, Filialen Opernringhof, SCS City Ringturm", *Jahrbuch für Architektur, Neues Bauen* 1980/81, Vieweg Verlag, Branschweig 1981, pp. 65-71.

"Essen und Ritual - Das Abendmahl", Proceedings of the IDZ Planning Seminar, Berlin, January 1981.

"Architettura nei paesi islamici", Contribution to the catalog, The Venice Biennal, 1982, p. 141.

"Introduzione - Walter Pichler", Venice Biennal 1982, Austria Catalog.

H. Hollein and W. Pichler, "Manifest über die absolute Architektur 1982", Stadt und Utopie, Berlin 1982, p. 105.

"Il Padiglione di Josef Hoffmann alla Biennale di Venezia", in "Josef Hoffmann - I 50 anni del Padiglione Austriaco", The Venice Biennal, 1984, pp. 11-12+16-17.

"Introduzione - Attersee", Venice Biennal 1984, Austria Catalog.

"L'ora di ginnastica", Exhibit Catalog, Monchengladbach Museum Editions, September 1984.

"Hans Hollein", Catalog "Arte Austriaca 1960-1984", Bologna 1984, pp. 104, 108, 132.

"Hans Hollein", *L'Architettura*, n. 5/1984, pp. 368-369.

"Das Konzept zur Präsentation der Austellung 'Traum und Wirklichkeit-Wien 1870-1930'", Exhibit Catalog, Vienna, March 1985, pp. 36-37.

"Zur Austellung Friedrich Achleitner-Schriften und Werk", Exhibit Catalog, Vienna, March 1985, p. 3.

H. Hollein, G. Düriegl, D. Steiner, ecc., "Wien 1870-1930", *du* 6/1985, Zurich, pp. 16-19.

"La relazione fra uomo e oggetto", *Gran Bazaar* 4/5, 1985, p. 96.

"The Gym Lesson", *International Lighting Review* n. 3, Amsterdam 1985, pp. 107-109.

"Introduzione - Max Peintner", Venice Biennal 1986, Austria Catalog.

"Introduzione - Karl Prantl", Venice Biennal 1986, Austria Catalog.

"Lugano. Concorso per l'ampliamento della Galleria von Thyssen-Bornemisza", *Domus* 678, December 1986, pp. 78-79.

"Hollein on Hollein", *Jidai no Kenchikuka*, Tokyo 1986, pp. 143-160.

"Wettbewerb Nationaltheater Tokyo", *Architektur und Wettbewerbe* n. 127, September 1986, pp. 30-32.

"Eine neue Galerie für die Sammlung Thyssen-Bornemisza", Electa and Thyssen-Bornemisza Collection Editions, 1986, pp. 44-51.

Bibliography on Hans Hollein's works and projects

Konrad Wachsmann, "Studium im team", *Bauen + Wohnen* 10, Munich 1960, p. 379.

Joseph Esherick, "Forms and Design by Hans Hollein and Walter Pichler", *arts & architecture*, Los Angeles, Ca., August 1963, pp. 14-15.

"Projekt Einfamilienhaus Direktor O.L., Wels", *der aufbau*, Vienna, November/December 1964, pp. 478-479.

"Candleshop by Hans Hollein, Architect", *arts & architecture*, Los Angeles, Ca., April 1966, pp. 24-25.

"Candle Shop in Vienna", *Domus* 438, Milan, May 1966, pp. 15-18.

Friedrich Achleitner, "Das Kerzenfachgeschäft am Kohlmarkt", p. 3, "Kerzenfachgeschäft Retti", pp. 37-41, Bau 3, Vienna 1966.

"Keyhole Shop", *The Architectural Forum*, New York, June 1966, pp. 33-37.

"Magasin Retti à Vienne, Autriche", *L'Architecture d'aujourd'hui*, Paris, June/July 1966, pp. 78-81.

"*Kerzenfachgeschäft* Retti am Kohlmarkt", *planen-bauen-wohnen* 20, Vienna 1966, pp. 22-23.

"Kerzen-Boutique in Wien", *Neue Laden* 4, August 1966, pp. 15-17.

"Kerzenfachgeschäft in Wien", *db Deutsche Bauzeitung*, Stuttgart, December 1966, pp. 1044-1047.

"Architectural Landscape", *Domus* 450, Milan, May 1967, pp. 4-5.

"Hans Hollein Boutique CM-Christa Metek", *architektur aktuell*, Vienna, June 1967, cover + pp. 30-32.

"Negozio a Vienna: la sigla è la facciata", *Domus* 456, Milan, November 1967.

"Boutiques – a new world of color – CM", *Progressive Architecture*, Stamford, Conn., December 1967, pp. 123-125.

"Boutique in Wien", *db Deutsche Bauzeitung*, Stuttgart, December 1967, pp. 972-974.

"Kerzenfachgeschäft Retti", der aufbau 6, Vienna, April 1968, pp. 214-215.

"Bold Boutique", *Design* 236, London, August 1968.

"CM-Boutique", *Bauwelt* 33, Berlin, August 1968, pp. 1032-1033.

"CM-Boutique", *Building Progress*, Cedar Rapids, Iowa, July 1968, cover + p. 2.

"Austriennale", *The Architectural Forum*, New York, September 1968, cover + p. 40 and ff.

"14th Triennal", *Domus* 466, Milan, September 1968, p. 26.

Kurt Jirasko, "Austriennale", *bauforum* 9/10, Vienna 1968, p. 11.

"Die grosse Zahl-Herausforderung aus der Zukunft", *db Deutsche Bauzeitung* 10, Stuttgart, October 1968, pp. 800+804-805.

"Austriennale", *Bauwelt* 37, Berlin, September 1968, p. 1159.

"Austriennale", *The Architectural Review* 860, London, October 1968, p. 304.

"Mode-Boutique in Wien", *md moebel interior design* 11, Stuttgart, November 1968, p. 96.

"Austriennale", *Neue Läden* 6, December 1968, pp. 19-20.

John S. Margolies, "Art Machine for the 70's", *The Architectural Forum*, New York, January/February 1970, pp. 44-51.

Don Raney, "Architectural Fabergé", *Progressive Architecture*, Stamford, Conn., February 1970, pp. 88-95.

Kenneth Frampton, "Richard L. Feigen & Co.", *Architectural Design*, London, March 1970, pp. 129-133.

"Richard L. Feigen Gallery, New York", *planen-bauen-wohnen* 38, Vienna 1970, pp. 35-43.

Jeremy Fisher, "Closely observed curves", *Design* 256, London, April 1970, pp. 42-47.

"Galleria d'arte a New York", *Domus* 485, Milan, April 1970, pp. 37-45.

"Wettbewerb der Siemens AG in München-Perlach", *db Deutsche Bauzeitung* 5, Stuttgart, May 1970, p. 318.

"Hollein: Eternit-Ausstellung", "Hollein: Ausstellungs-System", *Bauwelt* 17, Berlin, April 1970, p. 645.

"Richard Feigen Gallery, Hans Hollein", *L'Architecture d'aujourd'hui* 151, Paris, August/September 1970, p. 73 and ff.

"Boetik in Wenen", *Bouw* 52, Rotterdam, December 1970, pp. 2004-2005.

"Sistema per allestimenti", *Domus* 495, Milan, February 1971, pp. 20-21.

"Forum Olympisches Dorf", Transparent 4, Vienna, April 1972, cover + pp. 4-7.

"Venedig-Biennale", *art aktuell* no. 11, Cologne, June 1972.

"Media-Linien Olympisches Dorf München", *bauforum*, Vienna, July/August 1972, pp. 36-40.

Tommaso Trini, "Monaco: Media-Linien nel Villaggio Olimpico", "Venice, Biennale 1972", pp. 48-49, *Domus* 513, Milan, August 1972.

Wilfried Skreiner, "L'architettura trovata", *Casabella* 371, Milan, November 1972, cover + pp. 25-27.

"Work and behavior – life and death – everyday situations", *Studio International*, London, November 1972, pp. 192-193.

"Nel cuore di Vienna, un negozio", *Domus* 517, Milan, December 1972.

"Hans Hollein", *SD Space Design* 5, Tokyo, May 1973, pp. 5-79.

"Furniture showroom, Vienna", *The Architectural Review* 915, London, May 1973, pp. 307-310.

"Wertlos wie wertvoll", *md moebel interior design* 11, Stuttgart 1973, pp. 58-61.

Paulhans Peters, "Eine Industrie als Gastgeber", *Baumeister*, Munich, December 1973, pp. 1557-1564.

"Project on dresses", *IN* 10/11, Milan, June/September 1973, pp. 45-50.

"Magasin de meubles à Vienne", *L'architecture d'aujourd'hui* 169, Paris, September/October 1973, p. XIII and ff.

"Studie Landstrasse", *architektur aktuell* 39, Vienna, February 1974, pp. 34-39.

"Die Kunst der Ungleichheit-Gästeräume der Siemens-Hauptverwaltung in München", *db Deutsche Bauzeitung*, Stuttgart, June 1974.

Franco Raggi, "Vienna Orchestra", *Casabella* 392/393, Milan, August/Sept. 1974, pp. 41-42, 47-48.

Masayuki Fuchigami, "Schullin Jewelery Shop, a recent work by Hans Hollein", *a + u Architecture and Urbanism*, Tokyo, December 1974, p. 9.

"2nd Iran International Congress of Architecture", *Art et Architecture, Revue Internationale* 22-24, Teheran, May/November 1974.

"Schullin", *The Toshi-Jutaku* 701, January 1975, cover.

"Neue Läden", *architektur aktuell* 45, Vienna, February 1975, cover + pp. 29-31.

Produkte: "Ensemble Diagonal", p. 9, Berichte: "Bergkirche auf der Turracher Höhe", pp. 32-33, *architektur aktuell* 46, Vienna, April 1975.

Karl Wimmenauer, "Media-Linien im Olympischen Dorf München 1972", *Bauwelt* 16, Berlin, April 1975, pp. 483-484.

Peter M. Bode, "Design", *Der Spiegel* no. 18, Hamburg, April 1975, p. 142-145.

"Stadtisches Museum Abteiberg, Mönchengladbach", pp. 393-397, "Museum in der Villa Strozzi", pp. 414-416, *Baumeister* 5, Munich, May 1975.

"Sala de Exposiciòn en Amsterdam de Hans Hollein", *Arquitecturas BIS* 8, Barcelona, July 1975, p. 17.

Joseph Rykwert, "Ornament is no crime", *Studio International*, London, Sept./Oct. 1975.

"Laden als Kunstwerk", *db Deutsche Bauzeitung* 6, Stuttgart, June 1975, cover + p. 21.

"Hans Hollein: Il nuovo museo di Mönchengladbach", "Ristrutturazione di Villa Strozzi a Firenze", *Domus* 548, Milan, July 1975, pp. 16-22.

"Lichtblicke in Paris, Wien, Sao Paolo und anderswo", *LW-Lichtwerbung/Lichtarchitektur/Lichtinformation*, Stuttgart, July/August 1975, p. 5.

Claude Franck, "Critique/Criticism - Derniers travaux de Hans Hollein", *L'Architecture d'aujourd'hui* 180, Paris, July/Aug. 1975, pp. 95-106.

"Hans Hollein: Media-Linien a Monaco", *Domus* 550, Milan, September 1975, pp. 1-4.

"Fassadenjuwel für Wiener Schmuckschatulle", *Granit International* 5, Munich, Sept./Oct. 1975.

Wilhelm Schmidt, "Extravaganter Ladenbau für edle Steine", *moderner markt mit neuen läden*, Frankfurt, September 1975.

"Städtisches Museum Mönchengladbach", *Kunst-Bulletin des Schweizerischen Kunstvereins*, no. 9, Lucerne, September 1975.

"Neuerwerbungen deutscher Museen-Hans Hollein: Skyscraper, 1958", *Jahresring 74/75, Literatur und Kunst der Gegenwart*, DVA, Stuttgart, 1976.

Sokratis Dimitriou, "Juweliergeschäft Schullin", *bauforum 51*, Vienna 1975, pp. 12-14.

"Hans Hollein", *Arquitecturas BIS 10*, Barcelona, November 1975.

"Teilprojekt für den Umbau der Villa Strozzi in Florenz zu einem Museum", *glasforum 6*, Schorndorf (Germany), Nov./Dec. 1975, pp. 27-31.

"Wiener Bauten 1965-1975", baufachverlag GmbH, Vienna 1975, pp. 30-31, 34-35.

"Städtisches Museum Abteiberg Mönchengladbach", *Transparent 10/1975*, Vienna, December 1975, pp. 5-28.

Competition "House for a Superstar", *The Japan Architect*, vol. 50, no. 12, Tokyo, December 1975, pp. 148-149.

"Winners in the Shinkenchiku Residential Design Competition 1975, 'House for a Superstar'", *The Japan Architect 228*, Tokyo, February 1976, pp. 24-25.

"Kavaliershaus Nymphenburg, München", *DLW-Nachrichten 59/1975*, Bietigheim-Bissingen.

"Quinto Itinerario Domus", *Domus 556*, Milan, March 1976.

"Junge Architekten in Osterreich", pp. 118-120, "Alles ist Architektur", p. 21, *Bauen + Wohnen*, Zurich, April 1976.

"Hans Hollein: Intervento a Mosca/Intervento a Monaco/On paper a Vienna", *Domus 561*, Milan, August 1976, pp. 24-29.

Charles Jencks, "Fetishism and architecture", *Architectural Design*, vol. XLVI, London, August 1976, p. 492.

Pedro Cuedes, "Art Net Rally", *Riba Journal*, London, October 1976, p. 419.

"The Rally", *Art Net* no. 3, London 1976, pp. 4+8.

"Architektur-Architekt Hans Hollein: Macht müde Maurer munter", *profil* no. 45, Vienna, November 1976, pp. 56-58.

"Design Ausstellung 'MANtransFORMS' in New York", *Der Spiegel* no. 47, Hamburg, November 1976, p. 235.

"MANtransFORMS", *SD Space Design* no. 12, Tokyo, December 1976, cover + pp. 41-52.

"Art 7'76"-Abb. Kriemhilds Rache", *das kunstwerk*, Stuttgart, Sept. 1976.

Richard Pommer, "The New Architectural Supremacists", *Artforum*, New York, October 1976.

Amei Wallach, "Today in Newsday: Where Deisgn Meets Art; A grand new home for the Art of Design", *Newsday*, 17/05/1976.

Robert Mehlman, "The 'Coming of Age' of Design in America", *Interiors*, New York, August 1976, pp. 84-89.

"A new splendor", *New York Magazine*, New York, September 1976, pp. 50-51.

Grace Glueck, "Reborn Cooper - Hewitt Museum has New Home", *New York Times*, New York, 20/09/1976.

Robert Mehlman, "At Cooper - Hewitt Design Comes to Life", *Industrial Design*, New York, September/October 1976, pp. 58-64.

Jane F. Lane, "Long-awaited Opening Due for Cooper-Hewitt", *Park-East*, New York, September 1976.

"MANtransFORMS at Cooper-Hewitt Museum Oct. 7", Newtown, Connecticut, 24/09/1976 (weekly).

Thomas Hine, "New Cooper-Hewitt Tries to Stimulate Greater Sensitivity", *Philadelphia Inquirer*, 24/10/1976.

Ada Louise Huxtable, "The Miracle of Cooper-Hewitt", *New York Times*, New York, 03/10/1976.

Sarah Booth Conroy, "In Celebration of the Decorative Arts at the Cooper-Hewitt", *The Washington Post*, Washington DC., 03/10/1976.

Benjamin Forgey, "A Museum of Design for the 20th Century", *The Washington Star*, Washington DC., 06/10/1976.

"Hollein-Ausstellung im neuen New Yorker Museum of Design", *Die Presse*, Vienne, 07/10/1976.

"Hans Hollein für New York", *Kurier*, Vienna, 08/10/1976.

"Decorative arts museum gets new home", *The daily times*, Mamroneck, New York, 08/10/1976.

Peter Wynne, "The Design around us", *Bergen Record*, Bergen, USA, 08/10/1976.

Roberta J.M. Olson, "Cooper-Hewitt: The Oldest New Thing", The Soho Weekly News, New York, 07/10/1976.

"Hundert Brotlaibe in Plastik", *Arteiter-Zeitung*, Vienna, 08/10/1976.

Paul Goldberger, "Cooper-Hewitt's Gamble", *The New York Times*, New York, 08/10/1976.

Amei Wallach, "Some Grand Designs – The Cooper-Hewitt Museum's bold look at the world", *Newsday*, 08/10/1976.

Grace van Hulsteyn, "New Design for Carnegie Mansion", *East Side Express*, New York, 14/10/1976.

Douglas Davis, "Grand Designs", *Newsweek*, New York, 18/10/1976.

"Hollein-Schau für New York", *Neue Kronen-Zeitung*, Vienna, 18/10/1976.

Jane Alisson, "Museum Opens Decorative Arts", *The Indianapolis News*, 19/10/1976.

"The talk of the town – Cooper-Hewitt transformed", *The New Yorker*, New York, 25/10/1976.

Ray Smith, "Cooper-Hewitt turns the tide on design neglect", *The Village Voice*, 25/10/1976.

"Cooper Open to Fanfare", *Art/World*, New York, 30/10/1976.

Martin Filler, "DESIGN/The Cooper-Hewitt Museum of Design", *Avenue*, New York, October 1976.

Hermann Czech, "Exhibition: Austrian Architecture 1945-1975", *a + u Architecture and Urbanism*, Tokyo, October 1976, p. 7.

"MANtransFORMS - inaugurates reopening of Cooper-Hewitt", *American Fabrics/Fashion*, Fall 1976.

"Uberraschung und Schock", *Der Spiegel*, Hamburg, 15/11/1976.

Thomas B. Hess, "Design Neglect", *New York*, New York, 15/11/1976.

"The view from the castle", *Smithsonian Magazine*, Washington, November 1976.

Peter Blake, "Fun and dazzle rivaling Dadaism of the Twenties", *Smithsonian Magazine*, Washington, November 1976.

Barbara Lee Diamondstein, "The Cooper-Hewitt goes public", *Art News*, 1976.

Lin Harris, "MANtransFORMS", *Paris Passu*, 15/11/1976.

"New York and Washington Salute Cooper-Hewitt Opening", *Torch*, November 1976.

Johnny Douthis, "Cooper-Hewitt 'Gunmaking' attracts Media", *Torch*, November 1976.

"For Culture Vultures", *Audio-Visual Communications*, December 1976.

"Cooper-Hewitt will investigate the field of design", *Antique Monthly*, December 1976.

Ruth Berenson, "Ein Engelskäft eröffnet New Yorks neues Museum", *Die Welt*, Hamburg, 06/12/1976.

"Cooper-Hewitt Opening Draws Mixed Reactions", *Designer*, December 1976.

"MANtransFORMS", *SD Space Design*, Tokyo, December 1976.

Fernanda Pivano, "L'uomo trasforma - e poi?", *Casa Vogue*, Milan, January/February 1977.

"À New York: un musée vivant", *Crée*, Paris, December 1976.

Lindsay Stamm Shapiro, "Design as sign", *Craft Horizons*, New York, December 1976.

Ingeborg Hoesterey, "Alle Brote dieser Welt", *Süddeutsche Zeitung*, Munich, December 1976.

Suzanne Stephens, "Design deformed", *Art Forum*, January 1977.

"Des images de la production à la production de l'image", (Olivetti, Amsterdam 1969-1970), *L'Architecture d'aujourd'hui* no. 188, December 1976, p. 63.

Günther Feuerstein, "Gegenward-Möbel-Interieur-Austellung", *Wien gestern und heute*, Jugend &

Volk Verlag, Vienna 1976.

Marlis Grüterich, "Germany-Mönchengladbach", *Studio International*, London, January 1977.

"Kunst fürs Volk", *Profil*, Vienna, January 1977.

"Bergkirche auf der Turracher Höhe", pp. 44-45, "MANtransFORMS", p. 53, *Kunst und Kirche*, Linz, January 1977.

"Der Mensch muss nicht im Mittelpunkt stehen", *Siemens Data*, no. 1, Vienna, Jan./Feb. 1977, p. 9.

Dorothy Alexander, "Shullin-Jewelry Shop in Vienna", *Interiors*, New York, February 1977, pp. 70-73.

"Open your eyes" (MANtransFORMS), *House Beautiful's Home Decorating*, New York, Spring 1977.

John Stevens, "Bread - a matter of design", *Ladies' Home Journal*, USA, April 1977.

"Gestaltungswettbewerb mit Holz", *architektur und bau*, Vienna, Spring/Summer 1977.

"Undstillingens katalog - Alternativ arkitektur", *Louisiana Revy*, Humbleback, June 1977.

Ante von Kostelac, "The Dortmund Architecture Exhibition '76", *a + u Architecture and Urbanism*, Tokyo, May 1977, pp. 90-91.

"Actualités - Musée municipal d'Abteiberg, Mönchengaldbach", *L'Architecture d'aujourd'hui*, Paris, June 1977, pp. 20-21.

Jürgen Sembach, "Umgang mit dem Erbe des Klassizismus", *du*, Zurich, June 1977, pp. 40-49.

Adolfo Natalini, "Stanze e stili nei più recenti arredi di Hans Hollein", *Modo*, Milan, September 1977, pp. 21-26.

"Architektur", *Schaufenster-Die Presse*, Vienna, 02/09/1977, p. 2.

"Monuments Historiques - un palais classique: un siège social, Munich", *L'Architecture d'aujourd'hui*, no. 194, December 1977, pp. 26-27.

Alessandro Mendini, "Progetto 'Per', uno per uno, tutti per tutti/Analisi del progetto", Exhibit of Hans Hollein's works at the Colegio de Arquitectos in Barcelona, 1975, p. 23, *Modo 4*, Milan, November 1977, p. 23.

Günther Feuerstein, "Gestörte Form und Neo-Mannierismus", *Transparent 11/12*, Vienna 1977, p. 42.

Peter C. von Sedlein, "Architektur ohne Bauherr" (Competition), *Architektur-Wettbewerb 92* (Krämer-Verlag), Stuttgart, December 1977.

"A view of contemporary architects", "Hans Hollein-Museum Mönchengladbach", pp. 204-207, *a + u Architecture and Urbanism*, Tokyo, December 1977.

Michel Maek-Gérard, "Phantastische Fahrzeuge", Kultur + Technik, Zeitschrift des Deutschen Museums München, 1/1978, pp. 31-32.

Ugo La Pietra, "'MANtransFORMS', universo e pane quotidiano", *Modo 6*, January-February 1978, Milan, pp. 37-42.

"Rathaus Perchtoldsdorf", *architektur aktuell* 63/1978, Vienna, pp. 36-38.

Christoph Mäckler, "Hans Hollein", Publication in occasion of a conference of Hans Hollein at the Aachen/R.F.T. Polytechnic. Prof. Manfred Speidel, RWTH, Aachen, February 1978.

Kurt Lüthi, "Architektur: Hollein bau in Wien 'Ein Adler lädt ein...', 'Kunstszene Linz jetzt international", pp. 70-72, *Extrablatt*, Vienna, March 1978.

Ugo La Pietra, "Architettura radicale in Italia", *Domus 580*, Milan, March 1978, p. 3.

"Gebautes Fernweh: Osterreichisches Verkehrsbüro", *profil 12*, Vienna, March 1978, pp. 56-58.

Joseph Rykwert, "Ornament is no crime", *a + u Architecture and Urbanism*, Tokyo, March 1978, p. 68.

Peter M. Bode, "Die neuen Museen", *Westermann Monatshefte*, Braunschweig, April 1978, pp. 48-49.

"5 Arbeitersiedlungen im Revier (Reitwinkelkolonie, Recklinghausen-Grullbad)", *Bauwelt*, Berlin, April 1978, cover + pp. 564-566.

"Osterreicher im Ausland-Museum für Moderne Kunst, Florenze", p. 43; "Städisches Museum Mönchengladbach", p. 45; "Museum für Glas und Keramik", p. 49, *architektur aktuell 67/68*, Vienna, April 1978.

"Renovation und Umbau des Rathauses Perchtoldsdorf", *Bauen + Wohnen*, Zurich, June 1978, pp. 258-259.

Enzo Fratelli, "A Kassel l'utopia ha quattro ruote, ma non è un automobile", *Modo* 10, Milan, June 1978, p. 22.

Peter Rumpf, "Architektur als Geheimsprache", *Bauwelt*, Berlin, July 1978, pp. 971-972.

"Traumwelt", *Ladenbau aktuell* no. 8, Amstetten, July 1978.

"Osterreichisches Verkehrsbüro", *der aufben* 9/10, Vienna, September/October 1978, pp. 341-343.

Elke Trappschuh, "Architektur zwischen Pop und kultischer Hoheit", *Handelsblatt Düsseldorf*, September 1978.

Christoph Horst, "Ein neuer Mann für Wiens Kunsthochschule", *Profil* 37, Vienna, September 1978, pp. 54-56.

Erhard Stackl, "Stephansplatz-Gestaltung", *Profil* 41, Vienna, October 1978, p. 68.

P.P. Polte, "TW-Gespräch mit dem Wiener Architekten Hans Hollein", *Textil-Wirtschaft* no. 50, Frankfurt, December 1978, pp. 41-43.

Günther Bock, "Alles ist Architektur-Ist Architektur alles?", *Bauwelt* 43, Berlin, November 1978, pp. 1588-1591.

Friedrich Achleitner, "Osterreichische Architektur im 20. Jahrhundert", *Deutsches Architektenblatt* 11, November 1978, pp. 1204-1208.

"Reconversion - 'Kavalierhaus' - Fondation Siemens", *Technique & Architecture* 322, Paris, December 1978, pp. 57-58.

Charles Jencks, "Buildings in AD", *AD - Architectural Design*, vol. 48, No. 11/12, December 1978, p. 600.

"Hans Hollein - Austrian Travel Agency - Vienna, Austria", *a + u Architecture and Urbanism*, Tokyo, January 1979, pp. 31-46.

"Osterreichisches Verkehrsbüro", *Baumeister*, Munich, February 1979, pp. 154-156.

"Sonderthema: Stephansplatzgestaltung - 'Man schweight mein project tot'", *The Diplomat's and Manager's Magazine* 2, Vienna 1979, p. 24.

"Osterreichisches Verkehrsbüro", *moderner markt mit neuen läden*, Frankfurt, February 1979, cover + pp. 20-27.

"Osterreichisches Verkehrsbüro", "Rathaus Perchtoldsdorf", "MANtransFORMS", *db Deutsche Bauzeitung*, Stuttgart, March 1979.

"Rituali diversi in uno spazio circolare continuo", *Harper's Gran Bazaar*, Milan, March/April 1979, pp. 114-122.

"Osterreichisches Verkehrsbüro", pp. 134-136; "Stadtisches Museum Mönchengladbach", pp. 137-140, *kunst + kirche*, Linz, March 1979.

Horst Christoph, "Mit Säulen und Bögen gegen die Schachteln", *profil* 27, Vienna, July 1979, p. 57.

"Interessante Gestaltung eines Verkehrsburos mit Naturstein", *Naturstein*, Ulm, May 1979, pp. 406-407.

"Architektur ist Kunst", *Die Erste* 4, Vienna, June 1979, pp. 22-24.

"Von Semper bis Hollein", *Bauwelt* 25, Berlin, July 1979, pp. 1073-1077.

Lothar Juckel, "Konfrontation: Ein Bauwerk als Kunstwerk", *Neue Heimat*, Hamburg, August 1979, pp. 22-29.

"La Villa Strozzi à Florence , Italie", *Techniques & Architectures*, Paris, September 1979, pp. 68-71.

Charles Jencks, "Late-Modernism and Post-Modernism", *a + u Architecture and Urbanism*, Tokyo, October 1979, p. 68 ff.

"tot" "tod" - Redaktionsgespräch mit Hans Hollein, Ausstellung und Seminar zum Thema Tod, *werk und zeit* 3/79, Darmstadt 1979.

Karl Baur-Callwey, "Naturstein schafft Atmosphäre", *Steinmetz + Bildhauer*, Munich, October 1979, pp. 809-812.

Mark Mack, "Extracting and recombining elements", *Progressive Architecture*, Stamford/Conn., December 1979.

"Hans Hollein", *Wiener*, Vienna, October 1979.

Holger Schnitgerhans, "Hans Hollein - Ein Portrait des Wiener Künstler - Architekten und seiner 'Architektur der Zitate'", *Architektur und Wohnen*, Hamburg, January 1980, pp. 156-162.

"Zeitschriften - Ein Werkbundheft zum Thema 'tot'", *Steinmetz + Bildhauer*, Munich, February 1980.

"Art Galleries & Alternative Spaces", *Studio International* 195, London, 1/1980, cover + p. 1.

"IKG - internationales künstlergremium", *Zweitschrift* 7, Hannover, Spring 1980, p. 12.

Johannes Cladders, "Museum Abteiberg Mönchengladbach", *Architektur + Wettbewerbe* 101, March 1980, pp. 4-6.

Patrice Goulet, "Invitation aux voyages", *Crée*, no. 176, March/April 1980.

H. Haschek, "The Society of Friends of the Academy", *Austria today* VI, Spring 1980, p. 39.

"Musée municipal de Mönchengladbach, près de Düsseldorf, H. Hollein", *L'Architecture d'aujourd'hui* no. 208, Paris, April 1980, pp. 86-88.

James Stirling, "Hans Hollein, Vetrine di un'esposizione, *Domus* 607, Milan, June 1980, pp. 8-13.

"Eine Galerie in New York", cover + pp. 1142-1145; "Der Frankfurter Museums-Wettbewerb", pp. 1132+1137, *Bauwelt* 26, Berlin, July 1980.

Horst Christoph, "Wieder Säulen und Giebel", *profil* 32, Vienna, August 1980, pp. 42-50.

"Museum für Kunsthandwerk in Frankfurt - Ein 2. Preis", *Baumeister* 8, Munich, August 1980, pp. 767+774-775.

Gerald R. Blomeyer, "1. Biennale für Architektur in Venedig", *Bauwelt* 31, Berlin, August 1980, pp. 1344-1346.

Anna Piaggi, "Come è seducente, questa commedia", *Casa Vogue* 105, April 1980, pp. 234-239.

"Actualités: Musée des arts décoratifs, Francfort", pp. XIX-XX; "Syndicat d'initiative et agence de voyage, Vienne, H. Hollein", pp. 62-67, *L'Architecture d'aujourd'hui* 210, Paris, September 1980.

F. Jaeger, "Lernen von Palladio - Architektur - Biennale Venedig", *db Deutsche Bauzeitung* 9/80, Stuttgart, pp. 61-64.

"Marginalia - Post Modern in Venice", *The Architectural Review* 1003, London, September 1980, pp. 132-134.

"Magazine. En direct de la Biennale de Venice... A suivre, participer, voir, lire", *Crée* 179, September/October 1980, p. 17.

"La Torre di Babele", *Modo* 27, March 1980, Milan, pp. 30-32.

Andrea Banzi, "I post-romani a Venezia", "Breve rapporto sullo stato dell'architettura post-moderna alla Biennale di Venezia '80", *Modo* 34, Milan, November 1980, pp. 41-45.

Rainer Beck, "Wiener Diagnosen für diese Zeit", *Galerie der Künste, Connaissance des Arts*, Munich, November 1980, pp. 54-61.

"Hans Hollein, Verkehrsbüro in Wien, 1977", *Umbau* 3, Vienna, December 1980, pp. 24-26.

O. Kapfinger, D. Steiner, "Die Vergänglichkeit der Gegenwart", *Umbau* 3, Vienna, December 1980, pp. 59-69.

"The Glass Museum, Teheran, Iran", *The Architectural Review* 1006, London, December 1980, pp. 374-377.

"Musée de la Céramique et du Verre, Téhéran", *L'Architecture d'aujourd'hui* 212, Paris, December 1980, pp. 74-79.

"Dächer, Türme, Kuppeln", "Haus Molag, Isometrie", *Eternit - Impulse*, Vienna, November 1980, p. 88.

"Architektur - Biennale, Venedig '80", *SD Space Design*, no. 8012, Tokyo, December 1980.

Barnie Ott, "La Biennale '80 Venice", *Archetype*, vol. II, no. 1, San Francisco, Autumn 1980.

"Verkaufen und Werben", *Süddeutsche Zeitung*, Kalendar 1981, Munich.

"Architektur aus Osterreich", *Bauen und Wohnen*, Basler Magazin, Basel, 10/10/1981, p. 12.

Adolfo Natalini, "Frankfurt am Manhattan", *Domus* 613, Milan, January 1981, pp. 16-17.

Cleto Munari, "Silver for daily use", *Domus* 614, Milan, February 1981, p. 44.

Heinrich Klotz, "Die belle époque des Museumsbaus in Frankfurt/Main", Jahrbuch für Architektur, Neues Bauen 1980/81, pp. 20-21, Vieweg Verlag, Braunschweig.

Frank Werner, "Der Wettbewerb für das Museum für Kunsthandwerk in Frankfurt/Main", Jahrbuch für Architektur, Neues Bauen 1980/81, pp.22-52, Vieweg Verlag, Braunschweig.

"Möbelentwürfe", Jahrbuch für Architektur, Neues Bauen 1980/81, pp. 84-85, Vieweg Verlag, Braunschweig.

"Museum für Glas und Keramik, Teheran", *Domus* Calendar, August 1981, Milan.

"Osterreichisches Verkehsbüro", *a + u Architecture and Urbanism*, Tokyo, no. 125, February 1981, p. 8.

"The Venice Biennale Architectural Section", *a + u Architecture and Urbanism*, Tokyo, no. 125, February 1981, pp. 13-41.

"The counter-reformation in architecture - Reflections on the 1980 Venice Biennial", *AD Architectural Design*, London, January 1981 (supplement).

"Das Abendmahl", *Essen und Ritual*, IDZ Berlin, January 1981, cover + pp. 32-43+87.

"Western Artifice Celebrates Eastern Art", *Architectural Record* 5/1981, New York, pp. 88-95.

"Arbeiten von Hans Hollein", *Werk-Bauen + Wohnen* 1/2, 1981, Zurich, p. 56.

"Ein Architekt spielt Theater", *art* 3/1982, Hamburg, pp. 5-51.

"Städtisches Museum Abteiberg, Mönchengladbach", *Museum*, Brauschweig, May 1982.

"P/A Second Annual Conceptual Furniture Competition", *Progressive Architecture* 5/1982, Penton/IPC, Stamford/Conn., pp. 158-169.

"A Place for Art: Hans Hollein's Museum in Mönchengladbach", *Studio International* 995, London, June 1982, pp. 88-91.

"Mönchengladbach: Ein Tempel führt zur Kunst", *art* 6/1982, Hamburg, pp. 110-111.

"Mönchengladbach eröffnet", *Bauwelt* 24, Berlin 1982, p. 127.

"Pläne für ein deutsches Energiezentrum", *Bauwelt* 25, Berlin 1982, pp. 1048-1049.

"Attualità: Hans Hollein, oggetto consolle", *Modo* 51, Milan, July/August 1982, p. 7.

"Baukunst im wahrsten Sinne", *Stadt*, Hamburg, 8/1982, pp. 6-7.

"Kunst und Architektur", *Bauwelt*, Berlin, 3/1982, pp. 1192-1215.

"Hollein's 'Abteimuseum' eingeweiht", *Deutsche Bauzeitschrift* 8/1982, Gütersloh, p. 1143.

"Hans Hollein: Herausforderung zur MID-Arbeit", *Einrichten* 9/1982, Vienna, cover + pp. 52-53.

"Wie ein Träumer zu seinem Museum kam", *art* 1/1982, Hamburg, pp. 80-90.

"Museo di Arte Contemporanea a Mönchengladbach", *Panorama*, Milan, 04/10/1982, p. 20.

"Architektur für Kunst", *Werk, Bauen + Wohnen*, Zurich, 10/1982, pp. 32-42.

"Museum Abteiberg Mönchengladbach: Kunst, Architektur und Licht", *ERCO Lichtbericht* 15/1982, pp. 2-21.

"Hollein Fragmenta 1972-1982: la colonia d'arte sull'Abteiberg di Mönchengladbach", *Domus* 632, Milan, October 1982, pp. 2-17.

"Kommentar: Museumsbauten", *Baumeister* 10/1982, Munich, pp. 954-956.

"Museum Abteiberg in Mönchengladbach", *Baumeister* 10/1982, Munich, pp. 965-975.

"Hans Hollein: Il confronto - il museo municipale Abteiberg Mönchengladbach", *Gran Bazar*, Milan, November 1982, pp. 134-145.

"Das Museum auf dem Abteiberg in Mönchengladbach von H. Hollein", *Form* 98/1982, pp. 36-41.

"Das synthetische Kunstwerk", *db Deutsche Bauzeitung* 12/1982, Stuttgart, pp. 40-51.

"Stirling and Hollein", *The Architectural Review* no. 1030, December 1982, pp. 52-71.

"Angewandte Schizophrenie", *Wochenpress/Kurier*, Vienna, 28/12/1982, pp. 48-49.

"Eine neue Dimension in der Museumsarchitektur", *Architektur und Wohnen* no. 4, December 1982-March 1983, Hamburg, pp. 174-180.

"Hans Hollein: Il negozio incastonato", *Casa Vogue* no. 137, Milan, January 1983, cover + pp. 73-81.

"Annäherung an das Traumbild", *Kulturchronik* 1/1983, Bonn, pp. 30-31.

"Brighton lively", *House & Garden*, New York, January 1983, pp. 107-115.

"Hans Hollein's Municipal Museum", *art & architecture*, Institute of Contemporary Arts, London, January-May 1983, pp. 24-25.

"Hilfe, die Türken kommen", *Rendezvous Wien* 1/1983, Vienna, pp. 22-27.

"Building for the art of the 20th century", *Architectural Record*, February 1983.

"Golden Oases", *Der Spiegel*, 15/1983, Hamburg, pp. 243-245.

"Das Werden einer Freundschaft?", *Profil* 18/1983, Vienna, pp. 80-81.

"Hans Hollein - Portrait", *architecture intérieure*, Paris, April/May 1983, pp. 96-105.

"Kruzitürk'n die Türken", *Zeitmagazin* 23/1983, Hamburg, pp. 18-24.

"Fassadenlust statt Planungsfrust", *Profil* 26/1983, Vienna, pp. 57-58.

"Das Kühne Spiel mit Vieldeutigkeit", *Rendezvous Wien*, Vienna, no. 2/Summer 1983, pp. 76-79.

"Ornament is no crime", *Progressive Architecture*, Stamford, Conn., June 1983, pp. 76-79.

"1. Preis - Prof. Hans Hollein, Wien", *Der Magistrat der Stadt Frankfurt*, June 1983, pp. 13-18.

"Licht für die Kunst", Licht 8/1983, pp. 410-428 (Organ der Lichttechnischen Gesellschaft).

"Aktuell: Auf die Spitze getrieben", *db Deutsche Bauzeitung* 8/1983, Stuttgart, pp. 54-55.

"A Museum That is a Cluster of Eclectic Buildings on a Hilltop", *AIA Journal*, August 1983, pp. 128-133.

"A jewelry shop that is a sumptuous confection of rich ingredients", *AIA Journal*, August 1983, pp. 108-109.

"Museum für Modern Kunst", art 9/1983, Hamburg, p. 70 and ff.

"Light - Art - Architecture: Municipal Museum Abteiberg", *ilr* 3/1983, Eindhoven, pp. 61-66.

"Il museo fatto di luce", *Panorama mese*, Milan, September 1983, pp. 98-103.

"Projet de Musée d'Art Moderne à Francofort-sur-Le Main", *Architecture d'aujourd'hui*, no. 228, September 1983, Paris, pp. XI-XII.

"Trump Tower New York", *Gala*, Sept./Oct. 1983, pp. 26-33, Gala Verlag, Grünwald.

"300 Jahre: Die Türken vor Wien-Europa und die Entscheidung and der Donau 1683", ERCO Lichtbericht no. 17, October 1983, pp. 14-21, ERCO Leuchten, Lüdenscheid.

"AA Design", *AA/Architecture d'aujourd'hui* 230, September 1983, pp. 99-103.

J.F. Bizot, "La Maladie de Vienne nous menace tous", *Actuel*, no. 49, Paris 1983, pp. 102-105 + p. 147.

J. Tabor, "Das Kühle Spiel mit Vieldeutigkeit", *Rendezvous Wien* 2, 1983, pp. 10-13.

P. Rumpf, "Operation an offenen Herzen", *Bauwelt*, 46/47, 1983, pp. 1843-1847.

M. Pavesi, G. Ratti, "Tutte le novità sul mobile europeo", *Casa Vogue* 140, 1983, p. 240.

J. Rykwert, "Ornament ist kein Verbrechen", Ed. DuMont, Cologne 1983, pp. 177-178.

P.C. Santini, "Il Materiale Marmo", Catalogue "Tecniche e Cultura", Milan, December 1983, pp. 24-25.

"Hans Hollein", "Dal Cucchiaio alla città", Catalogue Triennal of Milan 1983, pp. 84-85.

D. Steiner, "Für Gold und Edelstein", *Bauwelt* no. 44, November 1983, pp. 1762-1764.

Hans Hollein - The Schullin Jewelry Shop", *GA Document* no. 8, October 1983, pp. 86-91.

"Actualités: Projet du Musée d'Art Moderne", *AA/Architecture d'aujourd'hui* no. 228, 1983, pp. XI-XII.

"Il letto verde", *Domus* 644, November 1983, p. 64.

A. Mendini, "Intervista: I Turchi a Vienna", *Domus* 645, 1983, pp. 1-7.

M. Emery, *Furniture by Architects*, New York 1983, pp. 132, 154.

"Recent work by Hans Hollein-Abteiberg Museum in Mönchengladbach", *SD/Space Design* 224, OS/83, pp. 62-78.

C. Jencks, "Hans Hollein-Städtisches Museum Abteiberg Mönchengladbach" *A.D.* no. 53, London, 7/8, 1983, pp. 110-121.

R. Miyake, "Architecture: beyond the secret objects", *GA Document* no. 6, Tokyo 1983, pp. 34-52.

"Art and Architecture, Ten New Buildings", ICA, London 1983, pp. 8, 13, 24-25.

O. Kapfinger, A. Krischanitz, "Schöne Kollisionen: Versuch über die Semantik in der Architektur", *Umbau* 8, Vienna, December 1984, pp. 5-6.

P. Rumpf, "Germania: Il miracolo dei musei", *Domus* 651, 1984, pp. 16-17.

W. Dechau, "Kaleidoskop: Auszeichnung für Hollein", *db/Deutsche Bauzeitung* 6, Stuttgart 1984, p. 4.

R.H. Fuchs, "Municipal Museum at Abteiberg Mönchengladbach", *a + u* 1/1984, pp. 27-58.

"Une collection d'espaces", Le Moniteur, Paris, December 1984, pp. 48-49.

B. Lazlo, "Hollein Monchengladbachi Muzeuma" *Mé/Magyar éptömüveszet*, Budapest, February 1984, pp. 51-53.

"Museum Boom West German vie for the best", *Tune* no. 16, Amsterdam, April 1984, p. 56.

P. Réstany, "La colline enchantée", *Décoration Internationale* no. 67, Paris, Dec./Jan. 1984, pp. 102-107.

"Evénement - Vienne bercau de la Modernité; Personalités", *Connaissance des Arts* 400, Paris, pp. 11, 33.

D. Mayhöfer, "Architekt des Jahres", *Architektur und Wohnen* no. 1, Hamburg 1984, p. 82.

A. Isozaki, R. Fuchs, "Recent Works of Hans Hollein", *a + u*, 1/84, pp. 27-72.

Y. Matsunaga, H. Hollein (interview), "Tradition and Contest", *JA/The Japan Architect* no. 330, October 1984, p. 8.

H. Klotz, "Die Revision der Moderne Postmoderne Architektur", Prestel-Verlag, Munich 1984, pp. 92-115.

H. Klotz, "Hans Hollein und die Wiener Architekten der Gegenwart", in *Moderne und postmoderne Architekten der Gegenwart 1960-1980*, Vieweg & Sohn, Braunschweig 1984, pp. 342-360.

M. Brix, "Hans Hollein - Architekturdesign", *Idea III* (cat.), Hamburg 1984, pp. 167-196.

R. Pedio, "Hans Hollein", in *Venti Progetti per il Futuro del Lingotto* (cat.), Fabbri, Milan 1984, pp. 94-103.

"Volksschule Köhlergasse", *Planen-Bauen-Wohnen* no. 105, Vienna 1984, pp. 36-39.

B. Pedretti, "Progetto inferno e paradiso", *Modo* no. 69, 1984, pp. 63-65.

K. Oshinomi, "From Alessi's latest works: Tea and Coffee Piazza. Modernism and Historism in a coffeepot", *SD/Space Design* no. 3, 1984, pp. 60-64.

A.J. Pulos, "Officina Alessi", *American Craft*, New York, June/July 1984, pp. 23-27.

"Forum Culturel Berlin", *AA/Architecture d'aujourd'hui* no. 293, 1984, pp. 80-81.

G. Glusberg, "Hans Hollein: Kulturforum West-Berlin 1983-1987", *Architectural Design* no. 54, 11/12 1984, pp. 56-59.

"Hans Hollein Projekt zum Museum für Moderne Kunst", *Parnass*, Linz, January/February 1984, pp. 18-21.

"300 years commemorative exhibition of the Turkish siege of Vienna", *a + u*, 1/84, pp. 66-72.

"Schullin Jewelry Shop 2", *a + u*, 1/84, pp. 59-65.

"Bijouterie Schullin II", *AA/Architecture d'aujourd'hui* no. 4, 1984, pp. 108-109.

W.F. Wagner, "Ein klein Castle", *Architectural Record*, New York, March 1984, pp. 146-151.

"Ludwig Beck (N.Y. USA)", *Nikkei Architectur* II, Tokyo, 1984, pp. 53-57.

"Documenta: Ludwig Beck a New York di Hollein", *Gran Bazaar* no. 4, 1984, pp. 115-118.

K. Khittl, "Messepalast: Hollein her", *Wochenpresse* no. 47, Vienna, 20 November 1984, pp. 47-48.

H. Klotz, W. Krase, "Städtisches Museum Abteiberg Mönchengladbach, Hans Hollein" in *Neue Museumsbauten in der BRD, 1985*, DAM, Frankfurt, pp. 91-104.

"Germany: The Städtisches Museum abteiberg (1983)" in *A Field Guide to Landmarks of Modern Architecture in Europe*, Prentice-Hall, Englewood 1985, p. 177.

P. Dyckhoff, "Neue Tempel für die Kunst", *Stern* no. 18, April 25, 1985, pp. 60, 62, 66.

P. Schneider, "Europe: la bataille des musées", *L'Express international* no. 1781, 1985, p. 13.

O. Oberhuber, "Museen: Was taugen die neuen Häu-

ser?", *Art* no. 8, Hamburg, August 1985, pp. 74-75.

E. Busche, "Präzise, streng und dennoch spieleisch", *Art* no. 11, Hamburg November 1985, pp. 11-12.

O. Tozzi, P. Portoghesi, "Collezione Cleto Munari", in *L'Idea in Forma* (cat.), Vicenza, September 1985, pp. 42-45.

"The Interviews: Hans Hollein", Transition, Melbourne, April 1985.

C. Guenzi, "Bergasse 19", in *Le Affinità Elettive* (cat.), Electa, Milan 1985, pp. 87-92.

M. Spens, "Comment Dream and Reality", *Studio* no. 1009, London 1985, p. 2.

F. Pasini, "Wien: Traum und Wirklichkeit", *Domus* no. 663, 1985, pp. 68-71.

C.W. Thomsen, "Wiener Weh, Berline Juchee", *Parnass* 4, Linz, July-August 1985, pp. 40-47.

M. Spring, "Vienna on the Couch", *Buildings* no. 18, London 3 May 1985, pp. 34-35.

M. Schmertz, "Fin de Siècle", *Architectural Record* no. 9, New York 1985, pp. 104-113.

M. Spens, "Hollein's Vienna", *The Architectural Review*, London, November 1985, pp. 58-63.

D. Roth, "Mélange eines Jahrhunderts", *Harper's Bazaar* 5, 1985, pp. 90-94.

I. Siebert, "Austellungsprundgang: Wer sind wir? Wind sir wer!", *"M" Das Magazin* no. 5, May 1985, pp. 8-13.

K. Andersen, "The art of joyful jam-packing", *Time Magazine*, Amsterdam, 15 April 1985, p. 49.

D.D. Boles, "Pritzker 1985: Hans Hollein", *Progressive Architecture*, May 1985, p. 21.

J. Tabor, "Ein Architekt aus Osterreich: Der moderne Mann", *Wiener* no. 61, Vienna, May 1985, pp. 114-119.

S. Boll, "Hans Hollein-Architektur und noch viel mehr", *Architektur und Technik* no. 6, Schlieren 1985, pp. 30-38.

"Hans Hollein - Alles ist Architektur", *a + u / Architecture and urbanism* no. 180, 1985.

"Projet lauréat du concours pour le musée d'art moderne, Francfort", *Techniques & Architecture* no. 359, Paris 1985, pp. 110-111.

M. Bédarida, "Formes Urbaines: Berlin-Rauchstrasse, un exercise de style", *AMC Revue d'architecture*, Paris, December 1985, pp. 63-69.

G. Schöllhammer, "Stadtvillen am Tiergarten: Berlin, Rauchstrasse", *Wettbewerbe*, Vienna, Nov.-Dec. 1985, pp. 82-83+91.

A. Hecht, "Grosse Parade der Baumeister von Heute", *Art* no. 4, Hamburg, April 1985, pp. 54-61.

U. La Pietra, "Speciale Salone: Linee di Moda", *Domus* 657, 1985, pp. 52-75.

P. Réstany, "Il Parnaso del design", *Domus*, April 1985, pp. 83-89.

A. Nemeczek, "Skulptur wird Möbel, Möbel wird Skulptur", *Art* no. 5, Hamburg 1985, pp. 48-57.

"Contemporary Landscape From the Horizon of Postmodern Design", Exhibit Catalogue Kyoto, September 1985, pp. 64-65.

K. Frampton, *Modern Architecture*, Thames & Hudson, London 1985, pp. 283, 308-309, 312.

G. Pettena, "Disciplinare Hollein", *D'Ars* no. 111, Milan 1986, pp. 80-83.

W. Pehnt, "Architektur als Collage", in *Hans Hollein-Museum in Mönchengladbach* 1986, Fisher Taschenbuch, Frankfurt 1986.

H. Schubert, "Mönchengladbach Museum Abteiberg", in *Moderner Museumsbau-Deutschland, Osterreich, Schweiz, 1986*, Deutsche Verlagsanstalt, Stuttgart 1986, pp. 137-139.

A.M. Printa, "Veneizia Wunderkammer", *Area* no. 31, 1986, p. 36.

H.H. Arnason, "Post Modernism in Architecture", in *History of Modern Art*, Harry M. Abrams, New York 1986, pp. 694-695.

H. Hollein, "Hollein on Hollein"; J. Rykwert, "Irony: Hollein's General Approach"; K. Frampton, "Hollein's Mönchengladbach: Meditations on an Aircraftcarrier", *a + u* 2/1985, special number on H. Hollein.

K. van der Marliere, "Hans Hollein im Gesprek", *Vlees an Beton* no. 5, Brussels 1986.

H. Klotz, "Revision der Moderne Postmoderne Architektur 1960-1980", Catalogue, National Museum of Modern Art, Tokyo 1986, pp. 52-56.

P.M. Bode, "Ein Star, der daheim lange nichts galt", *Art* no. 2, Hamburg 1986 pp. 106-110.

"Austria: Hollein", in *Encyclopedia of 20th Century Architecture*, Harry N. Abrams, New York 1986, pp. 30, 151-152.

M. Brüderlin, "Design und Zeitgeist", *Parnass* no. 3, Linz, May-June 1986, pp. 36-41.

"Le Design ouvre les portes", *Architecture & Techniques* no. 368, Paris 1986, pp. 15-157.

W.K. Albrecht-Schoek, "Banales als Thermometer der Kultur", *MD/Moebel Interior Design* 12, Leinfelden Echte 1986, pp. 52 56.

C. Desrues, "Wien, dämonisch", *Wochenpresse* no. 6, Vienna, February 4, 1986, pp. 44-45.

M. Pollak, "Vienne 1880-1938. L'Apocalypse joyeuse", *CNAC Magazine* 31, Paris 1986, pp. 60-63.

N. Bamberger, "Le Génie du Passé", *Jardin des Modes*, Paris, February 1986, pp. 60-63.

A. Hasegawa, "News", *SD/Space Design*, Tokyo, September 1986, pp. 166-167.

F. von Buttlar, "Würfel und Palazzo", *Baumeister*, Munich 1986, pp. 17-29.

F. Jäger, "Schein, Charme und Schabernack", *db/Deutsche Bauzeitung*, Stuttgart, September 1986, pp. 20-21.

P. Davey, "It's not the monument that matters"; P. Hannay, "Rauchstrasse 9", *The Architectural Review* no. 1069, 1986, pp. 23, 65-69.

S. Doubilet, "IBA Update", *Progressive Architecture*, February 1986, pp. 96-98.

D. Meyhöfer, "Rauchstrasse Berlin. Neuer Weg im Sozialbau?", *Architektur und Wohnen* no. 1, Hamburg 1986, p. 96-98.

"Opera de Tokyo", *AA/Architecture d'aujourd'hui* no. 247, October 1986, pp. 49-51.

F. Jollant Kneebone, "Concours pour l'Opera de Tokyo", *Archi/CRÉE*, Paris 1986, p. 20.

"The architectural competition for the new National Theater Tokyo", *Kokyo Kenchiku* 28/111, Tokyo 1986, p. 9.

"Second Place Winner: Hans Hollein", *JA/The Japan Architect* no. 352, August 1986, pp. 16-17.

J. Kräfner, "Wien muss weider den Mut besitzen, für sich zu lebenund zu gestalten", *Parnass* no. 3, Linz, May-June 1986, pp. 6-9.

U. Brunner, "Hans Hollein: Pro Wien, pro Hollein", *Umriss* 1, Vienna 1986, pp. 37-38.

V. Gregotti, "Ancora Stirling", *Panorama*, January 25, 1987, p. 19.

P. Fumagalli, "Fünf Themen-fünf Projekte", *Werk, Bauen, Wohnen*, Zurich, Jan.-Feb. 1987, pp. 4-9.

M. Barocco, "Nove ipotesi progettuali per una maniglia", *Domus* 680, February 1987, pp. 4-5.

P. Jodidio, "Hans Hollein entre en scene", *Connaissance des Arts* no. 421, Paris 1987, pp. 50-57.

J. Stirling, H. Hollein, "Galerie Thyssen-Bornemisza, Lugano", *Kunst und Kirche*, Linz 1/87, p. 43.

P. Kruntorad, "Die Welt ist ein Rätsel", *Nürnberger Nachrichten* no. 75, Nuremberg, March 31, 1987, p. 21.

F. Edelmann, "L'année critique", *Le Monde*, Paris, March 11, 1987, p. 20.

O. Boissiere, "Deux Architects à Beaubourg: Hans Hollein et Mies van der Rohe; le trivial et le sublime...", *Le Matin*, Paris, March 16, 1987, p. 19.

P.J., "Hollein: 'L'Architecture est sans but'", *Architects-Architecture* 176, Paris, April 1987, p. 3.

C. De Seta, "Dalla grande Vienna la maniera di Hollein", *Corriere della Sera*, May 31, 1987, p. 21.

F. Edelmann, "One ne choisit pas sa mère: Hans Hollein au Centre Pompidou", *Le Monde*, April 23, 1987, p. 15.

F. Metken, "Architektur als schöne Kunst", *Die Zeit* no. 17, April 17, 1987, p. 56.

P. Vaisse, "D'or et de sang", *Le Figaro*, April 14, 1987, p. 31.

M. Dezzi Bardeschi, "Sensuali Metafore da 'Object Trouvé'", *Il Sole - 24 ore*, April 5, 1987, p. 25.

V. Prest, "Hans Hollein: l'architecture n'a pas de but", *art press* no. 115, Paris 1987, pp. 4-7.

"Hans Hollein. Métaphores et Métamorphoses", *AA/Architecture d'aujourd'hui* no. 250, 1987.

ECM, "Premises of Thyssen-Bornemisza collection set for expansion", *AD/Art & Design*, London, April 1987, pp. V-VII.

M. Collins, "Post-Modern Design", *AD/Art & Design*, London, April 1987, pp. 11-13.

H. Cummings, "The Design Object, an international survey: Alessi Metalware" *AD/Art & Design*, London, April 1987, pp. 24-31.

"Hans Hollein", *AD/Art & Design*, London, April 1987, pp. 34-35.

"Swid Powell Ceramics", *AD/Art & Design*, London, April 1987, pp. 54-55.

"Jewellery", *AD/Art & Design*, London, April 1987, pp. 60-61.

W. Fischer, "Post-Modernism and consumer design", *AD/Art & Design*, London, April 1987, pp. 67-72.

Papadakis, "Post-Modern Performance Art: Hans Hollein", *AD/Art & Design*, London, April 1987, pp. 78-79.

B. Radice, *Gioielli di architetti dalla collezione Cleto Munari*, Electa, Milan 1987, pp. 33-44.

I. Novak, "Abgerundet: Das neue Haas Haus", *Architektur Aktuell* 118, Vienna, April 1987.

P. Bludwell Jones, "Where do we stand?", *a + u* no. 198, 3/1987, pp. 14-30.

H. Malotki, "Lugano: concorso per l'ampliamento della galleria von Thyssen-Bornemisza", *Domus* 678, 1987, pp. 78-79.

"Famosi architetti per orologi d'eccezione firmati Cleto Munari", *Vogue Italia* no. 449, July-August, 1987.

F. Palpacelli, "Hans Hollein and Richard Meier", Exhibit Catalogue, National Institute of Architecture, Florence, 1987, pp. 39-46.